Searching for Utopia

Searching for Utopia

THE HISTORY OF AN IDEA

Gregory Claeys

With 206 illustrations, 141 in color

Thames & Hudson

First published in 2011 in hardcover in the United States of America by Thames & Hudson Inc., 500 Fifth Avenue, New York, New York 10110

thamesandhudsonusa.com

Library of Congress Catalog Card Number 2010935146

ISBN 978-0-500-25174-4

Printed and bound in China by Toppan Leefung

PAGE 1   The Creation, as portrayed in the first words of Genesis in one of the earliest German translations of the Bible, printed at Nuremberg by Anton Koberger in 1483. A unicorn is present here, as Eve emerges from Adam's rib.

PAGE 2   Illustration of the Genesis story and the creation of Adam and Eve, as portrayed in an Ottoman Bible, 16th century, from the University Library, Istanbul. The snake is apparent in the third set of images, and the duty to labour following expulsion from Paradise in the fourth.

ABOVE   Jacopo Tintoretto, *The Creation of the Animals*, *c.* 1550. This is presumably the fifth day, on which God ordered: 'Let the waters bring forth abundantly the moving creature that hath life' (Genesis 1:20). Among the many animals, note the unicorn on the far right.

Contents

The Search for Utopia

The first page of the Hebrew *Sefer Yetzirah*, or 'Book of Creation', 15th century, though its origins are obscure, illustrating the description 'God created the earth, the planets and the stars of the sky'.

The concept of utopia in every age is some variation on an ideal present, an ideal past and an ideal future, and the relation between the three. Each of these may be mythical or imaginary, or have some actual foundation in history. The prehistory of the concept is chiefly religious, consisting of creation myths and a prospective afterlife, but may contain a speculative historical dimension, such as the all-encompassing flood first described in the *Epic of Gilgamesh* (*c.* 2000 BC). In the Western tradition, the Greeks' 'ancients' were Egyptians; their secular idealized present themselves, more or less epitomized by life in the *polis*, or city-state; their future, their afterlife, partly captured in the image of the 'Elysian Plain' of Homer's *Odyssey* (*c.* 9th century BC). The Romans' past was mostly Greek and partially Egyptian, but included various myths of an original 'golden age' or Arcadia; their future, as described in Virgil's *Aeneid* (19 BC), was a modified version of the Elysian ideal, to which the virtuous few were admitted. To medieval Christians, Genesis revealed a world in which Adam and Eve inhabited a bucolic Garden of Eden before being expelled, with a flood ending the earliest stage of history. In Asia, the Middle East and elsewhere, similar creation myths and golden ages appear in many forms. And today…we are confused. A great number of people still envision a scientifically shaped future in which experts provide solutions to all our problems without disturbing our ambitions. Many would today regard the present as the best so far attained; certainly it is so for the privileged. Far fewer would identify a point in the past as an ideal worth returning to. But some, however, do find in the past a period in which our needs were in harmony with nature, our population not overly burdensome and our consumption balanced with our production.

BELOW A detail from the painted sarcophagus of Butehamun, 21st dynasty, c. 1069–945 BC, illustrating an Egyptian Creation myth. In the act of creation, Geb, the god of the Earth, holds up Nut, the goddess of the Sky.

OPPOSITE *Mohammed's Paradise*, c. 1030, from a Persian School miniature in the Bibliothèque Nationale, Paris. It is not clear which figure is Mohammed; possibly the man with a green turban, though this is much debated. The depiction of Mohammed is in itself a rarity in Islam.

Whether our ideal lies in the past, the present or the future, the concept of utopia often has some bearing on how we conceive of this ideal. The three phases of development of utopian thought might loosely be considered as the mythical, the religious, and the positive (to paraphrase Auguste Comte)[1] or institutional. At each of these stages something akin to a concept of utopia functions to reinforce our sense of the communal bond and offer hope in an uncertain world. The first two stages also link the afterlife to this life, while the third mostly does not, though it may offer a secular equivalent to salvation. For most of our species-history we have been rooted in worlds beyond the domain of 'normal' or everyday consciousness, deriving meaning in life from an understanding of death and the afterlife. To give greater permanence to our brief lives we have imagined pasts and futures that suit the narrative of the present that we find most comforting. When our lives in this world deteriorate or are threatened, we react by cultivating a reinforced sense of familial harmony and ethnic, national and/or religious identity. Something approaching the concept of utopia, then, has functioned historically, from before the publication of Thomas More's famous work, *Utopia* (1516), to balance strife by privileging the communal, usually by making property and social classes much more equal. This equality is the crucial social dogma often regarded as definitive of the utopian agenda. Imagined or practised humanely, it can teach us the enduring value of love, respect, the cultivation of the individual, even the eccentric and unique.

Abused, it reveals darker passions, and may bear witness to an enraged mass, aroused by an ideology of extreme, vengeful egalitarianism, capable of blood-letting on an enormous scale.

The last phase of utopia, the more institutional or constitutional, is less concerned with imagining the ideal than with creating it, and reaches its apogee in modernity. While we tend to associate this with modern socialism, it would nonetheless be mistaken to omit liberalism from this story. Liberalism is often viewed as dealing in certainties, in sceptical and empirical, realistic statements of human possibility, not in fantasy, and not in idealized, much less increasingly socialized, futures. It is thus, in this view, quintessentially anti-utopian. Yet this story is misleading for four reasons: first, because liberalism itself presented a utopian vision of universal opulence, based on the division of labour and growth of trade, which remained credible for at least a century but then began failing to fulfil its promise. Second, liberalism eventually came to reckon with its failings, to see its future vision as deficient, and to prophesy the possibility of something better – of some compromise, in particular, between socialism and liberalism that might incorporate the better elements of both systems. Third, liberalism in several forms also promised an idealized democracy, even portrayed in terms of an 'end of history',[2] based on popular sovereignty as an alternative to monarchy, aristocracy and plutocracy. Often, however, it has failed to avoid governance by the few – usually the wealthy – over the many. In its most extreme form, these elements have been conceived as utopian when they are combined in the fantasy of an unregulated market that aims to supersede national sovereignty by a regime of quasi-omnipotent multinational corporations that imposes an economic, political and cultural strategy of globalization on the world's population.[3] Finally, liberalism has often promised that the good life consisted of maximizing individual liberty, autonomy and independence, and trumpeted the pursuit of greed or selfishness as the means of achieving them. As such it has often denigrated 'society', or the existence of any common or public good varying from the supposed sum of individual goods, and disparaged community and collective bonds and more altruistic forms of behaviour. Yet these elements or building-blocks of sociability are also constituent elements of individual happiness. People are happy being part of a neighbourhood as well as inhabitants of an apartment block; at belonging to the public as well as being detached from it. They are also generally happier when they do not live in fear of their neighbours, or, for that matter, in fear of illness and old age, because society shields them from their worst effects. These are a vital part of the lesson utopia teaches.

DEFINING UTOPIA

The study of utopia focuses on three domains: utopian thought; the narrower genre of utopian literature; and practical attempts to found improved communities. Whichever of these we consider, the range of expressions of aspirations for an ideal or vastly improved state of existence explored in this book is astonishing, and forces us to confront at the outset the problem of defining our central concept.[4] For the term 'utopia' to be meaningful, it cannot embrace every aspiration to social improvement: proposals to contain sewage emissions or extend public transport are not 'utopian'. Neither can utopia be reduced to a psychological impulse, dream, fantasy, projection, desire or wish, though these may underpin its creation or discovery. Nor does utopia mean the search for the 'perfect' life, though it is still frequently confused with this; 'perfection' is essentially

Lucas Cranach the Elder, *The Golden Age*, c. 1530. This depiction extends traditional views of the Golden Age, using nudity to symbolize peace and serenity in a natural garden setting.

a theological concept, which, while historically linked to utopianism, defines a state that is impossible for mortals to attain in this life.[5] In fact, utopia has often been attained or discovered (and as often lost again); many past ages were indeed the realization of earlier utopian visions; and, for some, every present is a past utopia. Yet each of these realized moments, too, contained fallibility, failure, the absence of perfection.

To provide a workable definition of 'utopia', then, is challenging. The breadth of the genre is bewilderingly large, encompassing positive ideals of much-improved societies; their negative satirical opposites, sometimes called anti-utopias or dystopias; various myths of paradise, golden ages and 'fortunate islands', and portrayals of primitive peoples living in a natural state; Robinsonades or shipwrecks; imaginary voyages to the Moon and elsewhere in space; and planned constitutions, model towns and various other visions of improvement. This list is far from exhaustive, but it forces us to narrow the range of the use of the term 'utopia' to avoid losing any meaningful application of it.

One way of doing so is to postulate that More's seminal text *Utopia* offers us a quasi-realistic account of a vastly improved society. Human nature here is not perfect, for crime still exists. Yet a more collectivist system of laws, manners and mutual consent ensures a vastly happier and better-ordered commonwealth. We can work outwards, then, from this 'realistic' core definition, which seemingly places less strain on human capability and credibility, to more elusive, dreamier, less likely scenarios of greater virtue, order and pleasure, to still more extreme fantasies and projections that bear little resemblance to any conceivable reality. Across the ages and the world these possibilities have appeared in a wide variety of mixtures. A number of these, however, promise wellbeing for some to the detriment of others. The discovery of an ideal society by an intruder – like a virus-ridden anthropologist – also often threatens the very existence of that society, as does the emergence of internal dissent from established or foundational

Painting of an elegantly clad Adam and Eve, from the *Manafi' al-Hayawan*, or 'The Usefulness of Animals', Maragh, Mongolian Iran, 1294–99. There is no 'original sin' in the Islamic portrayal of the first man and woman, who are instead forgiven after repenting their wrongdoing.

norms and beliefs. Repression can follow swiftly. Witches go to the stake, aristocrats to the lamp-post. The distance between utopia and dystopia can seem alarmingly close at times.

Let us distinguish at the outset, further, between three main variations on the utopian impulse. The first may be termed static as opposed to dynamic utopias: once formed, the ideal society seeks constantly to retain the purity of its original form; or, by contrast, it recognizes an inherent tendency towards historical development and constructs mechanisms for coping with such changes. Secondly, we may contrast ascetic to want-satisfying utopias. Ancient and early modern utopias virtually always accept the inevitable scarcity of goods and absolute insufficiency of resources. Needs are thus restrained by simplicity, and sumptuary laws frequently prohibit or restrict luxury. In the early modern period and later, this type begins to give way to concepts of regimes of abundance. Both liberalism and Marxism participate in this type. Finally, we may contrast hierarchical with egalitarian utopias. Many ancient and some later utopias (not to mention dystopias) have been hierarchical, and based on a belief in the inevitable inequality of humankind, with a select group of leaders enjoying a life of privilege and relative luxury. This view, often associated with Plato's *Republic*, was departed from in More's *Utopia*, where all men and women engage in farming and are trained to a craft. Most modern utopias, whether of the more or less primitivist type, include a substantial measure of equality. The dominant modern utopian ethos, epitomized in the egalitarianism of the American and French revolutions, and the still greater emphasis on equality in socialism, is effectively defined by this quality. The decline in religious belief accompanying modernity has thus displaced the search for equality in the afterlife by an enhanced desire to achieve it in this life. Creation myths have been, to a degree, supplanted by destination myths. Perfectibility is increasingly relegated to the afterlife, and when it is not, its pursuit often defines dystopia.

Modern utopianism, then, if largely unconcerned with the afterlife, retains some connections with both its mythological and its theological prehistory. But it places much greater weight on human efficacy in this life. In the ages of myth and religion, the gods and forces of nature

Embossed front cover of Jules Verne's *From the Earth to the Moon*, 1874. The plot follows three men in post-Civil War America, who build a large sky-facing Columbiad space gun. Note the three carriages – 'First', 'Second' and 'Third' class.

retain control over humanity. In the age of utopia, as it has emerged over the five hundred years since More's *Utopia*, humankind seizes its own destiny. It recognizes human deficiencies and attempts to contain them within a system of regulations and customs enforced by public opinion. Human beings, not gods, marshal these efforts and define their own systems of order. Their task may be rendered easier if they reduce their needs and if they live in a temperate climate: here the appeal of the primitive, of the life lived 'according to nature', has remained strong. Elsewhere utopia may be shaped by a constant struggle with a less than beneficent environment. In either case utopia is ultimately defined by the limits of humanity itself, though what these are have always been the subject of great debate. And, falling short of remaking the world, humanity may also create utopic moments of temporary harmony in time, as well as utopic places – such as planned communities – of harmony in space.

The quest for the ideal society, then, involves exploring a vast, dense, bewildering variety of terrains inhabited by some quite extraordinary beings. We will confront many extremes of imaginary creature, associated according to some very unusual rules, and located in some fairly strange places above, beyond, behind and far away from what we assume to be everyday reality. How far does it matter, in the end, where we imagine utopia to be located – on a far-flung island, on the Moon, beneath the Earth, on another galaxy, in a hidden valley encircled by misty peaks? Or how we get there – on a lengthy sea voyage, in a rocket, or by stumbling down a rabbit hole? Not much: the fictitious location is unimportant, as is, at one level, whether or not we use fiction to depict utopia. What matters, as far as defining the narrower utopian genre is concerned, is the plausibility of what we discover once we arrive. This is what differentiates science fiction from utopia, and indeed many of the sub-genres of utopia from utopia itself. It helps us to avoid reducing utopia to a psychological principle, a whimsical 'wish' or 'principle of hope', as well as to separate it from 'dreaming' of all kinds, for anything is possible in a dream, too. Such assumptions often confuse the motive that leads

Illustration from a publication of 1832 of the Saint-Simonian community at Ménilmontant, near Paris. Founded by Barthélemy Prosper Enfantin, the community was inhabited by about fifty persons at the time. Communism was practised, and a peculiar costume adopted.

some to seek utopia, with the object being sought, which is manifestly not 'hope', but rather its object or realization. The criterion of plausibility helps to narrow and specify utopia, as well as to conceive its realizability, and to separate it from the merely imaginary or the utterly impossible. Underground worlds are implausible; a society organized according to collectivist principles but merely fictionally located underground is not, necessarily, though the particulars of its details may be. We choose a dramatically different *topos*, or location, precisely in order to lend credence to an extended ideal of a better society. But if a projection is thoroughly unrealistic we may subvert any possibility of encouraging real social change, for form and content here bear a symbiotic relationship to each other. Demanding the impossible must always remain not only frustratingly tantalizing, but destructive of improvement.

Utopia, then, is not the domain of the impossible. In the lands of myth, almost anything is possible. And in religion spoken through the language of the apocalypse, of salvation and emancipation, of the final, the ultimate, the perfect, the complete, the total, the absolute, almost anything is possible. But utopia explores the space between the possible and the impossible. Tinged though it admittedly often has been with the desire for finality, absoluteness and perfection, utopia is nonetheless in this sense not 'impossible', indeed not even 'nowhere'. It has been 'somewhere' through much of history, even before the concept itself existed. It is a place we have been to, and sometimes fled from, as well as one yet unknown that we aspire to visit. Without it humanity would never have struggled onward towards betterment. It is a pole-star, a guide, a reference point on a common map of an eternal quest for the improvement of the human condition. Let us, then, begin the journey.

Chapter 1

The Classical Age

Myths, Golden Ages and Ideal Constitutions

Much like nostalgia for one's youth, many societies have creation myths that go hand-in-hand with the idea of a past golden age of purity, harmony and virtue. In Greece, Homer established this period as existing a thousand years before the Trojan War, when the first men were made of gold and were governed by the god Kronos. The idea was embellished by, among others, Hesiod (*Works and Days*, 8th century BC), who tells us:

> …they lived like gods, with carefree heart, remote from toil and misery. Wretched old age did not affect them either, but with hands and feet ever unchanged they enjoyed themselves in feasting, beyond all ills, and they died as if overcome by sleep. All good things were theirs, and the grain-giving soil bore its fruits of its own accord in unstinted plenty, while they at their leisure harvested their fields in contentment amid abundance.[1]

At this time the gods are generally portrayed as benevolent and as having a more direct relationship with mortals than is the case today. But the gods also punish human beings for betraying promises or agreements. For example, in Greek myth Zeus sends Pandora to Earth bearing a jar of miseries (including war, famine and sin), which are unleashed on humanity in punishment for Prometheus stealing fire from heaven.

According to Hesiod, the golden age is abandoned when the gods somewhat impulsively create a 'much inferior' silver race. Now the climate grows colder, food requires cultivation and humanity must shelter from the elements. When these people fail to honour the Olympian gods adequately, they too are supplanted – by a bronze race. This age is marked by growing human enmity, but is succeeded

The gods shown in this detail from Thomas Barker's Italianate portrayal of an *Arcadian Landscape with Deities* (*c.* 1793) include Hercules draped in light yellow and Olympus perched in a tree.

BELOW This mid-16th-century panel by Matteo Balducci depicts the story of Diana and Acteon, taken from Ovid's *Metamorphoses*. This narrative poem is one of the chief sources of Roman mythology, and recounts the creation and history of the world.

OPPOSITE ABOVE In *The Fight between Carnival and Lent* (1559), Pieter Bruegel the Elder's swarming panorama of 16th-century life, the excessive indulgence of Carnival – derived from ancient Saturnalia – is contrasted with the sobriety of Lent, as seen around the church.

OPPOSITE BELOW Pieter Bruegel the Elder's engraving, *Christ's Descent into Limbo* (1561), shows Christ liberating the just, the patriarchs, the prophets of the Old Testament, and Adam and Eve, from Limbo. The Gospel of Nicodemus describes these figures as having awaited his coming in the afterlife.

by a 'more righteous and noble' race of demi-gods, some of whom, after death, are permitted to dwell in the Isles of the Blessed. Next is the fifth or iron age, which is marked by warfare, greed, a breakdown in parental respect, and the spreading of envy and hatred. The gods intervene constantly to punish wickedness, and the pitting of good against evil comes to define human behaviour. The proto-utopia, once lost, is never regained, though the fault lies at least partly in the whimsy of the gods.

The Roman version of the golden age was taken up by Catullus, Horace, Seneca and Ovid, among others. It also portrays a state of harmony, abundance and peace, presided over by the god Saturn. Perhaps the most famous account of this age, in Ovid's *Metamorphoses* (AD 8), describes the gradual corruption of this state and the emergence of the silver, bronze and iron ages. To commemorate their loss the Romans invented the festival of Saturnalia, which re-created the golden age once a year (17–23 December). Slaves were permitted to dine with and speak freely to their masters, sometimes even ordering them to perform demeaning acts. Feasting, merry-making and a moratorium on harsh punishments took place. The Feast of Fools, or carnival, of the Middle Ages, was an imitation of Saturnalia and celebrated the theme of 'the world turned upside down'.[2] This marks the first appearance of utopia as an act of (pseudo-) historic memory and re-creation.

Such utopic moments would become increasingly rare, however, and most aspirations for real improvement remained displaced to the afterlife. Elysium, the Elysian Fields or the Islands of the Blessed were the various names given to the land inhabited by the blessed throughout eternity. As described in Hesiod's *Works and Days* and in Homer and Pindar, we envision a blissful land of beauty and abundance that is populated by heroic figures. For Hesiod, Hades was the home of dead souls, with a special dungeon, Tartarus, reserved for those who rebelled against the gods. For Plato, the

immortality of the soul implied the possibility of eternal punishment, though he allowed that the soul might achieve benefits in the afterlife by worthy deeds in this one. In later Roman versions (notably Virgil's *Aeneid*, *c.* 19 BC), the promise of health and eternal life is held out to all who have proven their moral worth, while manifold tortures await the unworthy below, as related by Aeneas. In Greek myth, Elysium was located variously in the Atlantic regions or closer to home; in Rome the Blessed Fields were a part of the underworld, or in a deep valley. Other lands also had their sacred places inhabited by the gods. Valhalla, the great hall of Odin, the supreme god in Norse mythology, is the final resting place of the bravest warriors; lesser mortals are received here, but then move on to another place, Niflheim, to pass eternity.

Around the 9th century BC Homer reported in the *Odyssey* the existence of the land of Aiaia, somewhere in the Mediterranean. Its only inhabitants were the sorceress Circe and her servants, whose visitors were often turned into wolves, lions and pigs. Homer also described Aiolio, the floating island of Aiolos Hippotades, king of the winds, whose six sons and daughters lived incestuously, and who gave selected visitors a bag of evil winds, which if opened would impede their return journey. Homer's text also talks of the island of the Cyclops (one-eyed monsters that devour human flesh) as well as the

This Roman fresco, dating from the 3rd century AD, shows Mercury in the Elysian fields, the Graeco-Roman paradise of the afterlife, where the heroic and virtuous spent eternity. Evil-doers went to Hades, the underworld.

Fortunate Islands, which welcome mortals and are inhabited by happy spirits; and in the land of the Lotus-Eaters, munching on lotus flowers causes worries to disappear and visitors to lose all desire to return home. In Lucian's account (2nd century AD), the Island of the Blessed, located somewhere in the Atlantic Ocean, was inhabited by bodiless, ethereal beings who lived in a capital made of gold, where the walls were of emerald and loaves of ready-made bread sprang from fields of wheat. Lucian also described Dionysus's Island, in the same region, which possessed rivers of wine and grapevines that resembled the upper part of a woman's body.

Atlantis was a powerful ancient archetype of the idealized society and was first described by Solon and Dionysius of Miletus. In the best-known account, Plato tells us that nine thousand years had elapsed since the great war between Athens and the kings of the island of Atlantis. Over 5,800 square miles (15,000 sq km) in size, the Atlantean nation was located somewhere beyond the Rock of Gibraltar. Its power as a prosperous empire threatened even Egypt and Greece until it was destroyed by a great earthquake that left just two parts of the country intact. Its capital, also called Atlantis, boasted great warehouses and

Apollonio di Giovanni's extraordinary narrative, *The Adventures of Ulysses* (1435–45), recounts various episodes experienced by Ulysses (Greek: Odysseus), the hero of Homer's *Odyssey*, on his journey home to Ithaca after the Trojan War. The foreground detail shows the blinding of the cyclops Polyphemus.

strong defences. In later literary glosses, Atlantean science enabled the production of artificial food and drinks, and telepathy permitted the projection of past memories. The Atlantean myth of a lost island or continent has proven astonishingly enduring and gives a discernibly realistic sense of one source of the utopian ideal.[5]

The ancients also developed various other motifs that would come to be wedded to utopianism through the ages. Aristophanes' *The Birds* (414 BC) is perhaps the best-known early farce or satire on Athenian imperial ambitions. Here, attempts to colonize Sicily are portrayed as Cloudcuckooland, depicted in part as a 'city in the sky' of birds, where vices such as hostility, violence and ambition have been banished. The epic voyage, which would become a key motif in utopian thought, included Virgil's *Aeneid*. In this text part of Aeneas's journey involves a visit to Hades, the underworld, and to Elysium, the paradise of heroes.

The tradition known as Arcadia, named after a region in the Greek Peloponnesus renowned for its supposed peacefulness, dates from a pastoral literature established as early as the 4th century BC in the work of Greek writers such as Theocritus. It was continued under Roman

authors, including Ovid and Virgil, and was then reinvented in the form of an idealized rural idyll in the works of Iacopo Sannazzaro (*L'Arcadia*, 1501), Sir Philip Sidney (*The Countess of Pembroke's Arcadia*, 1590) and others. Linked to images of the golden age, pastoral themes reappear frequently in utopianism throughout the subsequent period. In the early modern era they were sometimes associated with the reigns of particular monarchs, notably Elizabeth I, and were frequently taken up in dramatic form, as in Shakespeare's *As You Like It* (*c.* 1599), set in the forest of Arden. Robin Hood-style myths of virtuous, forest-dwelling peasants overlap with the imagery of arcadian virtue, simplicity, and antagonism to courtly pretentiousness and hypocrisy. Arcadian visions were, like many forms of monasticism and mysticism, often linked to ascetic or want-denying ideals of moral purification. While some images of medieval peasant life promote want-indulgence, or cornucopia, as in the land of Cockaygne, the renunciation of urban society is often portrayed as a return to rural primitivism, with morals becoming purified proportionately as needs are simplified.

The ancient world also created a variety of constitutional forms that were later regarded as 'ideal' in terms of social and economic stability, the division of land, the distribution of wealth, laws, manners and social relations. These would become one of the most direct sources for the 'realist' strand in utopian thought by the time Thomas More's

OPPOSITE ABOVE Title page of the third edition of *The Countess of Pembroke's Arcadia* by Sir Philip Sidney, 1598. Centring on the shepherd's life, Sidney's romance idealizes the pastoral, uniting classical images of the Golden Age with primitivist themes.

OPPOSITE BELOW One in a series of four paintings by the Dutch artist Pauwels Franck (also called Paolo Fiammingo), *Love in the Golden Age* (*c.* 1585–89) depicts erotic aspects of the pastoral motif and mythical Golden Age.

Lycurgus (9th century BC)

The semi-mythical lawgiver, sometimes assumed to have been a member of the Spartan royal family, provided the city-state's constitution and system of education. Virtually everything known of him derives from one source, Plutarch, writing in the 1st century AD, who himself tells us that his sources are dubious. Nonetheless, Lycurgus is supposed to have travelled widely in Asia and Egypt, studying different constitutions and modes of rule. Coming to power in Sparta, he created a constitutional balance between a group of kings and a senate, with a popular assembly possessing the power to ratify or reject whatever the former proposed, but not to legislate independently. Lycurgus rendered money valueless by abolishing silver and gold coinage and circulating only iron instead, which was too heavy to be practical and was not accepted elsewhere in Greece. Slaves were poorly treated, and there were restrictions on travel, with the aim of avoiding the corrupting influence of less virtuous societies.

Lycurgus, beating his wife

Utopia appeared. Sparta, and to a degree Crete, would come to exemplify, in later ages, a contempt for luxury and an intense devotion to the common good of the city-state. As recounted by Plutarch (*c.* AD 100), Lycurgus was a 9th-century BC reformer who created a dual monarchy and senate in Sparta that balanced the monarchy and popular assembly and approved all legislation. To solve the problems of poverty and social inequality in Sparta, land was divided up and redistributed fairly and equally. Simplicity in personal and household decoration became the norm; communal meals were introduced so that the rich, when obliged to dine with the poor, 'could not make use of or enjoy their abundance, nor so much as please their vanity by looking at or displaying it.'[4] Exercise, sometimes taken naked, was also communal. Married men and women slept separately, except when desiring intercourse. Lycurgus permitted relations between single men and married women with older husbands, but not other forms of adultery. Children were regarded as 'not so much the property of their parents as of the whole commonwealth'.[5] Those deemed unfit or unhealthy at birth were left to die on a mountainside. Educated in common, living in dormitories from the age of seven, shoeless, naked and with shaven heads, children were inured to climatic extremes, and were soon hardened to the necessities of military life.

Hilaire-Germain-Edgar Degas, *Young Spartans Exercising, c.* 1860. Lycurgus ordered Spartan girls to undertake wrestling contests. Here they are portrayed urging the boys to fight. It was common for participants to be naked or only partly clothed.

Plutarch's description of life in Sparta has become synonymous with bravery and self-sacrifice, but also with the militarized utopia (or dystopia), where individuality is sacrificed to the communal good and no price is deemed too high to secure submission to the demands of the state. Yet Lycurgus's aim was not to create an imperial, militarist state, it was to keep Spartans 'free-minded, self-dependent, and temperate'.[6] His description would become crucial to Jean-Jacques Rousseau in the 18th century, as well as to some socialists in the 19th century.[7] And today the last closed communist society, North Korea, can be seen as inheriting aspects of this tradition.

Plato's *Republic* (*c.* 370 BC) and *Laws* (*c.* 360 BC) also provided several possible models of utopian thinking that proved immensely influential through subsequent ages. One of his central propositions was that wealth concentrated in the hands of the ruling class would corrupt. In the *Republic*, as recounted by Plato, Socrates proposed that rulers should embrace a communal existence and avoid the pursuit of wealth, in return for which they would be maintained by the general population. Plato also described ritual festivals in which, as in Plutarch's Sparta, the most robust males and females met. Their children were, again as in Sparta, to be reared communally and educated in the ethos of public service. The text commends rule by the philosopher-king – whose love

Plato (428/427–348/347 BC)

The Greek philosopher was the author of the *Republic* and many other works. A native of Athens, he was a disciple of the greatest teacher of his day, Socrates, who was condemned for corrupting the morals of the young and committed suicide in 399 BC. After this, Plato left Athens, travelling widely over a number of years. He returned to Athens in 387 BC and, in a public olive grove on the edge of the city, founded his Academy. His preferred method of instruction was through dialogue, of which his *Symposium* and *Phaedo* remain among the best known. In *Timaeus* and *Critias* he offered an influential account of the former great empire of Atlantis. In the *Republic*, among other things, he developed two ideas that would remain profoundly influential throughout the subsequent utopian tradition: a plea for wise rule by a philosopher-king, and the maintenance of a ruling guardian caste that possesses community of both goods and wives. Plato also remains renowned for his theory that reality can be known only through pure 'forms', or ideas, accessible to the mind alone, material objects being mere reflections of these forms.

Plato's Academy

Map of the European provinces of the Roman Empire after Augustus, taken from *The Historical Atlas* by William R. Shepherd, 1911. The Roman empire was the largest in the ancient world, and established a paradigmatic ideal of the imposition of order and civilization upon barbarian peoples.

of wisdom best qualifies him for the task – and explains why other regimes, such as oligarchy, or rule by the rich, timocracy, or government by the military, and democracy, or despotism by popular demagogues, are doomed to fail. In his *Politics* Aristotle rejected Plato's communism, particularly with respect to community of wives and children, arguing that greater unity would not result from its practice. He continued to call for private ownership but common use of goods and for a reliance on education to create a viable sense of unity.

Rome, of course, would become the greatest empire of the ancient world. Like later imperial conquerors (and More's fictitious Utopians), it regarded the imposition of its laws, customs and order on the barbarians as the greatest possible favour. Some Romans, such as Seneca, believed in an original, natural condition of human equality, though conceded its inevitable evolution into a controlled and civilized

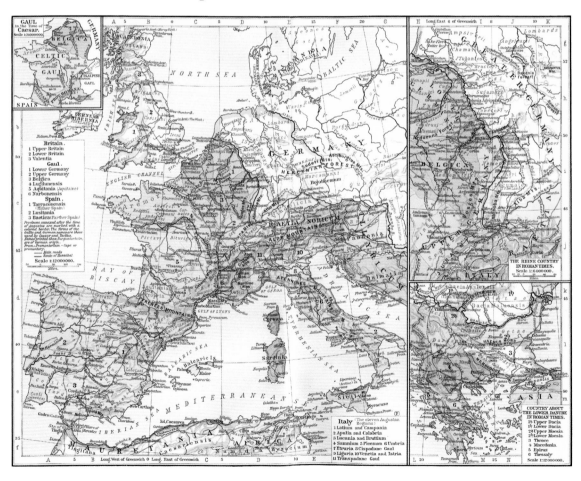

Fresco at the Temple of Bacchus in Pompeii, 79–55 BC, showing life on the river Nile in Egypt, with temple buildings and children playing. Even the ancients had ancients. Pompeii had a temple devoted to the Egyptian goddess Isis, who was associated with motherhood, magic and fertility. Such frescoes thus combined mythical, religious and touristic themes.

society. Many Roman versions of the earliest times, as formulated by writers such as Lucretius, downplayed any original advantages, instead praising order based on civilization. Cultural primitivism was not a utopian option here, though the Romans possessed pastoral and other spaces that formed utopic retreats from their increasingly urbanized lives. They frequently decorated their walls with paintings of past glories. At Pompeii, for example, these often portrayed Egyptian themes. But the Romans tended to regard their constitution as the best. Later generations, at least down through Gibbon in the 18th century, would consider that greed, pride, luxury, ambition, the over-extension of power and the loss of public virtue were among the reasons for Rome's downfall. A sense of a decline from its 'golden age' – often associated with the reign of the first Roman emperor, Augustus (27 BC to AD 14) – emerged. This was now caused not by the gods' arbitrariness but by the unwillingness to sacrifice self for country, which was induced, for writers like Seneca, by luxury in particular. Correspondingly, an image of Germanic warlike shepherds, successful because of their resilience, would also emerge in later Roman history, chiefly in Tacitus. And other shepherds, notably the Mongols, would achieve even greater renown, and suggest a similar moral lesson.

Chapter 2

Christian Archetypes

Heaven and Hell, Millennium and Apocalypse

Western utopianism is rooted firmly in Christianity as well as classical thought. In Christianity its aspirations rest on two images in particular: Eden, the original birthplace of humanity, and heaven, the believer's hoped-for final destination. The most famous Christian utopian was of course Jesus Christ. The possibility of his return has entranced believers throughout the ages, fuelling a variety of forms of millenarian belief, and eventually a post-millennial ideal of secular progress. Hell, in turn, whether reached through malevolent deeds or thought-crime of some form, has inspired many a later dystopia. In addition, the possibility of achieving near- or even perfect virtue in this life has underpinned many a Christian heresy through the ages, particularly various forms of antinomianism, or belief in a 'free spirit' or complete release from sin.[1] The suppression of such heresies, notably by the Catholic Inquisition, wedded the use of torture to the official enforcement of virtue long before the epoch of revolution, linking hell intimately to this life.

The Christian idea of Eden is derived in part from earlier Babylonian, Persian and other concepts of paradise (the word *edin* is Sumerian for 'plain'; the corresponding Hebrew term translates as 'delight'). Eden came often to be regarded as the idyllic image of the garden oasis of pastoral peoples for whom water, abundance of greenery and plentiful food contrast to the barrenness of a sandy desert landscape. The subsequent ideal of the bucolic garden, or rural or pastoral retreat, would thereafter provide a dominant theme within utopian thought. In the proverb 'God made the country, man the city', the country may be seen as embodying virtue, the city vice. As famously portrayed in Hieronymus Bosch's painting *The Garden of Earthly Delights* (1503–4), Eden is inhabited by a naked Adam (from

The left-hand panel of Hieronymus Bosch's triptych *The Garden of Earthly Delights* (1503–4) shows God blessing the newly created Eve before presenting her to Adam. The dragon tree in the background supposedly represents eternal life.

Jesus Christ (*c.* 4 BC to *c.* AD 30)

The Jewish sectarian and founder of the religion subsequently known as Christianity was born the son of a carpenter at Bethlehem, in what was then Roman-occupied Judea. He would eventually become the most influential religious leader of all time. While little is known about many aspects of Jesus's life (and speculation continues as to whether he survived crucifixion to die in old age in India), key events, such as the Sermon on the Mount, together with leading features of his teaching, notably on non-violence and charity, are adequately recorded. Jesus presented himself as a prophetic reformer within Judaism, but appeared as one among many pretenders to the role of the Jewish Messiah, or son of God. His supposed divine status remains a subject of controversy to this day. His leading disciples synthesized his doctrines into a manifesto or programme, which gained significant force with the conversion to Christianity of the Roman emperor Constantine in 313. Thereafter the most important developments in the religion were the split of Protestantism from Catholicism in the 16th century, and the growing secularization of many notionally Christian societies from the 18th century onwards.

The resurrection of Jesus

the Hebrew *adamah*: earth) and Eve, who oversee a lush garden populated with domestic and exotic animals. Genesis 2:11, which dates from about 1000 BC, tells us that God has included gold in his bequest. In the later book of Ezekiel (28:13) gold and precious stones are enumerated. In Revelation 22:1–2 there are descriptions of a 'tree of life' as well as a 'pure river of water of life'. Here hints are also laid down as to the attainment of paradise by the virtuous. The Bible thus portrays both virtuous innocence and sumptuous luxury as ultimate objects for eternal human aspiration. Much of this imagery would be embellished by later, particularly Roman, writers, such as Irenaeus and Josephus.

In Genesis, God is described as creating the first man, Adam, and then the first woman, Eve. He gives them dominion over nature and the promise of infinite plenty, with one caveat: not to eat from the Tree of the Knowledge of Good and Evil. However, the Garden also contains a snake, or dragon, which is the fallen angel Lucifer in disguise. He entices Eve to eat fruit from the tree, with the promise that both she and Adam would then be 'as gods, knowing good and evil' (Genesis 3:5). Adam is subsequently able to blame Eve for this extraordinary lapse in discipline. Thereafter women were often held accountable for the divine retribution that followed – the rapid

Lucas Cranach the Elder's *Adam and Eve* (1533) depicts the fatal moment of the Fall, when Eve tempts Adam to partake of the forbidden fruit of the Tree of Knowledge, resulting in the expulsion of both from the Garden of Eden. This account of succumbing to temptation formed the foundation for the Christian idea of 'Original Sin'.

expulsion of both from Paradise. To live by the sweat of one's brow is the subsequent earthly fate of all humankind. Redemption can occur only in the afterlife, following the final day of judgment. Original Sin, often misconceived to be sexual intercourse, is thus virtually unavoidable.

The story or allegory is beset by paradox. Why would a benevolent god provide such temptation in the first instance? Why would an all-powerful god permit Lucifer to escape or continue to exist in order to permit such a lapse to occur, much less allow his disguised entry into Eden? These elements appear to have been introduced into the narrative for dramatic effect, without recourse to logical or theological consistency, and morally, to satisfy the all-important question of the origins and persistence of evil in a notionally monotheistic – but really dualist – system.

Besides Eden, the Bible describes a variety of idealized locations, including Beulah (Isaiah 62:4–5), where humans are 'married' to God in a symbolic embrace of religious dogma analogous to the process of baptism. The antitheses of good and evil are represented in the urban images of Jerusalem and Babylon, the City of God and the City of Man, lightness and darkness, the virtues of the spirit and the sins of the flesh. The Tower of Babel (Genesis 11:1–9), built to 'reach unto heaven', is a potent image of the folly and ambition of humankind. All peoples at this time are described as speaking one language but, in punishment for their arrogance in trying to build a tower that would reach to heaven, God 'confounded' their speech, making them incomprehensible to one another thereafter.

Map of Jerusalem by Franz Hogenberg, c. 1590. The famed 'city on a hill' is sacred to Christians, Muslims and Jews, and provides the basis for imagery of the 'New Jerusalem', or perfect city, where, as described in the Book of Revelation, the virtuous will live in perpetuity with God.

One of the most famous images of mankind's propensity for folly, the Tower of Babel, here painted by Lucas van Valckenborgh (1594), shows humanity speaking one language and living in a tower high enough to reach heaven. Divine retribution would soon follow, scattering humanity and imposing a 'babel' of tongues upon them.

Punishment for earthly sins is also represented in the Bible by the great flood, which only Noah and his family survive (there is a Greek counterpart and other flood myths, some of which incorporate ideas of divine retribution for human malfeasance). More importantly, in the final book of the New Testament, Revelation (c. AD 90), the Old Testament idea of the apocalypse, or end of time, is invoked. Coinciding, perhaps, with the second coming of Christ, the world is riven with floods, earthquakes and other evils, as the good prepare for salvation and the evil anticipate everlasting torment. God succeeds in restraining Satan, but the promise of a New Jerusalem, in which the tree of life grows from God's throne, is delayed by the threat of a thousand years of conflict between good and evil. Then, at least in John's view, the City of God (in the form of a cube with sides 1,500 miles, or 2,415 km, long) would house the resurrected dead after the Last Judgment, its centre being occupied by the thrones of God and Christ, next to the river and the tree of life. Some variant on this image would remain the model for many a later ideal city.

Eden remains the greatest Christian myth of all, and the fount of much of the Western utopian tradition. It is reinforced primarily by descriptions of the afterlife, which in Christianity are typified by ideas of heaven and hell. In a vision inherited from Judaism and

Zoroastrianism, among other sources, and incorporated into the Old Testament, heaven was first closely associated with Eden. It then was increasingly imagined theocentrically as the holy residence of God somewhere above the world. While Eden had a more or less precise and earthly location, heaven has also been understood to be a metaphysical rather than a real state, and a spiritual locus for the unity of the human soul with the divine.[2]

By the time of the New Testament, heaven is typically portrayed as light, high above the Earth, and populated by God himself, with Jesus Christ usually shown seated on a throne at God's right hand. Also present are the archangel Gabriel and a variety of angels, seraphs and saints (some of whom enjoy important bureaucratic functions, such as St Peter, the gatekeeper), beside an ever-growing plenitude of normally virtuous mortals. Sectarian views differ greatly on the question of who should be admitted to heaven, but almost every version of heaven excludes not merely infidels and heretics but also non-believers in specific dogmas. Mormonism, however, proposes the eventual salvation of all human beings, including pagans.

The problem of how to occupy oneself throughout eternity has proved troublesome in Christianity: with so many tempting vices outlawed in the afterlife, profane entertainment is reduced to a minimum. Heaven is often popularly depicted as including copious harp-playing, presumably to accompany the constant hymn-singing ('eternal hallelujahs', as the Puritan minister John Cotton put it). Yet it has been viewed in many different ways. One 17th-century French theologian, François Arnoux, imagined heaven to be a 'Louvre of the blessed', where 'laughter never ceases'.[3] A complex heavenly scheme, like that of the 18th-century mystic Emanuel Swedenborg, permitted a wide variety of interactions. Some Renaissance images of heaven also inherited a much livelier classical sense of how time would pass in paradise, permitting friendship and even erotic love in a bucolic natural setting adorned by plants and animals. Mormonism, in keeping with its polygamous practices, would also later extend the institution of familial love into the afterlife, with offspring being reproduced until the end of time. However, many more puritanical visions of heaven proscribed idleness in particular. Some envisioned mandatory

The central panel of Hans Memling's triptych *The Last Judgment* (1467–71) shows Jesus sitting in judgment and the archangel Michael sending souls to hell. In Catholic belief good souls and bodies would be reunited in heaven, while the bad would go to hell.

collective sport. But of course this is all relative – after a life that has been short, brutish and nasty, it is possible that endless hymns and even callisthenics in front of a telescreen would have appeal.

Both heaven and hell have also always been conceived as organized and structured, after a fashion. The heavenly hierarchy, at least as constituted by the medieval period (accounts vary), consisted of three spheres of angels: seraphim, cherubim and thrones; dominions, virtues and powers (the keepers of history – in one account Satan is

Detail of Giotto's fresco *The Last Judgment* in the Arena Chapel, Padua, 1304–5. At the top we see heaven, with Jesus in the centre, flanked by apostles. The lower part shows the elect who will enter heaven, and the damned who are sentenced to hell. The archangels Michael and Raphael hold the cross in the middle.

their chief); and principalities, archangels and angels. Cherubim have four wings covered with eyes, and ox's feet; they guard the tree of life, among other functions, and are assisted by beryl-coloured, wheel-shaped ophanim, who have hundreds of eyes.[4] Archangels guard individual nations: Michael, for example, protects Israel. Seraphim continually shout 'Holy, holy, holy, is the Lord of hosts. All the earth is filled with His glory', in what must be the most tedious task of all.

In hell things are slightly different. Unlike the Babylonian underworld, which was morally neutral insofar as it contained all the dead, the Christian hell is inhabited only by evil-doers and their torturers. The wicked may toast in unquenchable fires of sulphur and brimstone (their bodies, Augustine claimed, were saved from destruction only by divine, miraculous intercession). But here, too, there is work to be done. Satan is assisted in hell by a multitude of other rebellious angels, who have been enumerated, most famously, by John Milton in *Paradise Lost* (1667). In this account of angelic insurrection we witness the first seeds of dystopia being laid. A third of the angelic hierarchy, led by Satan, mutinies against God, conducts a mighty war and is expelled. Among the rebel angels is Mammon, perhaps the first dystopian, or the proof of the worm in the original metaphorical apple. He is portrayed by Milton as being, even in paradise, always 'downward bent/admiring more/The riches of Heaven's pavement, trodden Gold/Than aught divine or holy else enjoyed/In vision beatific.'[5]

Not all, however, feared that their own future entailed a coming age of sulphur and brimstone. The anticipation that divine intercession might render the Earth heavenly was to become a powerful current in Christianity. Most millennialists have heeded the predictions laid down in Revelation 20:4–6, where the second coming of Christ heralds a

Pieter Bruegel the Elder, *The Fall of the Rebel Angels*, 1562. Here the key figure in golden armour is the archangel Michael, surrounded by rebel angels and fighting animals such as the seven-headed dragon. For some the theme demonstrates free will, but also the folly of angels who were created good but embraced evil.

reign of a thousand years, after which Judgment Day occurs. Among the major variations on this theme, pre-millennialists believe that Christ would appear before this period, while post-millennialists anticipate the prior golden age to occur before the New Jerusalem was constructed in some earthly location. From the 16th century onwards such aspirations were linked to the new world. In the 17th century the Puritans who emigrated there greatly reinforced this vision. By the 19th century, many looked to the young United States as God's chosen land, a 'city on a hill' or 'redeemer nation', not only a haven for the righteous, but destined to save all other nations from unrighteousness via battles that for some continue to the present, and may indeed terminate only with Armageddon.[6] Many of the chiliastic or millenarian aspects of Christian doctrine would re-emerge with regularity across the centuries of the medieval and early modern epochs into the modern era. Inheriting a Jewish apocalyptic tradition (one part of which is evidenced in the biblical book of Daniel), a variety of heretical Christian sects, like the medieval Cathars, or neo-Manichaeans, subscribed to one or another variations on the theory that an increasingly evil world would eventually be overthrown. A godly state would then be reintroduced in which saints or elect, godly or earthly, might rule for a time prior to the defeat of the Antichrist (the man of sin) and the Messiah's advent.

The idea of the kingdom of the saints runs so closely parallel to that of utopia that they are often confused. In the writings of the 14th-century monk Joachim of Fiore the search for an earthly and a heavenly paradise are intimately linked, and an imminent Third Age of Humanity is posited that corresponds to that of the Holy Spirit. During the Reformation, Thomas Münzer, most famously, would claim to have been penetrated by the divine will. The prophets of the 14th-century English Peasants' Revolt, John Wycliffe and John Ball, and the fomenters of the 15th-century Hussite rebellion, discovered that the poor, freed from the vices of avarice and luxury, were the new elect, the saints or chosen ones – a theme taken up by Karl Marx some three centuries later. Millenarianism would also define many of the most enthusiastic moments of the English Revolution of the 17th century. Both during the revolution, and under the rule of the Lord

Protector, Oliver Cromwell, a variety of sects entertained egalitarian and sometimes communistic ideals of an Anabaptist bent. The Fifth Monarchy Men believed that Christ would personally return to rule the world and revive the institutions of Mosaic law. Gerrard Winstanley's group, the Diggers, aimed to recreate a community similar to that which had existed before the Fall. They cultivated untilled land in Surrey (a third of the nation's soil remained unenclosed by private owners at this point) in order to 'work in righteousness and lay the foundation of making the earth a common treasury for all, both rich and poor',[7] until they were rudely driven off. Winstanley believed that the coming battle was to be 'fought between the two powers, which is property on the one hand, called the devil or covetousness, or community on the other hand, called Christ or universal love'.[8] Winstanley was the author of an important Commonwealth utopia, *The Law of Freedom in a Platform: or, True Magistracy Restored* (1652), which included proposals for nationalization of royal, clerical and common and waste lands, the abolition of buying and selling the labour of others, and a system of mandatory universal labour.

Thomas Münzer (*c.* 1490–1525)

This German prophet and millenarian was a communistical reformer of the early Reformation. He emerged as a radical leader closely associated with the Anabaptist heresy amid the Peasants' War of the early 16th century. Biographical details respecting his early life are scarce, and coloured by his enemies' prejudices. He is believed to have been born at Stolberg in the Harz Mountains (now Saxony-Anhalt) in 1490 or 1493. He obtained a doctor's degree, worked for a time as a teacher, and then emerged as a preacher in Zwickau in 1520 on the recommendation of Martin Luther. Here he became associated with a group of journeymen weavers in their struggle, religious as well as social, against rich priests and their benefactors. Defeated in this struggle, he fled to Prague, and eventually settled in Saxony. Increasingly radical in his beliefs and by now completely at odds with Luther, in 1524 he was one of the leaders of a series of insurrections (known as the Peasants' War): at Mühlhausen in 1525 his involvement led to the dissolution of the town council, the confiscation of Church property and the creation of a communistical community. However, the uprising was savagely repressed, and Münzer was tortured and executed. His attempt represented, nonetheless, an impressive experiment in Christian communism, and influenced Marx and other socialists.

Other groups, like the Ranters, believed that divine inspiration might free a minority from the sentence of Original Sin, and permit an antinomian, libertine freedom of action in a state of grace. Here, as free spirits, or what Norman Cohn has famously described as 'an elite of amoral supermen' (the remote predecessors of de Sade, Stirner and Nietzsche, the utopian egotists),[9] they proclaimed themselves to be released from the trammels of earthly morality and were thus able to indulge in any behaviour whatsoever. Some groups, like the Quakers, led by George Fox, insisted on egalitarianism, plainness of dress and speaking, and a strong communitarian orientation. Their fervent opposition to war would mark their conduct decisively across the coming centuries. Quakers would provide some of the most notable proposals for international peace in the modern period, including plans by William Penn for a European parliament to arbitrate disputes.

The idea of the sharing of property, usually in imitation of Christ and of apostolic practice, has thus characterized many such heretical Christian sects, including the Waldenses in 12th-century France. They distinguished between the 'perfect', who adopted communism and celibacy, and novices, who led a more traditional life. The Taborites in 15th-century Bohemia and the Lollards in Britain embraced similar ideals. The Hussite sect of Adamites also adopted nudity and

Engraving by François Morellon la Cave of Adamites in their community house. Originally an African Christian sect dating from the 2nd century, the Adamites termed their church 'Paradise', adopted nudity and rejected marriage as un-Christian.

community of wives. At the time of the Reformation, Thomas Münzer as well as the Anabaptists with whom he was associated, produced a series of bold, social experiments that were bloodily suppressed. Various mid- and late-17th-century sectarians, such as the Dutch cult, the Family of Love, founded by Henry Niclaes, adopted community of goods. However, by the early 18th century millenarian and apocalyptic ideas had greatly declined in elite, literate culture, though they never disappeared entirely.

Christianity has also always included a desire to practise less extreme forms of virtue in this life. The most famous portrayal of the ideal Christian society in the early centuries of the religion was St Augustine's *The City of God* (413–26). Writing against the backdrop of the decline and fall of the Roman Empire, Augustine contrasts the evils of the City of Man, epitomized by Rome, with the virtues of the City of God. In the latter he describes a recapturing of the innocence, harmony and peace of Eden. This image has two functions: it proposes an idealized Christian community of pure religion and practical virtue, towards which believers may aspire, and which, in the ideal of the New Jerusalem, might be created in this life, or recaptured through vanquishing heathen foes. It also gives a sense of the life that may be expected following Judgment Day, after believers have entered their final state of existence. It thus exhibits a dualism endemic throughout the utopian tradition (here represented partly by Augustine's embrace of Manichaeism): the doctrine of the omnipresence of two principles, good and evil, neither able to dominate the other. Some have viewed this as essential to Christian dogma ever since the introduction of the devil figure, Lucifer or Satan.

Christianity was also capable of being united to various forms of pagan mysticism, as in the medieval, and especially Arthurian, legend of the quest for the Holy Grail – a cup or dish used by Christ at the

Illumination showing St Augustine of Hippo, whose early 5th-century book, *The City of God*, was profoundly influential throughout the Middle Ages, and portrayed a stark contrast between the corrupt life of mankind, as epitomized by the Roman empire, and the virtuous state of the afterlife.

Last Supper that was believed to contain some of his blood from the Crucifixion. This quest would be reinvigorated as late as the 16th century in the search for the Fountain of Youth in the new world. The domain of the miraculous remains a utopic dimension in Christianity to the present.

In the Renaissance and early modern period, Christian mythology was restated in a number of immensely powerful and influential texts. Three of the best-known authors were Dante, John Milton and John Bunyan. Dante's *Divine Comedy* (1320) recounts a descent into a hell populated by criminals, heretics, pagans and atheists. There are further journeys to purgatory (where penance is undergone for a variety of sins), via, for some, limbo, where the unbaptized and others, like Socrates, dwell; and then, eventually, onwards to paradise, which is inhabited by God's elect – mainly great leaders, saints and angels.

The most famous literary expositions of the loss of Eden, Milton's *Paradise Lost* (1667) and its successor, *Paradise Regained* (1671), lament

the rupture of the soul's unity with God as a consequence of Satan's corruption of Eve. Bunyan's *The Pilgrim's Progress* (1678) is the leading Christian allegory concerning the search for salvation. Here numerous hardships test the faith of the pilgrim, Christian, on his perilous journey. But faith eventually triumphs and he reaches the land of Beulah and, thereafter, heaven, where he is relieved of the curse of Original Sin. Paradise is described chiefly in terms of the Celestial City, which guards the tree of life and is built of pearls and precious stones, with streets of gold and flourishing gardens.

Such a scenario might also be imagined not allegorically, but in terms of a promised land destined by God to be granted to a chosen few. In the book of Exodus, the Jews were offered such a place by their god Yahweh. Here they would be reunited as a people, peace and plenty would prevail, the wolf would dwell with the lamb, and so on. In other accounts a prophet would lead his peoples to this sacred respite from worldly cares. In the early centuries of Christianity, and notably during the Crusades, this idea of the promised land was often conceived of in terms of the resettlement of the Holy Land. Thereafter the New Jerusalem might be located elsewhere, most notably in the new world, later in the United States, and also became associated with the foundation of the state of Israel. One major sect of Protestants, the Mormons, took such a claim from Joseph Smith's *The Book of Mormon* (1830). This was supposedly based on revelations as old as 600 BC from the angel Moroni. They were revealed once again to Smith in 1823. This led to the establishment of the Church of the Latter-day Saints, the leading Protestant sect to arise in the United States in the 19th century. The Jehovah's Witnesses share a similar millennialism, as do a variety of non-Western groups, such as the Melanesian 'cargo' cults.

Frontispiece from John Bunyan's immensely popular *The Pilgrim's Progress from This World to That Which is to Come* (1678), which recounts the progression of a pilgrim from the sinful City of Destruction to salvation in the City of God.

Chapter 3

Extra-European Visions of the Ideal Society

Nowhere, Elsewhere

It has often been suggested that 'utopia' is a specifically Western tradition that rests in European classical thought and Judaeo-Christianity.[1] However, comparative studies on the subject are few and far between and provide a slender basis for generalization.[2] It could be claimed, albeit tautologically, that Christian Europe alone possesses a 'utopian' tradition because it is here that sufficient textual and semantic material has accumulated to result in an established intellectual niche or genre, particularly in literary form. In this view, Thomas More's *Utopia* established utopianism quite simply because it defined the concept's terms of reference. Hinduism has been described as generally not producing 'dreams of blissful utopias'.[3] The case for discounting a Chinese utopianism seems to be weaker *prima facie*. But as far as the possibility of a more universal, extra-European concept of utopia is concerned, the focus must rest principally on examination of relatively advanced non-European civilizations that have extensive literary traditions and complex political histories. Primitive societies have far less need for the concept of utopia because they already possess the prerequisites for an ordered, utopian-style existence.

Primitive peoples live, so to speak, in their own golden age, and to be nostalgic about the present would be paradoxical. Their land has not yet been stolen by aristocrats or overrun by sheep. Their priests and fathers have not yet been deposed. Such societies provide discernible utopic spaces and events in terms of communal living arrangements, feasts, dancing, rituals, religious ceremonies, processions and observances. The great ancient religious monuments of the world, such as Stonehenge, Angkor Wat, Easter Island and the Acropolis, still evoke this sense of sacred space. Parallels to the Roman festival of Saturnalia have been found in the Ainu festival of the bear and the

Sultan Muhammad, 'The Prophet's Ascension', *c.* 1540, from the *Khamsa of Nizami* (1539–43, Tabriz). During the *Miraj* (the Prophet Mohammed's ascent into paradise), he was led by the angel Gabriel and mounted on Buraq, his human-headed horse.

Hindu celebration of Holi, among many examples. Aboriginal concepts of time and space may also encompass a more communal idea of the cosmos. In their 'Dreamtime', for example, native Australians exhibit a seamless connection between the creation, daily existence and the afterlife, in which the dead continue a stewardship over the living. Individuals in such societies usually suffer far less alienation and isolation from the group, with patriarchal government by elders (generally men) assisting obedience to custom. Historians in the 17th and 18th centuries often believed that most, if not all, primitive societies possessed some form of communal property. Many later writers, such as Lewis Henry Morgan in *Ancient Society* (1877), also described the slow emergence of inheritance in land from tribal ownership and the avoidance of individual ownership of houses or lands throughout the Americas;[4] as did Karl Marx, when he explained the 'Asiatic Mode of Production' as the first major stage of property.[5] In the 16th century such forms of society were often conceived to define the heart of the utopian enterprise, and in this sense utopia is itself born of a non-European source.

Most non-Christian accounts of the origins of the cosmos overlap with images of a semi-mythical golden age or ideal past. Various sources of the Christian creation myth are themselves 'non-Western', or at least 'pre-Western', as in the Sumerian classic, the *Epic of Gilgamesh*, which recounts the exploration of the underworld in a manner later taken up by Homer, Ovid and others. The classic Egyptian account of the afterlife, the *Book of the Dead*, dates from around 1400 BC and describes how the spirit of the deceased is thought to wander the corridors of the underworld until it is brought before Osiris, god of the dead, who judges former sins.

Variations on heaven and hell also exist in Norse, Native American, Islamic, Hindu and other traditions. Most of these depict the inhabitants of the afterlife as either gods themselves, or hero-figures in earthly life who have earned their just

OPPOSITE This Mughal miniature, attributed to Govardhan and dating to *c.* 1635, depicts the spring festival of Holi being celebrated during the reign of Emperor Jahangir and his favourite wife, Noor Jahan.

BELOW Detail of the *Book of the Dead*, Papyrus of Hirweben, Thebes, 21st Dynasty, 1075–945 BC. Overseen by the two protective Eyes of Horus, the sun's rays illuminate a solar barque, and then the mummy lying underneath. The *Book of the Dead* was intended to assist the deceased in making the transition to the afterlife.

Buddha in Nirvana, Tibet, 18th century. *Nirvana* is described as a state of the 'highest happiness', in which karmic rebirth has been surpassed, and the individual is free from desire, anger and other disturbances.

rewards or, more democratically, people whose moral worth merits eternal beatitude. Heaven is often high above the clouds but may lie across the seas; hell is usually beneath the earth. Native Americans typically portray the afterlife in terms of bountiful hunting grounds, but there is sometimes mention of resurrection and the re-creation of a peaceful community on Earth. In Norse mythology the magnificent hall of Valhalla is home to the chief god Odin and the resting place of dead warriors; ordinary beings reside in other heavenly mansions that are accessed from Earth via the red band of the rainbow. In Hinduism virtuous souls exist forever, in the company of Vishnu, in a heavenly state among the stars after having achieved *nirvana* (enlightenment). In Buddhism several forms of afterlife, including punishment for evil-

doers and a state of bliss for the virtuous, temporarily interrupt the process of karmic rebirth, which results from past deeds. In the lower levels of some Buddhist versions of heaven, carnal desires may be sated.

Chinese Daoism sometimes describes a Pure Land where pain is unknown. In this faith the search for a balance between positive and negative forces, or yin and yang, particularly through the practice of virtue and harmony with nature, certainly evokes utopic qualities. In the Islamic paradise, *houris*, or attendant virgins, await the hero's command and the virtuous dead are permitted resurrection prior to divine judgment. Satan also exists in the form of Iblis in the Islamic holy book, the Quran, where he is expelled from paradise, tempts believers from the course of true duty and offers constant torments in hell for the damned, though some are permitted purification and a possible entry to paradise.[6] In the Quran there is a description of paradise as a garden, similar to that in parts of the Christian Bible, and the promise of unbounded wealth without labour, of gold, pearls and silk, good and bountiful food without end, and perpetual youth, with a day of judgment and resurrection of the dead.

In Celtic mythology, the Otherworld served as a halfway house prior to reincarnation, while the Land of Life, or Tir-na-nóg, was one of the realms of permanent afterlife. Here, too, every 31 October (now celebrated as Hallowe'en or All Hallow's Eve) the dead were permitted to haunt those who had wronged them on Earth. In many portrayals of the afterlife, corporeal corruption following death is reversed at an appointed time of resurrection.

It is evident, therefore, that none of the grand themes of European paganism and Christianity that flow into utopianism and provide its mythical basis, lacks a parallel in non-Western traditions. The claim that 'non-Western' or non-Christian utopianism does not exist appears to rest largely on the assumption that a chiefly non-religious, often literary

This 16th-century illuminated Islamic manuscript depicts angels paying homage to Adam, as observed by Iblis, or Shaytan, the Devil. The Quran describes man as created out of clay, and the Devil out of 'smokeless fire'.

Confucius (left) with the Daoist Laozi and a Buddhist arhat

Confucius (551–479 BC)

Best known of the ancient Chinese philosophers, and founder of the system known as Confucianism, which has dominated Chinese official and administrative thinking through much of the country's history, Confucius was born to a poor family in Lu state, in the province today known as Shandong. He married at nineteen, and was employed as a minor official. Moving to Qi in 517 BC, he gained some success as a teacher, then for some fourteen years wandered from state to state seeking patronage. At the age of sixty-seven he returned to Lu, where he died five years later.

The chief collection of his teachings, *The Analects of Confucius*, was compiled by his followers and published after his death. Two of his most famous later disciples were the philosophers Mencius and Xunzi. Confucius's system focused on the need to return to what he saw as the pure values of past traditions and customs. Though associated with the promotion of ritual, rote learning and memorization, and giving great emphasis to filial piety and submission to parental authority, Confucianism also enjoined a sense of responsibility on the part of the ruler towards the populace.

component did not emerge outside Christian Europe to any marked degree in an independent manner prior to the impact of European thought on the non-European world.

Nonetheless, it is sometimes conceded that virtually every major strand of non-European political thought possesses some utopic elements, or an account of an ideal society, and that this often has secular rather than religious foundations and includes some concept of a lost golden age of justice and virtue. This is notably the case in China. *The Analects of Confucius* propose a harmonious society where rulers enforce justice, subjects pay taxes, authority and age are revered, and ritual observance of the principles of order and the will of heaven binds society together. Writers such as Mozi indicated the heightened virtue and wise policies of 'the sage kings of ancient times'.[7] Confucius's ideals were officially adopted by various Chinese emperors from 206 BC onwards, and Neoconfucianism was reinforced thereafter at various points in Chinese history before being virtually eradicated under Mao Zedung. As Zhang Longxi has argued, Confucianism was not only a consciously secular tradition, subordinating concern for the afterlife to the search for good order in this. It also idealized the ancient kingdom of Zhou under King Wen, which Confucius sought to emulate by means of both individual and collective moral self-rectification.[8] Mencius, among others, embellished this ideal, envisioning a 'humane government' in which the people were well clothed and fed, the young nurtured and educated, and the elderly sustained. Laozi's description of Daoist beliefs also referred to an ideal past, before warfare and poverty became overwhelming.

In the early modern period, particularly in China, the fusion of Confucian, Daoist and Buddhist philosophies also produced literary utopianism. Among the better-known texts is Tao Yuanming's *Peach Blossom Spring* (c. AD 400), famous for its description of a hidden community of peace and harmony. This was echoed in Wang Wei's *The Ballad of Peach Blossom Spring* (8th century) and in the even more daring 11th-century work of the same title by Wang Anshi, which imagines a community organized on the basis of kinship, without any hierarchy between ruler and ruled. A later example, Li Ruzhen's *The Mirror of Flowers* (1828), is notable for its depiction of female rulership.[9] The work of Kang Youwei and other 20th-century Chinese intellectuals was based on the concept of *datong*, or grand harmony, which was thought to be rooted in a real, pre-Confucian ideal past (c. 2300 BC), a time when communal property was the norm and 'possessions were used, but not hoarded for selfish reasons'.[10]

Sichang Wang's Song Dynasty painting, *Peach Blossom Spring* (c. 1531), illustrates the fisherman Tao's rural idyll in the mountains. In the poem and story he unfortunately mentions its existence, and is consequently never able to return to it.

The notion of an ideal, wise ruler is described in the Dharmashastra tradition within Hinduism, part of which passed into Buddhism. Once supposed (often in contrast to ancient Greece) to rest solely on a religious and metaphysical foundation, Hinduism is now believed to have produced a 'realist' wing, as exemplified in the writings of Kautilya (*c.* 300 BC), who is often likened to Machiavelli. The endorsement of a divine origin for the caste system in Hinduism can certainly be seen as a priests' and warriors' utopia, a fantasy of power that has proved to be the most successful of all fixed status systems.[11] Unlike most religions, Buddhism, founded by Siddhartha Gautama (*c.* 563–*c.* 400 BC), though originating in part as a reform movement within Hinduism, does not enjoin belief in any gods. It portrays earthly life as dominated by suffering, which originates in desire. According to this tradition, freedom from *karma* (the process of continual rebirth that results from past actions) can be achieved by *nirvana* (enlightenment) or through *moksha*, salvation by integration of the individual into the cosmic whole. (The Buddhist notion of *nirvana* is equivalent to the Christian idea of epiphany, or illumination by divine light.) Buddhism enjoins the peaceful spread of such beliefs and practices in this life. Its utopic qualities include a powerful monastic tradition, with strong injunctions to charity, and the assumption of the attainment of a substantial degree of inner as well as communal harmony in this life. Rulers are enjoined to justice and peace. In Japan, aspects of Daoism, Confucianism and Buddhism were filtered through the indigenous belief-system of Shintoism to provide a series of powerful images of the cosmos, including a golden age, visions of the ideal state and a paradise beyond the sea known as Tokoyo no Kuni (The Eternal Country), whose inhabitants never die. The ideal land in turn became fused with the mythology of the first divine emperor and with concepts of the final resting place of the dead. From the late 19th century onwards Western utopianism made a considerable impact on Japanese thought, producing, it has been argued, a distinctive and enthusiastic engagement with the futurological aspects of the genre.[12]

Islam has also produced idealized images of the polity.[13] Some of these are based on concepts of the rule of Sharia law as personifying good order and religious observance. Islamic utopianism has not generally utilized imaginary travel accounts or fantastic ideal societies to depict such ideals, though the collection of folk tales known as *The Thousand and One Nights, or Arabian Nights Entertainments*, first collected around the 9th century, has utopic elements. Islam has focused instead on the first Caliphate in Medina (632–34) as the most just and egalitarian period in its history, and thus the golden age of Islamic polity. This 'Utopian vision of enormous influence' and 'great emotive power'[14] became a major source for later fundamentalist aspirations, and was followed in importance by the Umayyad Caliphate (661–750). The mechanisms of social control proposed in various Islamic texts parallel those that can be identified with Christian European utopianism. Most notably, the injunction against usury in the Quran as a means of suppressing social inequality has remained profoundly important in differentiating Islamic perceptions of modernization from those rooted in Western capitalism.

The most important theorist of the ideal Islamic society, Abu Nasr al-Farabi described 'The Virtuous City' (*c.* 940) as exhibiting 'most excellent good and the utmost perfection', chiefly by promoting mutual co-operation, justice and proportionate equality.[15] Al-Farabi upheld the regulation of employment, supporting doctors and the very ill alike

Abu Nasr al-Farabi (*c.* 870–950)

The early origins of this Islamic philosopher and interpreter of Plato and Aristotle, sometimes referred to as the 'second teacher' after Aristotle himself, are disputed. He may have been a soldier's son of Turkish origin, and was possibly born in Wasij in Turkestan. He was long resident in Baghdad; early employed as a day labourer, he was self-educated, studying Islamic jurisprudence and music. He eventually moved in high court circles in Aleppo, and died in Damascus. He became thoroughly acquainted with the major Greek philosophers and their subsequent interpreters, possibly studying in Constantinople, then going to Egypt. His interest in mathematics led to commentaries on Euclid and Ptolemy, and he wrote extensively on music. His chief philosophic work was *The Philosophy of Plato and Aristotle*, a commentary that included a wider study of Plato's *Laws* and Aristotle's *Nicomachean Ethics*. Al-Farabi is usually described as the first Islamic thinker to confront the challenge of philosophy to religious orthodoxy, indeed to subordinate religion to philosophy, and is often viewed as the founder of Islamic political philosophy as such, through his focus on the effects of the secular organization of the city upon the happiness of its citizens.

from public funds, and the cultivation of enlightened, philosophic rulers whose moral achievements could enable them to live without doctors or judges. (An antinomian strain would characterize some other forms of Islamic utopianism as well.) Later writers such as Ibn Sina (Avicenna, 979–1037) enjoined government to banish idleness and unemployment, abolish gambling and usury, and regulate marriage and child-rearing. Many Muslim societies retained public landownership, and though a growth in the idea of fixed social ranks became increasingly common after around 1000 throughout the Islamic world,[16] such measures can be seen as indicative of one form of Islamic utopianism.

As discussed, many non-Western ideals rest upon some conception of a past or lost golden age (for instance, the Krita Yuga or first epoch of perfection in Hinduism), or a state of nature (sometimes conceived largely negatively, as for Kautilya) and/or of the ideal law ('Dharma', as exemplified in the *Laws of Manu*; 'Li' in Confucianism; the 'Dao' in Daoism). Many use myths or epic tales to describe this past: the Hindu

sacred text the *Mahabharata* refers to the Vedic ages, while Aztec priests sang of Tulan, from which their race sprang, a 'land abounding with limpid emeralds, turquoises, gold, and silver',[17] where food grew of its own accord.

Today, some still propose returning to a reconstructed ideal of this past. In the modern period, in face of modernization, urbanization, individualism, the eradication of traditional forms of authority and the generally bewildering onslaught of Western culture, the appeal to renew declining patriarchal and religious authority may be considerable. Groups like the Taliban in Pakistan and Afghanistan may relatively easily portray themselves as the party of virtue in the face of regimes widely perceived to be corrupt, and in addition backed by 'infidel' foreigners. Injunctions to restore the Caliphate are warmly heeded by those to whom regimes in Washington or Kabul offer little or nothing. The reward for so doing may often be described in terms of paradise, but it is equally often perceived more tangibly as the renewal of community, sometimes conceived locally, as often, particularly in an era of post-communist, anti-imperialist nationalism, as a community of believers. Their 'principles, honor, and purity', to give one description, are contrasted (in the words of Osama bin Laden) with 'the immoral acts of fornication, homosexuality, intoxicants, gambling, and usury' indicative of a Western outlook.[18] They may demand or aspire to a return to an international *status quo ante*, or earlier state of affairs – in some cases stretching back centuries.

Such examples indicate a revival of utopian aspiration in non-Christian traditions that increased markedly in the 19th century, in much the same way as European utopianism arose partly in response to the decline of more egalitarian and communal forms of peasant proprietorship and their replacement by a more merciless, large-scale, export-driven feudalism. Chiliastic movements of resistance to imperialism were common from the 18th century onwards. In 1781 a messianic Peruvian *mestizo*, José Gabriel Condorcanqui, claimed to be a lost Incan king and led a rebellion of thousands against Spanish rule. In Africa, the Mahdi opposed British rule in the Sudan against the background of a resurgence of fundamentalism, condemning religious decadence as 'due to a luxurious mode of life and contact with Christians.'[19] The late 19th-century Native American invention of the 'Ghost Dance' as a means of countering white expansionism invoked a lost age of plenty. Maori resistance to British incursions sometimes assumed similar forms. The Indian Mutiny (1857–58) had a 'revitalizing' utopian element.[20] In China, the Taiping Rebellion (1851–64) and Boxer Rebellion (1900–1) also resolutely pitted an image of China's past against Western imperialist occupation.[21] In the 20th century Ayatollah Khomeini's vision of post-revolutionary Iran was associated with similar ideals.

Many of these movements are sometimes described in terms of 'millenarianism'. But they clearly also possess utopic elements in the sense of visualizing a pre-imperial past when indigenous peoples retained control over their lands and destinies. Anti-colonial revolutionary movements often produced utopian impulses, sometimes, as in the case of Frantz Fanon, intimately linked to ideas of racial identity, especially of negritude; to ideas of Afrocentric essentialism; or to memories, real or phantom, of a lost regime of village or tribal democracy, or of a harmonious engagement with nature. Specific visions of African socialism have been proposed by Julius Nyerere, Léopold Senghor and Aimé Césaire, among others.[22] Post-colonial literatures, too, sometimes echo such concerns. In Africa, for example, a variety of works, including Ben Okri's *Astonishing the Gods* (1995), focus on such themes.[23]

In the 20th century, by far the most important such anti-imperial vision was that provided by the Indian leader Mohandas Gandhi, whose prolonged campaigns to secure equal rights and to resist British occupation were crucial to securing India's independence in 1948. Gandhi was influenced by the non-violent approach to resistance of Tolstoy and others, as well as by Hindu ideas of the golden age. His image of India's future was often resolutely anti-modern, relying on a proposed rejuvenation of the 700,000 villages that then composed the nation, which were to become self-sufficient, and reinforcing the traditional framework of village councils that provided order at the local level. Regarding private property as a trust held by its owners, Gandhi proposed that the wealthy should utilize only what they required, administering the remainder in the interests of the community, with inheritance being limited. Heavy industry was to be nationalized and owned by the state, as was the land. Here anarchist decentralization and socialistic ownership and management policies thus co-existed cheek by jowl.

To what extent, then, do such concepts echo or mirror the utopianism explored so far in this book? Idealized kingship or theocracy are not 'utopian' as such. Nor is the wish or hope for improvement, despite efforts to define utopianism simply as a desire for a better life, which have been used to argue for the universality of the utopian concept.[24] Religion, conceived as the search for both salvation in the afterlife and perfectibility in this, needs to be distinguished from the quest for utopia in principle. But utilizing idealized versions of the past points in a more utopian direction. According to this view, utopia does not rest on a Christian basis, or upon any idea of paradise as such, but upon a concept of property and society, indeed a particular construction of the communal, in which poverty and scarcity are avoided by restricting inequality, greed and injustice. Thus many pre-modern societies already possess substantial utopian elements. From this perspective, then, rather than from that of any universality of a desire for improvement as such, the utopian construct is indisputably a global one.

Mohandas Gandhi (1869–1948)

Often known by his honorific, Mahatma ('Great soul'), this Indian political leader and social reformer is usually considered responsible for engineering India's independence from Britain in 1948. Born the son of the chief minister of Porbandar in northern India, he was educated locally until in 1888 he moved to Britain to study law; he was called to the bar in 1891. Unable to obtain work in India, he moved to South Africa, where he lived until 1914 and became active in opposing racial discrimination against Indians. Increasingly religious in orientation, Gandhi came to describe his views in terms of an ideal named *satyagraha*, or 'truth force', which involved, in practical terms, non-violent resistance to oppression and unjust laws, self-renunciation, and the acceptance of suffering on the part of the resister. From his return to India in 1915, his policies of non-cooperation included strikes, resistance to taxation, fasting and marches, culminating in the Quit India movement (1942). Gandhi was assassinated in 1948 in Delhi by a young Hindu fanatic.

Chapter 4

A Genre Defined

Thomas More's Utopia

The mystery of Thomas More's *Utopia* has entranced generations of readers since the book's first appearance in Latin at Louvain, Belgium, in 1516 (English translation, 1551). The very title of the work was a pun on two words: *eutopia*, 'good place' and *utopia*, 'no place' (the first Italian edition was entitled *Eutopia*). Since the publication of the book, the word 'utopia' has become synonymous with paradise, the ideal, the unrealistic and unattainable. Luminaries such as John Ruskin have described More's work as 'perhaps the most really mischievous book ever written'.[1] But the tradition established by the text, or at least reinterpreted by it, in fact represents not the perfect society, only a radically improved one. This means that however greater order and improved morals are achieved (which is chiefly by enforcing equality and community of property), human behaviour is not portrayed as being so substantially modified as to be unbelievable. Utopia thus constrains rather than abolishes vice. It recognizes, but resists, the possibility of decadence and moral degeneration. Crime and criminals persist, even if, as portrayed by More, the fetters worn by offenders are made of gold. 'Utopia' in this understanding is not about perfectibility, which, as already discussed, can be relegated as a quasi-theological category to millenarianism and other fantastic sub-genres of the imaginary or ideal society. Utopia remains attainable, indeed has in some senses been attained, though the price exacted may be one many are unwilling to pay.[2]

The narrative takes the form of a three-way conversation between 'More' himself, his friend Peter Giles and a traveller, Raphael Hythlodaeus, or Hythloday (the name in Greek implies a 'recounter of nonsense'). Hythloday has recently returned from travels in the new world, where he accompanied the Italian explorer Amerigo Vespucci,

Hand-coloured woodcut version of the frontispiece of Thomas More's *Utopia*, 1516. One of the most iconic of all images of utopianism, it depicts the island described in More's definitive text as a balance of isolation and good order.

spending five years on the island of Utopia. He appears to uphold ideals of natural human goodness, rationality and the possibility of planning a good society. But both the narrator and More infuse elements of doubt, scepticism and satire into such assumptions. More's 'real' intentions, then, are left in some doubt, and many a reader emerges from the text uncertain as to what has been recommended and what has been satirized.

But a social critique is undoubtedly offered in *Utopia*. The immediate context for More's text was the displacement of thousands of peasants from small farms in order to make way for large-scale sheep farming.[3] The result was increasing unemployment and rising food prices. The rural poor were forced to wander the countryside begging. The wealthy and their town-dwelling dependents, waxing in luxury and growing increasingly idle, heaped ever crueller punishments on the poor to restrain their resistance to change (including imprisonment for vagrancy). Their own morals were degenerating, particularly with the proliferation of gambling, brothels and alehouses. More was clearly alarmed at these developments and observed that 'it would have been much better to provide some means of getting a living, that no one should be under this terrible necessity first of stealing and then of dying for it'.[4] The key question is whether he intended the social and

Thomas More (1477–1535)

The consummate English Renaissance scholar and humanist, and a leading political figure of his time, Thomas More is the central figure in the history of utopian thought. Born in London on 7 February 1477, he studied classical languages and law, and considered the priesthood, living for two years among Franciscan friars. In 1516 he journeyed to Bruges on a diplomatic mission and met Peter Giles, friend of Erasmus, in conversation with whom he conceived the dialogue that would emerge as *Utopia*. The text functions as a critique of the growing contemporary oppression of the poor, but More left doubts, by challenging key facets of utopian life, such as community of goods, as to whether he actually subscribed to Utopia's central ideals or thought them practicable in the England of his day. He later wrote, though did not finish, a history of King Richard III, and became a member of parliament and, in 1529, lord chancellor. Although he was a close associate of King Henry VIII, Henry's divorce from Catherine of Aragon occasioned a breach between the two. More was tried for treason and beheaded on 6 July 1535.

LEFT Map of Utopia, c. 1595, by Abraham Ortelius, the Flemish cartographer and geographer who is usually regarded as the creator of the first modern atlas, and the first to conceive that the continents had once been joined.

BELOW The chief economic and social context underlying More's *Utopia* was the displacement of thousands of peasants to make way for sheep-farming. Here, illustrating the text of Psalm 94, a ploughing team is portrayed, the man leading the horse being followed by a slinger to frighten the crows (c. 1325).

political structure described in the text to be a realistic solution to the problem, or whether he thought such a solution unattainable, and even regarded the evils of England as irremediable. The ambiguity present in these alternatives has bedevilled generations of readers.

Hythloday recounts the discovery of an extraordinary crescent-shaped island republic some 200 miles (320 km) broad. Established by a conquering king, Utopus, around 1,700 years earlier, and guided by the principle of living according to nature, it exhibits all of the characteristics of 'the best state of a commonwealth'. The population is evenly distributed across the nation in fifty-four city-states, 'all spacious and magnificent, identical in language, traditions, customs,

and laws', and 'similar also in layout and everywhere, as far as the nature of the ground permits, similar even in appearance'.[5] They are separated by no more than a day's journey on foot.

The cities in Utopia are uniform in design and appearance. Flat-roofed houses are built of stone or brick to a height of three storeys, with luxuriant gardens behind. The cultivation of these gardens was one of the greatest pleasures of the Utopians; the image of the garden as utopic space would thereafter grow ever more powerful. Individual households are not allowed to accumulate wealth, and houses are exchanged by lot every ten years. Streets are wide, and cities are divided into four quarters, each containing its own store, market, meeting hall and hospital, where free public healthcare is provided. The capital, Amaurotum (recognizably modelled on London), is fortified.

In the cities, Utopian households are governed by the eldest member of the family. Families are entitled to take whatever goods they require from public storehouses. Dining is communal, with refectories serving thirty families at a sitting: private dining, although allowed, is usually considered inferior in quality. Women do the cooking, helped by slaves, and wait on their husbands. Children assist their parents. Mealtimes involve music and conversation, and are followed by games and reading.

The economic system of Utopia is organized centrally. All citizens pursue agriculture, with each person also learning another skill (usually in wool, linen, metalwork or carpentry). Most follow the trades of their fathers, though transfer is possible. Women generally engage in lighter occupations. The working day is six hours long, and leisure is plentiful. In the cities, produce is delivered to one of four markets. In the country, farms consist of some forty labourers (and two serfs or slaves) sent in rotation from the cities for two years' service. Those who enjoy rural life may remain longer. (More does not force the view that life in the city may be superior to life in the country.) Delegates from each farm are sent to the cities on an annual basis to learn the latest agricultural techniques. Two years' supply of food is maintained at public expense to safeguard against famine. Equality of distribution ensures that everyone receives plentiful supplies. At harvest time citizens emerge from the cities to reap crops. Farms generally produce a surplus of grain and cattle, which is given away, without exchange, just as goods needed from the city are provided freely. One seventh of exported foodstuffs are reserved for the poor of the receiving country. Such regulation of the market goes beyond medieval ideas of the 'just price', the restraint of usury, a measure of contempt for covetousness, and a promotion of the need to subordinate commerce to other social

Illustration of blacksmiths at work, mid-14th century, from a treatise on the Signs of the Zodiac, southern Netherlands. From More's time onwards, utopianism was often associated with a more equitable distribution of work, and in particular the sharing of manual labour and abolition of idleness.

ends, but not so far as to be unrecognizable or foolishly extreme; the imaginative distance to later generations, and to us, of course, is proportionately much greater. Nonetheless most of More's contemporaries presumed that community of property as a universal principle had only suited humankind before the Fall.

The political system of Utopia is essentially democratic. Farms are ruled by a master and a mistress, 'serious in mind and ripe in years'. Each year, groups of families choose an official, a 'phylarch', whose chief task is to curtail idleness. Ten such magistrates are ruled by a 'tranibore', who is also elected annually but not usually removed. Three citizens are sent from each city every year to Amaurotum, where a deliberative assembly is held.

Hythloday and More agree that Plato's ideal of the philosopher-king would be the best form of government. Yet Utopia is no tyranny: its leader serves the people, rather than the reverse; republican virtue seems to prevail, with minimal loss of liberty. A total of two hundred magistrates elect by secret ballot, from a list of four candidates provided by the citizens, a governor deemed 'most useful'. He holds office for life, unless suspected of tyranny, and is mandated to uphold simplicity – a mere sheaf of grain is carried before him to denote his office. Much of the burden of government consists in transferring surpluses in some districts to mitigate scarcities in others.

The legal process is simple. Trials are conducted by a judge and the parties to the case; lawyers do not exist at all. Gambling is proscribed. Permission to travel, though restricted by a system of internal passports, is readily granted but is limited by the need to work when resident longer than a day anywhere. Wandering idly without permission is punished. The death penalty is enforced for those who attempt to usurp power, but the usual punishment for serious crimes is slavery. Slaves perform heavy labour as well as some special tasks, such as the slaughtering of animals, which Utopians find distasteful.

Utopian society is well ordered. The regime's central principle is to place life before work and to ensure that 'as much time as possible should be withdrawn from the service of the body and devoted to the freedom and culture of the mind'.[6] Instructive amusements, such as public lectures, frequently occupy several hours a day. Although there is a surplus of goods, great variety is unknown, and 'vain and superfluous' crafts are considered to minister 'only to luxury and licentiousness', as evident in societies in which 'money is the standard of everything'.[7] Clothing is simple and durable, and is differentiated only between the married and unmarried. It consists of a leather working costume covered by a woollen cloak. Utopians do not attempt to 'excel others by superfluous display of possessions', nor do they 'pay…divine honors to the rich'. Such behaviour is unknown in the fictional state.[8]

Women may marry at eighteen and men at twenty-two. Prospective marriage partners are allowed to view one another naked to inspect for abnormalities. Divorce is permitted, but adultery is punished by the strictest form of slavery. Surplus children are given to childless couples, and new colonies remove any pressure of overpopulation. Here Plato's scheme of community of wives for the ruling caste is prominently rejected.

According to Utopian philosophy, pleasure is the 'whole or the chief part of human happiness'. Its pursuit is limited by religious injunctions on extravagant self-indulgence, which reduce aspiration to what is 'good and decent'. Religious practice is left broadly private, and a variety of sects exists, but the more extreme are the most devoted to hard labour. All share in the worship of one God, Mithras, and all are expected to believe in the immortality of the soul. Women may become priests. Knowledge of the classics, particularly Greek philosophy and history, is well established. Public hospitals, plentiful common meals and relative freedom of movement seem to ensure widespread content. People are said to be 'easygoing, good-tempered, ingenious, and leisure-loving'. The price to be paid for this appears to be the renunciation of vice. There is:

> …nowhere any pretext to evade work – no
> wine shop, no alehouse, no brothel anywhere,
> no opportunity for corruption, no lurking

Certain types of work were reserved for slaves in More's *Utopia*, such as the slaughter of animals, here illustrated in an early 16th-century manuscript illumination from the *Livre d'heures de la vierge* showing the killing of a pig.

hole, no secret meeting place. On the contrary, being under the eyes of all, people are bound either to be performing the usual labor or to be enjoying their leisure in a fashion not without decency.[9]

In Utopia kings do not hoard gold, and there is a general ethos of equality. But it is not a perfect society. Crime, idleness and the desire for luxury, although rare, do exist. Slavery is constrained but remains essential to Utopian ease. War also takes place, sometimes to overthrow despots in other lands (indeed, tyrannicide is actively encouraged). If the population grows too large, people are sent to establish utopian colonies on the nearby mainland. Once there, if the original inhabitants 'refuse to live according to their laws, they drive [them] from the territory… If they resist, they wage war against them.' The Utopians consider it a 'just cause for war when a people which does not use its soil but keeps it idle and waste nevertheless forbids the use and possession of it to others who by the rule of nature ought to be maintained by it'.[10] This imperialist tendency could be viewed as one of *Utopia*'s most significant weaknesses: similar justifications would underpin widespread European domination over indigenous peoples for the next five centuries.[11]

How should we interpret this central, definitive text to which generations of readers have returned in search of an answer to the problem of how to construct the ideal society? Utopia is clearly

Frontispiece engraving from the 1518 edition of *Utopia*, showing a garden scene with, from left to right, the servant John Clement, Raphael Hythlodaeus (Hythloday), Thomas More and Peter Giles. Much of More's text assumes the form of a conversation between the author himself and key figures in his social circle.

intended to be contrasted to the England of More's day, where the enclosure of land in particular was causing widespread unemployment and social upheaval. But is the text a critique? A recipe? A lament? A satire? No single narrative perspective within *Utopia* is given greater authority than any other. This encourages the reader to attend to the various arguments presented. Even when Hythloday recommends that all nations adopt the rule of the Utopians, we are left in some doubt as to the wisdom of his enthusiastic outburst; the level-headed More seems to be the corrective to his radical idealism. So when Hythloday insists that communism alone can permit justice and happiness to flourish, More responds that without the hope of individual gain, men will become lazy. Some critics believe this to be his most persuasive objection to the Utopian constitution.[12] We trust Peter Giles, of whom we are told that 'no one is less given to deceit'.[13] But even if the Utopian commonwealth is the 'best state' possible, this does not mean that all might or could adopt it. It is the manners of the Utopians that make their constitution workable. Nonetheless, More portrays the Utopians as pagan, even if they seem to practise a purer Christianity, and act with greater reasonableness, than most. But did More expect his contemporaries to be capable of such standards of behaviour? He recognized that 'pride is too deeply fixed in men to be easily plucked out', and that although the Utopian commonwealth was undoubtedly desirable, introducing it anywhere would be problematic at best.[14] The last lines of *Utopia* are More's wistful, if enigmatic, reflection that, although he cannot agree with everything that has been said, 'I readily admit that there are very many features in the Utopian commonwealth which it is easier for me to wish for in our countries than to have any hope of seeing realized.'[15]

The central issue in *Utopia* is the problem of poverty and how to solve it. And here, it is safe to say, More expressed his own deep, personal concerns. As its leading interpreters have stressed, *Utopia* was clearly indebted to a humanist tradition of advising Christian princes as to their moral responsibilities. And stringent penalties were not uncommon where the capacity for self- or communal regulation seems to have been doubted. In Johann Eberlein von Günzburg's *Wolfaria* (1521), for example, drunkards are to be drowned and adulterers publicly executed.[16] The key question is not More's sympathy, but his apparent proposed solution: a 'common life and subsistence – without any exchange of money' – a practice he may have believed existed in more primitive parts of the world, particularly in the Americas. More has also been linked to the tradition of Christian communalism. His friend Erasmus, who supervised the first, Latin, edition of *Utopia*, was acquainted with Waldensian and other medieval communistical experiments. Thomas Münzer knew of Plato, and *Utopia* was discussed by the Anabaptists. Nineteenth-century communists, such as Karl Kautsky, also recognized the obvious links between their early-modern predecessors and their own movement, and particularly the Paris Commune of 1871. They believed that More's 'socialism made him immortal'[17] by virtue of his recognition that equality was the basis of a well-governed state. But More also became a Catholic saint, and to his orthodox interpreters this is heresy.

Utopia is sometimes taken to be a quintessentially 'humanist' text. More's 'pity for the undeserved misery of the exploited poor', in one account, balanced by a typically Renaissance humanist response that their condition might by remedied by human effort, produced 'an

Loyset Liedet, *Feast in Honour of the Marriage of Regnault de Montauban to Clarisse, his Bride*, 1470. Marriage was a key theme in More's text. Most European marriages in this period were arranged, not made from free choice.

apocalyptic vision of the best earthly state possible – Utopia'.[18] In this view, the text lies within a clearly discernible Renaissance revival of thinking about the ideal city-state.[19] But, if so, why the jokes and irony? And, if so, More may still not have believed that people could modify their behaviour sufficiently to practise Utopian norms: the example of Jesus was, after all, not sufficient to make all people good Christians.

Utopia does, then, portray one image of the best life, though it is not necessarily one More thought most humans could emulate. And if the text is not, fundamentally, intended as both serious social criticism and the provision of a remedy, but is a satirical *jeu d'esprit*, wherein lies its hope? In the afterlife? If Plutarch, Plato, Christian communalism and indigenous American custom provide the substantive constitution of the Utopians, are not the Aristotelian and other criticisms of the viability of communism compelling, and aimed to convince? Plato's communism had only been elitist; Christ's, too, had been bounded by the circle of his disciples. That of the Utopians is universal. Did More intend this to be an obvious violation of one potentially acceptable norm? Erasmus thought Utopia a 'holy commonwealth' that all Christians should imitate. More also viewed Utopia as a speculative exercise in exploring how a society based on friendship might operate. In this view, the text is essentially a defence of some monastic and some Platonic ideals and practices, but not a recommendation that they were nationally applicable in any other than an ethical sense. Most commentators have concluded that the widened communism lauded in *Utopia* was thought by More only to be suitable to a state of grace. The correct moral answer to society's problems does not provide the correct social and economic answers. Mercy and charity are suitable to this life, complete happiness only to the next. More becomes a great Catholic rather than, as for Karl Kautsky, a great communist.[20] But this interpretation will not suit all readers. Like Utopia itself, More remains an enigmatic, perplexing figure, rich in suggestion, in ambiguity, pointing towards doubt, but also towards promise, hope and faith. The debate goes on…but the enormous, tantalizing influence of his vision, at least, remains undisputed.

Portrait by Hans Holbein the Younger (1523) of More's close friend, the famed Dutch Renaissance priest, theologian and humanist, Erasmus, who was the author of *The Education of a Christian Prince*, also published in 1516, another text in the 'best commonwealth' tradition.

Paradise Found?

Voyages of Discovery to the New World and Beyond

A s any tourist knows, a worthy voyage is a mixture of fantasy, anticipation and delight in the discovery of novelty. And the more exotic the better, as far as both adventure and bookselling are concerned. To Europeans, until relatively recently, even the known world was enchanted – that is, inhabited by gods, elves, fairies, leprechauns, trolls, spirits of nature and fabled creatures. These beings not only threatened unknown horrors but also, occasionally, held out the promise of untold blessings, like a crock of gold at the end of a rainbow. The unknown world has always suggested still more wonders, and has been the subject of innumerable projections and fantasies. The mythical, fabulous or extraordinary voyage is nearly as old as travel itself, and the lines between religious narrative, legend, fantasy, mariner's tale and downright lie are often impossible to draw.[1] Pilgrims, who formed a substantial portion of medieval travellers, set off on their journeys brimming with expectation and assumption. They believed they would encounter the marvellous in some form, either on reaching the Holy Land or on their way there. Many still thought that the Garden of Eden was physically located somewhere on Earth, perhaps awaiting rediscovery.

They also continued to suppose that distant, unknown places were not necessarily inhabited by beings resembling themselves. Dystopian spaces have thus often lurked on imaginary maps, holding out the prospect of terror to unwary travellers. Sir John Mandeville's *Travels,* a composite of earlier fantastic voyages, published in 1499 but written in the mid-14th century, reported the existence of peoples with eyes in their shoulders and others who walked on their hands or had only one foot, albeit large enough to provide shade.[2] The 9th-century *Book of Diverse Types of Monsters* described headless creatures on an island in Egypt whose senses were attached to their bodies. Such monsters and

This detail from a 15th-century illuminated manuscript shows Marco Polo setting sail from Venice in 1271. His twenty-four-year journey, taking him as far as China, was recounted in *The Travels of Marco Polo*, commonly known as *Il Milione*.

'monster-lands', as Shaftesbury later termed them, would remain a staple of travel narratives for many centuries.

Among later fantastic lands was an animal nation described by the French writer Nicolas Perrot d'Ablancourt in the mid-17th century, which was ruled by a phoenix and had lions and tigers as soldiers. In the same period the Duchess of Montpensier's *Account of Imaginary Island* (1659) portrayed a world governed by greyhounds and served by foxes, lions and monkeys. Islands or countries in which animals and humans mingle in appearance are also discovered, notably in Margaret Cavendish's *The Blazing World* (1666); Gabriel de Foigny's *A New Discovery of Terra Incognita Australis* (1676; English translation, 1693), which has ape-like men; and Nicolas Restif de la Bretonne's *Australia Discovered* (1781), which has bear-men, ape-men and otter-men. Charles de Fieux Mouhy's *Lamekis* (1735) described Trisolday, an underground land of worm-men who gather the world's precious minerals. The Marvellous Islands, described in a 16th-century French text, contained ape-men, centaurs, creatures covered with eyes and ears, and other marvels. The search for the unicorn, which in legend could only be tamed by a virgin and whose horn was reputed to possess magical powers, entranced many an explorer. Animals, too, then, could possess utopic qualities.

When the age of discovery began in earnest, such myths were not simply jettisoned. On the contrary, the 'new world' was from the outset as much a projection of European fantasy as Utopia itself would be. Long before the Americas became known, the Atlantic was dotted with reputed or imaginary places infused with mythical content. Around 1000 BC, Norsemen imagined that the natives they encountered in Vinland might be trolls or supernatural beings (contact with whom was proscribed by their church). The Celts speculated about Avalon, or 'apple island', a kingdom somewhere beyond the horizon of the Atlantic Ocean whose inhabitants were believed to live without death, fear or woe. An island named 'Bresal', later called Brazil, is identifiable as early as the 5th century. Soon after, St Brendan is said to have embarked on a quest to discover an earthly paradise, the Promised Land of the Saints. The exceedingly delightful and fertile Fortunate Isles, possibly the Canaries, are mentioned by 1100. A map of 1367 showed the Fantastic Islands off the shores of America.

Other parts of the world possessed similar spaces. Amazonia, supposedly located somewhere near the Caspian Sea, was reported in Mandeville's voyages in the 14th century as the abode of fearsome warrior women who propagated only at an annual festival, and then expelled males from their domains. He also described the Dondum Islands, where one group of headless peoples – thought to have descended from the union of women with devils – had eyes in their shoulders; and Pentixore, where gold and the richest gems adorned the emperor's palace. He hinted, too, at the existence of the 'Paradise Terrestrial', the highest

This engraving, from *Nova typis transacta navigatio* by Caspar Plautius, Abbot of Setenstetten (1621), shows the legendary St Brendan in search of the Promised Land of the Saints, west of the coast of Africa. The legend of Abbot Brendan originated in Ireland, but wedded pagan, Christian and classical themes.

Map of the fabled lands of Prester John, 1603. Circulating from the 12th century onwards, the medieval legend of Prester John described a Christian monarch ruling over a kingdom located in Asia or Africa and abounding in wealth and great marvels. Here it is positioned south of Egypt.

place on Earth, containing a well from which all rivers were derived.

The vast Catholic kingdom of Antangil, to the south of the Indian Ocean, was described in early 16th-century France as being defined by democracy and community of property. But here only the female children of the nobility were educated. Further east, there were 12th-century reports of the fabled lands of the legendary Christian ruler Prester John, a supposed medieval 'Emperor of Ind'. And in the late 13th century Marco Polo excited great interest with his (possibly fictional) account of the Mongol empire of China, whose merits he praised highly. Beyond that, or so 16th-century travellers presumed, lay the reputedly wealthy island of Japan, located near the Islands of Gold and Silver, sought by Abel Tasman in the early 17th century. Further south, it was

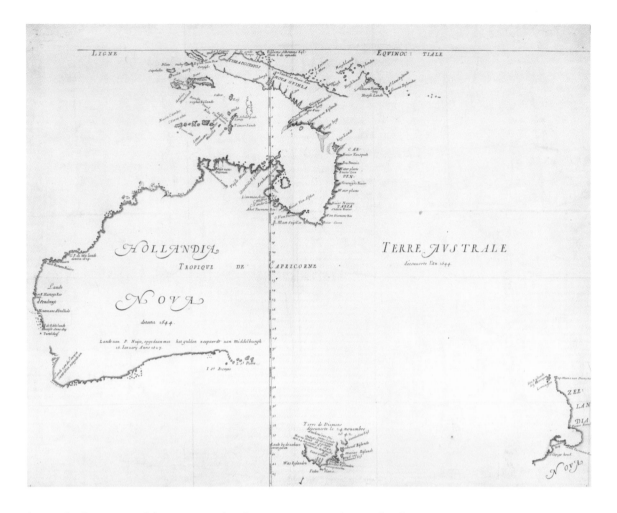

increasingly supposed, lay a vast antipodean mass or continent, the Great
South Island, called New Holland and Terre Australe by the late 17th
century. Although its supposed riches failed to materialize, some thought
it was inhabited by the lost tribes of Israel, others by Atlanteans or, in
Fijian legend, émigré Africans. Further speculation focused on other,
sunken continents, such as Zealandia.

The period of the first serious exploration and subsequent conquest
of the new world and other parts of the globe follows the mythic voyage
and precedes the age of modern travel. Henceforth the imaginary
would fall increasingly by the wayside and the anthropological would
come to the fore. By the time Richard Hakluyt's *Principal Navigations,
Voyages and Discoveries of the English Nation* (1589) was published, scientific
and economic interests were becoming predominant. The great

'Hollandia Nova detecta 1644;
Terre Australe découverte l'an
1644', printed in Melchisedech
Thevenot's *Relations de divers
voyages curieux*, published in
1663. Suspicions regarding a
mysterious southern continent
persisted for decades.

Christopher Columbus (1451–1506)

The Italian navigator and explorer of the Americas made four voyages to the 'new world'. These took place between 1492, when he reached San Salvador Island, Cuba and Haiti, and 1504, when he landed at Honduras and Nicaragua. (The other journeys, between 1493 and 1496, were to Guadeloupe, Montserrat, Antigua, Puerto Rico and Jamaica, and 1498, when he reached Trinidad and the mainland of South America.) Born in Genoa, Columbus took to the sea at an early age and for a time was employed in Portugal as a mapmaker. In the belief that a route to the spice-rich Indies could be found to the west, he set off with the support of Ferdinand and Isabella of Spain in 1492. He was also strongly motivated by religious principles and associated his epochal trip with biblical prophecy as well as the active will of God, who he thought had destined him to deliver humanity by effecting the conversion of all non-Christians, thereby heralding the second coming of Christ. He became embroiled in controversy with Spanish colonial administrators and eventually died in poverty.

Christopher Columbus, a man obsessed with God and gold in about equal measure (though the latter seems to have assumed the upper hand earlier in his life), may have been looking for a new spice route when he set sail on his voyages to the new world. But also he believed that King Solomon's mines, of biblical repute, lay there (near Panama). He saw himself as being both inspired by the Holy Spirit and fulfilling the destiny of ancient prophecies.[3] Columbus also knew of Plato's account of Atlantis.

At first landfall Columbus reported that there were no better people or soil anywhere in the world.[4] Thereafter the significance of his discoveries and/or inventions was constantly ratcheted up. In a letter written in 1498 concerning his third voyage, he claimed to have discovered the terrestrial paradise (which Vespucci also thought lay in the new world). This was affirmed by the sweetness of a river he encountered (the Orinoco), which he dared not enter without God's permission. (Juan Ponce de León would later seek the Fountain of Youth in what is now Florida; and in the 17th century, Antonio de León Pinelo would attempt to prove Columbus's theory in *El paraiso en el nuevo mundo*, or 'Paradise in the new world').

The indigenous peoples of the lands that were 'discovered' by Columbus – some of whom, in their turn, thought the Spaniards had come from the skies – soon became objects of fascination for the European explorers.[5] Many travellers thought them comparable to the first peoples of the lost golden age. Columbus described 'a very gentle race, without the knowledge of any iniquity; they neither kill, nor steal, nor carry weapons', and 'set no value' on gold as such, only when it was crafted into ornaments.[6] (Tacitus had noted a similar disdain for precious metals among the ancient Germans.[7]) Yet doubts were evident from the outset. What true virtue could these people really possess as non-Christians, some conquerors wondered? Others simply found them vicious, 'stupid and silly', lacking any respect for justice or 'truth, save when it is to their advantage'.[8] Some were soon found to be cannibals. And the natives would thus, inexorably, find themselves swept rapidly through the cycle of degeneration as their inability to sustain such hopes of primitive innocence left them open to forcible conversion to the one true religion. The price to be paid was the pillage of their valuables and the spilling of their blood. Questions of origin and innocence aside, their possession of gold was quickly established and came to define the purpose of the European enterprise. Columbus would write that gold is 'the most precious of all commodities' and 'he who possesses it has all he needs in this world, as also the means of rescuing souls from purgatory and returning them to the enjoyment of paradise'.[9] The richest irony of the newly rediscovered golden age, as soon became evident, was the negligible attention it paid to gold.

'A council of State between the chiefs and principal councillors', from Theodor de Bry's *Indorum, Floridam provincian imhabitantium excomes*, Frankfurt, 1591. The natives here appear to be unarmed, the Europeans prepared for action. Though De Bry made many engravings of native Americans, he never visited the new world himself.

Hand-coloured German woodcut from 1505, showing New World cannibals roasting body parts over a fire, supposedly based on Amerigo Vespucci's description in the *Mundus Novus* of peoples he encountered in Brazil. The existence of cannibalism was a crucial justification for the right of conquest.

The new world was, then, invented just as much as it was discovered, and Columbus can rightly be claimed as the inventor of modernity.[10] Following Columbus, a variety of 16th- and 17th-century speculators continued to wonder whether the Native Americans were a pre-Adamic people created separately by God (a theory later termed 'polygenesis'); or perhaps a race inhabiting a condition closer to what God intended for humanity; or descended from the Jews or Atlanteans. The earliest account of how they lived – indeed, the first history of the new world (1504, but compiled as early as 1493) – was by an acquaintance of Columbus's, a fellow Italian known as Peter Martyr Anglerius.[11] This text described the natives as inhabiting a 'golden age' where 'amongst them the land belongs to everybody, just as does the sun or the water. They know no difference between *meum* [me] and *tuum* [you], that source of all evils.'[12] It is very likely that Thomas More knew this text.[13] Certainly his imaginative excursion into Utopia was intimately bound up with Vespucci's account (itself at least partly fabricated by later editors) of his four voyages to the Americas between 1497 and 1504. This text, which More had devoured eagerly, reported finding peoples whose property was communal, having 'no trade, they neither buy nor sell', holding 'as nothing' precious metals, each being 'his own master'. (Later narratives would indicate they placed a lesser value, at least, on such materials – this often angered their conquerors, for they then failed to amass them in sufficient amounts.[14]) J. H. Hexter regards this account as instigating a 'decisive leap' in More's imagination.[15] And such assumptions would be carried into later epochs. Michel de Montaigne also believed that the Americas demonstrated the golden age far more vividly than Lycurgus or Plato. His essay 'The Cannibals' (*c.* 1580) described a land off Brazil, apparently only recently inhabited, where the peoples required no laws or civilization to maintain themselves. Families lived harmoniously in communal houses, sharing meals, and despite their apparent anthropophagy, or practice of eating human flesh, the natives are contrasted favourably to Europeans. Shakespeare was impressed and incorporated the idea into *The Tempest* (1611).

But there was in fact no reliable or consistent information on how the natives of the new world were organized or what their true character was. In some versions of Vespucci's narrative – those now classed among the forgeries – women as well as men were inordinately lustful, laws were few, and each was 'lord of himself',[16] and lived in a supposed primitive condition of liberty that many perceived to be vicious and barbaric in the extreme. The Incas of Peru, not known by Europeans until some fourteen years after More wrote *Utopia*, would provide a very different model of society that would come to be associated with aspects of More's text. Garcilaso de la Vega's *Commentaries on the Incas* (1609–17) described a far more complex, highly regulated and well-ordered society defined by paternal rule and efficient state organization. It was a model that would be taken up in many later utopias. Precious metals were largely regarded as 'superfluous' since they were not used in coinage, though shells and precious stones were valued. Enough land was assigned to each household to provide its maintenance.[17] Pedro Pizarro and others described the organization of Inca society according to labour quotas, the all-pervasive role of supervisors, and complete care for the individual in illness and old age.[18] Gold was used only by the Inca rulers, chiefly for adornment, and not by the general population. Later writers, such as William Prescott, stressed this, adding that since they had little property or trade, very few laws were required, and the Inca 'agrarian law' was even 'more thorough and effectual' than that of

'Levantose por rei Inga Mango Inga'. A depiction from Felipe Guaman Poma de Ayala's chronicle (*c.* 1615) of the newly crowned emperor Manco Inca Yupanqui (1516–1544) on his ceremonial throne at Cuzco.

Lycurgus. The Incas were mainly farmers, though a small proportion became craftsmen. The occupations of those who were employed by the government were rotated to allow individuals to maintain their own households. The relief of poverty, including the state supply of clothing, was generous and unstinting.[19]

Elsewhere in the Americas, the tribal property of the Aztecs of Mexico was divided by clan. But they had no money and also placed little value on gold. The Maya have also been linked to More.[20] And after *Utopia* was published in 1516, a variety of experiments in the new world attempted to apply his ideas to native life. Among those that followed the Spanish explorer Hernán Cortés to Mexico, at least one Franciscan friar, Mendieta, believed that the unacquisitive nature of Indian society (which he believed to be Jewish in origin) heralded a new golden age for a regenerate European Christianity, when it would be possible to live 'virtuously and peacefully serving God, as in a terrestrial paradise'.[21] In the Jesuit missionary experiment in Paraguay in the 17th and 18th centuries (which Voltaire likened to Lycurgan Sparta), the absence of private property in Guarani society was opposed by the Spanish, who attempted to introduce private possession. But communal property remained important to the Guarani, 'private' land was not heritable and money was not used by most of the Indians, who enjoyed a 'half-Arcadian, half-monastic' existence.[22] The Jesuits did not covet or amass gold, or enslave their subjects, and ultimately left their 'very weak' sentiment of property largely undisturbed. They were eventually expelled and their work undone in just two years. Here, then, as everywhere else in the new world, utopia once found was soon lost or destroyed.

Yet such accounts indicate that the Spanish described something like Utopia before More wrote of it, and that he, and others, believed that something like Utopia, or facets thereof, existed in the 'Mundus Novus' (new world) and perhaps elsewhere. Narratives of the new world presented by later explorers did not fundamentally alter this understanding, and *Utopia* reinforced it. 'Utopia' was therefore somewhere before it was 'nowhere', a real entity before it became a fictional one. If this was the case, might or could it be imitated by 'civilized' Europeans? Or had they degenerated too far to entertain such a possibility? At one level, of course, it matters less whether such descriptions were true than that people thought them to be so, and acted upon the assumption. But we have seen that there is real evidence that utopian societies of both the primitive and complex types were believed to exist. Did their success lie in their proximity to the natural state or in cleverly designed constitutions? If they were truly virtuous, which was sometimes disputed, how could such societies possibly be pagan? And did it matter if they were willing to surrender their gold rapidly? Here was surely scope for fruitful speculation on the part of the most intrepid, and certainly the greediest, traveller.

Of these two facets of the myth of the Americas – gold and innocence – the former came quickly to predominate. The search for the fabled city of Manoa, capital of El Dorado (the 'Golden Kingdom'), would eventually be wedded to a more generalized lust for other precious metals, for the treasures of ancient empires like those of the Incas and Aztecs, for conquest and dominion, and for access to eastern trade routes. Where having a white skin meant possessing *carte blanche,* avarice almost immediately incited practically limitless plunder, goaded on, as in so many later empires, by wholesale terror.

Bartolomeo de Las Casas, Vasco de Quiroga and others would adopt a more enlightened humanist approach towards governing the natives, in the hope of moulding them into primitive Christians.[23] But to little avail. They could not stem the mass death, partly by murder, often by suicide, but mostly by disease, that resulted from European conquest. The native Caribbean population would be reduced from somewhere between two and eight million (estimates vary) to only 100,000 in the twenty years after 1492, when Columbus first arrived in the region. (The natives also began refusing to procreate in order to avoid begetting slaves.)

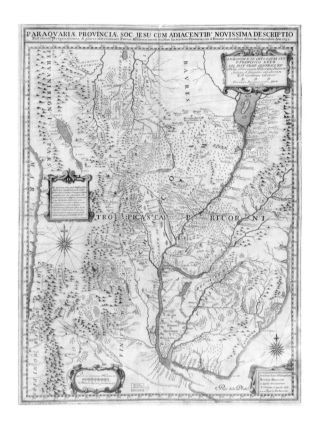

This map, made in Rome in 1732 by Giovanni Petroschi, shows the chief missions and missionary journeys in the Jesuit province of Paraguay and neighbouring areas.

Yet the Americas would continue to signify what the Pacific came to symbolize in the 18th and 19th centuries: a place of primitive moral purity, of closeness to the original state of nature, peopled by noble savages living in greater harmony with their environment than their 'civilized' descendants. 'In the beginning all the world was America,' wrote John Locke in 1690,[24] and generations thereafter continued to debate whether this meant a condition of rude but peaceful co-existence, or Thomas Hobbes's war of all against all, a fierce scramble for scarce resources in which the devil took the usually darkly coloured hindmost. The moral trope would nonetheless long continue to be popular, and to be satirized. Voltaire's portrayal of El Dorado in his famous satire *Candide* (1759) focuses on the kingdom's ideal religious dimensions – here all priests live in harmony and are engaged in continuous worship. This text is just one example of his many accounts of journeys that expose the sorrows, follies and misdeeds of humanity, and particularly the widespread war and violence of his epoch.

The empires of the new world were thus intertwined with utopian and dystopian ideals on a number of levels. What was utopian for Europeans was, of course, usually dystopian for the conquered indigenous peoples, as well as for their successors – slaves imported from Africa. More's Utopians were zealous imperialists and, as in the case of the nation as an 'imagined community',[25] the concept of empire can be seen as a subset of utopia in the sense that it promotes an ideal of order imposed on conditions in which government was regarded as minimal or absent. Empires also impose a set of qualities – Christianity and commerce foremost among them – that go under the rubric of 'civilization'. From the late 15th to the 20th centuries this concept of empire, which usually involves a magnification of the virtues of the conquering nation as well as of the vices of the conquered, resulted in the immense expansion of European domains. By the early 17th century, colonies in North America, such as Virginia, were being invested with similar millenarian, arcadian and other hopes intermixed with expectations of rapid enrichment. Religious persecution drove thousands of Protestant sectarians from Europe in the 17th century, investing northern America with the symbols of the promised land or 'city on the hill', whose 'chosen people' were destined

'The arrival of the Englishmen in Virginia', as depicted in a hand-coloured version of Theodor de Bry's engraving of English ships reaching North America, published in Thomas Hariot's *A Briefe and True Report of the New Found Land of Virginia* (1588). The hazards of the journey are stressed by the portrayal of the five ships closest to the coast as sinking.

to triumph over their enemies, as is evident in John Eliot's *Christian Commonwealth* (1659). Hopes for godly rule among either natives or emigrants were often as speedily dashed. A century later the focus would shift towards Asia. In some cases, such as British India, the large-scale public ownership and/or management of land was involved in imperial administration. Some later utopias, including that of Louis-Sébastien Mercier, would subsequently announce the renunciation of empire in the future.[26] But for the most part, the new world's golden age gave way to its age of gold without protest by Europeans.

Real voyages did not, however, by any means destroy the popularity of more fantastic journeys; indeed, the public's appetite for both was unbounded. As exploration expanded swiftly in the 17th century the locations of fantastic destinations also became more extensive. Among the imaginary voyages of this period were Henry Schooten's *The Hairy-Giants, or, A Description of Two Islands in the South Sea* (1671), which revealed the island of Benganga, an absolute monarchy of giant devil-worshippers; and Joshua Barnes's *Gerania: A New Discovery of a Little Sort of People* (1675), which describes a pygmy people reposing in arcadian simplicity. Set in Surinam, Aphra Behn's extremely popular *Oroonoko* (1688) blended an anti-slavery narrative with a well-crafted 'noble savage' ideal. In France, Foigny's *A New Discovery of Terra Incognita Australis* (1676), was the most important of the early imaginary voyages to select Australia as its destination.

OROONOKO.

Mr. SAVIGNY in the Character of OROONOKO.
Oro. I'll turn my Face away, and do it so.
Published Nov.r 23. 1776 by J. Lowndes & Partners

This 18th-century engraving shows the actor John Horatio Savigny in the role of Oroonoko, from the novel of the same name about slavery in Surinam by one of the earliest female British novelists, Aphra Behn.

At the beginning of the 18th century, travellers reported the existence of the kingdom of the Abdalles, off the coast of north Africa, where there was a golden stream that cured all wounds. At the same time, George Psalmanazar's *An Historical and Geographical Description of Formosa* (1704) invented a bogus language as well as a travel narrative. On Paradise Island, as recounted in *The Adventures, and Surprizing Deliverances, of James Dubourdieu* (1719), shipwrecked Europeans were regarded contemptuously by the natives, whose wives and property were held in common. Not all such places were pleasant: the Island of Boredom, described in an 18th-century French text, was populated by poisonous plants and venomous animals that attacked visitors. Nor were the natives always friendly; Captain Cook was a famous real-life victim among explorers.

By this time the standard trope of a European explorer or merchant surviving a storm and shipwreck, encountering untold marvels and then achieving a miraculous or redemptive escape, was becoming well established. Not all the discoveries were of more virtuous peoples. In Thomas Artus's *Les Hermaphrodites* (1605) the inhabitants lacked all the manly qualities, and were beset by vice; it has been noted that unisexuality is associated with a variety of earlier Christian sects, including the Adamites. Foigny described a hermaphrodite society (all single-sex children having been killed) without rulers, centralized power or inequality. The society's 'glory' resided in 'appearing identical and equally cultivated in all things.' As with Plato, children are educated in common and divided by age. All dine together and live in apartments of four persons.[27] Another well-known text, Denis Vairaisse d'Allais's *The History of the Sevarites or Severambi* (1675), also set in *terra Australis*, wedded detail from a single narrative maritime voyage to Spartan and Morean themes. In the society described here precious metals are not traded and have little value beyond adornment or use as utensils. The government is despotic but democratically elected. The state maintains individual welfare through adequate food distribution. Children are educated communally from age seven, and social equality is greatly prized. Private property is absent, eating is in common, clothing is uniform in appearance and labour is well organized. Religious toleration is also enjoined. Lawyers are admitted but carefully confined.[28] Although set in the Mediterranean, François Fénelon's *Adventures of Telemachus* (1699) adopted similar themes, using more classical references as well as descriptions of the Indians to promote a contempt for luxury, ambition and 'civilization' in general. The inhabitants are chiefly shepherds and do not live in cities.

Other texts also took up classical utopian themes. *A Voyage to Tartary* (1689) by one 'Heliogenes L'Epy' discovers a colony descended from Greek philosophers, where the laws emulate Plato's commonwealth and primitive Christianity, and community of property is upheld. The inhabitants practise the utmost frugality and enjoy perfect health. As in More's *Utopia*, the entire population passes chronologically through the same course of social development, being educated, working on the land from the age of eighteen until thirty, then returning to the city, where all over the age of thirty govern through a general assembly. Another literary utopia from this period that promoted a return to a primitive, patriarchal, purified state of Christianity was Francis Lee's *Antiquity Revived: or the Government of a Certain Island Antiently Called Astreada* (1693). Among the most popular supposed desert island narratives of the epoch was the oft-reprinted *The Isle of Pines* (1668), by the republican Henry Neville. This fantasy recounts a shipwreck, after which one man populates a remote island with the assistance of four 'handsome' women, one of whom was black. He dies at the age of ninety-four, having produced some two-thousand descendants living under his benign Christian rule. Tyranny was avoided here, though speaking evil of the governor was punished by beating and expulsion. Other republican utopias published at this time included *The Free State of Noland* (1696), a neo-Harringtonian tract (see p. 100) in which, as J. G. A. Pocock, J. C. Davis and others have argued, demands for civic participation were integrated into schemes for constitutional balance.[29] Around this time science was beginning to furnish its own utopian variant, with Francis Bacon's *New Atlantis* giving rise to a number of imitations.

Chapter 6

The Age of Defoe and Swift

Satires and Desert Islands

Two books published in early 18th-century Britain would come to have an enduring impact on utopian thought and writing: the famed shipwreck novel, *Robinson Crusoe* (1719), by Daniel Defoe, and the best known of utopian satires, Jonathan Swift's *Gulliver's Travels* (1726). Each would be widely imitated and give rise to new sub-genres of the literature – Robinsonades and Gulliveriana.

Beloved by children and adults alike, Defoe's *Robinson Crusoe* remains perhaps the most popular fantasy work of all time. The story was modelled, at least in part, on a true narrative, the account of a Scottish mariner, Alexander Selkirk, who was shipwrecked on the island of Juan Fernández, off Chile, from 1704 to 1709. (Today it has been renamed Robinson Crusoe's Island.) The story may also have been indebted to a Dutch narrative, Hendrik Smeeks's largely anti-utopian parody, *The Mighty Kingdom of Krinky Kesmes* (1708).[1]

Robinson Crusoe is not, strictly speaking, a utopia, for while one individual, the marooned Crusoe, imposes order on an uninhabited island, the reconstitution of society – the central, definitive utopian issue – is not here germane, even after the introduction of Crusoe's man-servant Friday. Defoe's work is much closer to the pastoral and Edenic retreat of the mythical golden age than it is to the tradition of the well-ordered commonwealth. It is also a psychological study within a Bunyanesque Christian tradition of the search for salvation, for Crusoe's order is, crucially, imposed upon himself, by sheer willpower. Yet the text sits so securely within the genre of imaginary voyages, and of the association of primitivism with virtue, that no account of utopia would be complete without considering it. To be 'king and lord' of his island with an 'inheritance as compleatly as any lord of a manner in England'[2] is the ultimate bourgeois individualist utopia, and perhaps

This colour lithograph and watercolour by Oskar Woite, 1882, shows the shipwrecked Captain Lemuel Gulliver extinguishing a fire in the castle of Lilliput in Jonathan Swift's *Gulliver's Travels* (1726). Though often bowdlerized and read as a children's book, the work is a complex satire on British society in its day.

Daniel Defoe (*c.* 1660–1731)

Best known for *Robinson Crusoe* (1719), the most influential and imitated shipwreck novel of all time and a major influence on the development of the novel generally, Defoe was born in Cripplegate, London, the son of a butcher. He became a tradesman in hosiery, travelled widely, and participated in the Monmouth Rebellion of 1685. In 1703 he was jailed briefly for his support for Nonconformists and satirical attacks on the Church of England, notably in *The Shortest Way with Dissenters* (1702). One of the most prolific of all British writers, Defoe was the author of more than five hundred works. His later novels included *Captain Singleton* (1720), *Colonel Jack* (1722), *Moll Flanders* (1722), *A Journal of the Plague Year* (1722) and *Roxana* (1724). He died on 26 April 1731.

OPPOSITE ABOVE An illustration of the Scottish castaway Alexander Selkirk with British sailors, taken from *Tales of Travellers, or A View of the World*, published in 1838. Selkirk, who spent four years on an uninhabited island off Chile, is usually assumed to have inspired Daniel Defoe's seminal novel, *Robinson Crusoe*.

OPPOSITE BELOW This hand-coloured lithograph (*c.* 1874) shows Robinson Crusoe with his man Friday, whose introduction into what is often regarded as the first English novel alters its complex psychology dramatically by introducing issues of race, power and empire.

the ultimate psychological retreat into interiority. Crusoe's fantasy is centrally one of power, both of self-mastery, largely attained by religious conversion, and of power over nature, achieved through a focused application of the work ethic.[3] For many later political economists the text epitomized the emergence of humankind under God's providential direction from the state of nature into well-ordered society defined by private property and settled government. It is, after a fashion, an allegory of empire, if not of modernity itself.

The narrative of *Robinson Crusoe* is familiar to most readers. Born in York, the runaway Crusoe is stranded off Trinidad in the Caribbean in September 1659. Thanks to his extraordinary ingenuity and his ability to rescue his ship's supplies, Crusoe, despite moments of doubt, is able to transform a potential disaster into something like – were it not for his isolation – a tolerable existence. With excruciating, methodical care, his life is planned around securing safety and plenitude. But nature has been kind: melons, grapes and other forms of sustenance abound. And when providence provides him with a man-servant, Friday, his prayers are answered. Piety, endurance and hard work are rewarded, and a tropical paradise is transformed into the microcosm of the British empire. Crusoe's fantasy of power over others, doubtless that of every imperial adventurer, is satisfied.

This vision had immense appeal and imitations of Crusoe were plentiful across the entire range of European national literatures, especially Germany, where some forty Robinsonades appeared

between 1722 and 1769, the most interesting being J. G. Schnabel's *Die Insel Felsenburg* ('Felsenburg Island', published in four parts between 1731 and 1743). Some of these are primarily 'sea novels' or 'travel novels' without substantial didactic content, or fabulous voyages of the most imaginative type. Others, however, come closer to the more traditional definition of utopia discussed in previous chapters. One of the later examples of this type during this period, Thomas Spence's *A Supplement to the History of Robinson Crusoe* (1782), counsels the ownership of all land by the nation and its management by the parish. The work was praised by Jean-Jacques Rousseau in *Emile* (1762) as an instructive moral fable, and would undergo many other mutations. One of the better known of these was Johann David Wyss's *Der Schweizerische Robinson* ('The Swiss Family Robinson', 1812).

The second equally influential text in the genre to be published in 18th-century Britain was a satire. Jonathan Swift's *Gulliver's Travels* ('Gulliver' being a possible amalgam of 'gullible' and 'traveller'), first published in 1726, remains perhaps the greatest ever satire on the human aspiration to lead a life according to the principles of reason. This text echoes repeatedly down subsequent ages, through William Godwin to Aldous Huxley and George Orwell in the 20th century. It has given the English language several memorable terms, including

Thomas Spence (1750–1814)

The Newcastle-born Scottish pamphleteer is best known in this context as the author of *A Supplement to the History of Robinson Crusoe* (1782). Born to a poor family of nineteen children, Spence was, like William Godwin, raised as a Sandemanian Baptist. He first proposed his 'Land Plan' to the Newcastle Philosophical Society in 1775, and virtually all his subsequent writing is a variation on the theme of rendering land communal, under parish management, in order to eradicate poverty. In this scheme land was to be rented to the highest bidder, the proceeds being applied to parish expenses. Spence is best located intellectually in terms of the development of a neo-Harringtonian position respecting the restriction of land ownership. He regarded himself as more radical than his famous contemporary, Thomas Paine, through his extension of the idea of an agrarian law towards what would later be broadly termed 'land nationalization'. Spence's ideas were developed through the Society of Spencean Philanthropists by Thomas Evans in particular, and later picked up by the socialist H. M. Hyndman.

Jonathan Swift (1667–1745)

This Irish writer, satirist and cleric is best known for *Gulliver's Travels* (1726), the most famous utopian satire of all. Born in Dublin, Swift went to Trinity College, Dublin, in 1682, where he failed to shine. In 1688 he moved to England, where he became secretary to the diplomat Sir William Temple. He was ordained as a priest in 1694 and moved between England and Ireland, in 1699 becoming prebendary at St Patrick's, Dublin; he would become dean in 1713. Increasingly active politically, he wrote various pieces upholding the Tories' defence of the Church of England against Whiggish interference and Nonconformity, exploring such themes satirically in *The Tale of a Tub* (1704), and during the same period wrote *The Battle of the Books* (published 1704). In a later satire, *A Modest Proposal* (1729), he suggested that poverty might be solved by eating the children of the poor. *Gulliver's Travels* scrutinizes a wide range of contemporary follies, including scientific and financial as well as political speculation. Its influence on later utopian writers was considerable, notably with respect to the inadequacy of the power of reason to solve humankind's problems.

'Lilliputian' and 'Yahoo', and was frequently imitated throughout the period. *Memoirs of the Court of Lilliput* (1727) and *The Travels of Mr. John Gulliver, Son. to Capt. Lemuel Gulliver* (1731) were two early instances; as late as 1796 *Modern Gulliver's Travels* took up the themes of monarchical and courtly corruption and the burden of heavy taxation on the poor.

The text consists of four voyages by Captain Lemuel Gulliver from Bristol to the East Indies between 1699 and 1710. The first two voyages essentially satirize early 18th-century British politics: the initial trip is to Lilliput, where a minute, infantile people possess worthy qualities (such as only raising the number of children they can support, who are reared in state nurseries); the second is to Brobdingnag, inhabited by gigantic and massively vulgar people. The third voyage, chiefly to the flying island of Laputa, mocks the highly speculative bent of scientific projectors of the epoch, where the practical application of science to agriculture is spurned in favour of projectors' schemes, such as extracting used sunlight from cucumbers.

BELOW This drawing by E. C. Broch, from the 1894 edition of Swift's *Gulliver's Travels*, shows Gulliver awakening to find himself a prisoner of the tiny Lilliputians, during the first voyage recounted in the book.

Frontispiece to Samuel Johnson's popular novel *Rasselas: Prince of Abyssinia*, first published in April 1759 and reprinted almost continuously thereafter. Though the work portrays idyllic life in a 'happy valley', it is usually regarded as a satire on utopian aims.

The fourth, most utopian and controversial, voyage is to the land of the Houyhnhnms, horse-like creatures governed by reason – their name means 'perfection of nature'. They live in virtuous simplicity and have no names for dishonesty, punishment, law, government or power. Their manifestly superior ordering of life is contrasted to the extreme vulgarity and passionate nature of the Yahoos, who are sometimes thought to represent the Australasian aborigines, following accounts of them given by William Dampier during his travels to the region. However, it is often supposed that Gulliver himself, referred to as a Yahoo, symbolizes humanity in general. In the religious context of Swift's thought the contrast is instructive. For a pessimistic Tory like Swift – paradoxically a great admirer of More – the life of reason is not suited to fallen humankind, and to expect that the world will ever be peopled with anything other than ordinary mortals results from an infatuated, hubristic delusion. A similar perspective would be evident in Samuel Johnson's famous *Rasselas: Prince of Abyssinia* (1759), subtitled 'The Choice of a Life', much of which was set in an idyllic 'Happy

Valley' in order to contrast the unsatisfactory nature of temporal as compared to eternal life. Such texts, then, represent one strand of the Christian counterattack on utopia and particularly on assumptions about a life lived according to the principles of reason, which failed to take account of the naturally and fatefully sinful nature of humankind. It now appears evident to some commentators that literary texts in this period begin to take a sceptical, pessimistic turn in a dystopian direction.

Both Defoe and Swift, then, touched on the contrast between a life of simplicity (lived, in some sense, according to nature) and that of an increasingly complex European civilization. In an age prone to trumpet the virtues of progress, scepticism about its unalloyed advantages often took the form of nostalgia for earlier and purer forms of social and political institutions. By the time Rousseau began to explore the theme, in the middle of the century, the combination of the appeal to simplicity and radical, usually republican, politics (often inspired by Sparta, sometimes by More) had become an explosive mixture. Crowds flocked to witness Omai, the famous Otaheitan who toured Britain after Captain Cook's voyages to New Zealand, while other stories of 'wild children' raised by animals captivated thousands.[4] Such enthusiasm would doubtless help to fuel a revolutionary impulse. The moment was almost nigh when utopia would come to be widely perceived as realizable in the here and now, by the unaided power of reason, and at least partly cast as the image that the poor might enjoy much the same enviable life as the rich.

Omai (Mai) (Mai), Sir Joseph Banks and Daniel Charles Solander, by William Parry, *c.* 1775–76. The portrait shows Joseph Banks and Dr Daniel Solander, who accompanied Captain Cook on his first voyage to the South Pacific in 1768. They assisted the Tahitian Omai when he visited Britain in 1774.

The simplest explanation for the growing urge for 'simplicity' is the sense of nostalgic loss of the slower rhythm of agricultural life, which increasingly urbanized European populations began to lament throughout this period. The fascination with the 'primitive', original state of humankind can be explained, in part, by the fact that scientific progress ran parallel with a revival of religious belief, in which return to a golden age or Garden of Eden was still thought possible. At the same time, however, natural law theorists such as Hugo Grotius and Samuel Pufendorf secularized Christian accounts of the creation to explain an original state of primitive community of goods, and generally commended the emergence of private property and commerce as inducing a vastly superior state of society.

The widespread, corrosive effects of the growth of luxury remain so pervasive a theme in the utopias of the 17th and 18th centuries that it is difficult not to acknowledge a sense of nostalgic regret for the vanishing worlds of primitive, more contented peoples, and the widespread perception of decadence and degeneration in modern society, which would be echoed in later Victorian angst about species decline in the wake of the Darwinian debate. In the anonymous *Private Letters from an American in England to his Friends in America* (1769), luxury,

TOP Portrait of the natural law theorist Hugo Grotius by Michiel Jansz van Mierevelt, 1631. Grotius was a highly influential jurist and philosopher, whose theories would lay the foundations for the political economy of Adam Smith.

ABOVE Portrait of the natural law theorist Samuel Pufendorf by Joachim von Sandrart, 17th century. Pufendorf built upon the ideas of Hobbes and Grotius, among others, to provide a widely praised account of the origins of modern ideas of rank, commerce and property ownership.

profligacy, vanity and idleness are shown to have corrupted Britain to such an extent that its government is transferred to America. Robert Paltock's *The Life and Adventures of Peter Wilkins* (1750) also portrays a complex dialogue between civility and primitivism, and warns that once people have been introduced to superfluities they would sooner give up life itself than return to their original state. In one of the most extensive explorations of this theme in late 18th-century Britain, *The Travels of Hildebrand Bowman* (1778), Bowman's narrative is constructed around visits to four countries at various stages of economic development. In Bonhommica, modelled on the Tudor era, consumption of delicacies is moderate and honesty and virtue predominate. But in Luxo-Volupto, ruled by King Gorgeris (George III), expanding commerce has refined tastes and weakened morals.[5]

Here, as in many utopias of the period, the emulation of the rich by the poor is remarked upon as distinctive to the epoch. Whereas social rank had once been legally formalized by clothing, and enforced by sumptuary laws, now such obvious distinctions do not exist. A new atmosphere of equality appears to follow the passion for trade and commerce. This is often portrayed as an unsettling process.

Centrally, thus, we witness the emergence of the proposition that modernity entails greater unease, disorder, unhappiness and malaise, both psychological and physical. The creation of wealth instils, the texts of the period repeatedly insist, a sense of continually unfulfilled longing, where the satisfaction and commodification of desire are merely aggravated by the accumulation of wealth and possessions. So, too, the alienation and isolation of the modern individual – increasingly pitted in competition with others, increasingly divested of the props and rudders of the extended family, the clan, tribe, village and priest, which would be among the great themes of 19th- and 20th-century psychology and sociology – would emerge at this early stage in utopian form.

In utopian literature the great contrast to this increasingly confused sophistication remained the discovery of some form of 'natural society' where greater contentment prevailed. In James Dubourdieu's *The Adventures & Surprizing Deliverances of James Dubourdieu* (1719), for example, we encounter the nation of the 'children of love'. Here animals mingle harmlessly among the naked, unembarrassed human population, and the lust for wealth does not exist; there is no government or courts and rule is by the eldest male heads of families, who direct all public assemblies and make crucial decisions concerning marriage and protocol. 'A Description of New Athens in Terra Australis Incognita' (1720, author unknown) describes a Christian state that is focused on charity; wages and prices are regulated, the oppression of the poor is eliminated and, as in More's *Utopia* (and many others), lawyers are banned. Simon Berington's *The Adventures of Sig. Gaudentio di Lucca* (1737) portrays a land in the interior of Africa with plentiful food and an advanced civilization, where equality is maintained under the benign rule of patriarchal leaders who ensure a just distribution of property. An 'inverted' world, in which the wealthy are held in contempt, is discovered in Baron Holberg's *Journey to the World Under-Ground* (1741). Writers and readers often tended to expect that peoples encountered via the imaginary voyage could only be virtuous if they practised a purer form of Christianity. Thus John Kirkby's *The Capacity and Extent of the Human Understanding; Exemplified in the Extraordinary Case of Automates* (1745) describes an island ordered by uncorrupted Christian practice:

Denis Diderot (1713–84)

This leading French Enlightenment philosopher was also editor of the enormously influential *Encyclopédie* (1751–72), the definitive intellectual treatise of the epoch. The *Encyclopédie* would eventually reach thirty-five volumes, and included contributions by Voltaire, Rousseau, Holbach, Turgot, Raynal and others, not least Diderot himself. Known philosophically for his materialist and mechanistic approach to the natural world, Diderot had an interest in primitive societies that was instigated in part by his friendship, eventually to sour, with Jean-Jacques Rousseau, for whom the contrast of artificial to natural man formed a central theme in many of his writings. Diderot's concerns prompted his highly speculative *Supplement to the Voyage to Bougainville* (1772). This took up the proposition that the Polynesians were among the least corrupted by sin or vice of all primitive peoples, and also focused on the centrality of sexual freedom, including polygamy, promiscuity and incest, and the avoidance of hypocrisy, as leading utopian themes, here substantially anticipating the speculations of Charles Fourier several decades later. Diderot was also known for other works, including *Rameau's Nephew* (begun in 1761), *The Dream of d'Alembert* (1769) and the *History of the Two Indies* (1772–81).

to conceive of the inhabitants' virtue as emanating from another source would have been far more subversive.

Following the voyages of captains Cook and Bligh, the South Pacific became a favoured destination for such accounts. Among the important later texts of this period in this respect was Denis Diderot's *Supplement to the Voyage to Bougainville* (1772), which firmly established Tahiti as the epitome of the South Pacific tropical paradise, 'a prelapsarian Arcadia, biblical and classical',[6] as one writer has put it, perhaps following a 1766 British landing there in which sailors had been offered women in propitiation after a bloody battle. Written in dialogue form, the *Supplement* contrasts French customs of private property and religious hypocrisy to the community of property and wives in Tahiti. One of the leading religious critics of the age, Diderot used such descriptions chiefly as a form of attack on the hypocrisies of Catholicism. The *Voyage* has been seen as an elaboration of Rousseau's critique of civilization, with the primitive native portrayed as 'innocent and gentle whenever his peace and security are left undisturbed'.[7] By the end of the 18th century the cult of the 'noble savage' was well-rooted in European thought. Yet this reflected, as has already been discussed, a dialogue between primitivism and progress within the

William Godwin (1756–1836)

The founder of English philosophical anarchism is best known as the author of a major treatise of political thought, *An Enquiry Concerning Political Justice* (1793). William Godwin, raised as a Sandemanian Baptist and destined for the ministry, forsook his religious beliefs in the 1780s and turned to journalism and literature for his livelihood. *Political Justice* established his reputation as a defender of individual liberty: the text resolutely rejects all forms of interference with the individual's right to form his or her own judgment. Though subsequent editions modified some of his more extreme formulations in this respect, and *The Enquirer* (1797) placed him more firmly on the side of civilization in contrast to his previous apparent embrace of primitivism, Godwin influenced Robert Southey, William Wordsworth and Samuel Taylor Coleridge to contemplate a 'Pantisocratic' experiment of communal living and working, which was projected at one point as a settlement on the banks of the Susquehanna River in what is now Pennsylvania. The experiment failed to materialize, but Godwin achieved renown as a novelist, notably through *Caleb Williams* (1794), and later became adviser to the founder of British socialism, Robert Owen. He married Mary Wollstonecraft and was the father of Mary Shelley.

utopian genre that had been established much earlier. The image of the primitive was also intimately linked to satires of the civilized. The milder satires of the period invoke a purer period of national politics, before trading wealth had come to corrupt the political process. Thus *The Voyages, Travels & Wonderful Discoveries of Capt. John Holmesby* (1757) attacks Whig corruption as underpinned by financial and trading interests from the perspective of more virtuous landowning Tory magnates. In Britain many such texts invoked the Bolingbrokian figure of a 'patriot-king' arbitrating between the sparring factions increasingly emerging as modern political parties, and banishing venality from the land. Patriarchalism is often commended as a remedy for political strife. This period also produced an extensive variety of other satires that focused most notably on the theme of social and political corruption. Some of the best known also lampooned emerging ideas of utopia itself. Among the most impressive of these was Edmund Burke's *A Vindication of Natural Society* (1756), which contrasted 'artificial' or 'political' society with a simpler, happier ideal of the state of nature. So successful was the effort that it was later commonly read (for example, by William Godwin) as an advertisement for the merits of the latter state.[8]

The growing equality of 18th-century society was also reflected in the utopian portrayal of women as securing a greater degree of control over their lives than had hitherto been the case. In *The Island of Content* (1709), women achieve 'Precedency in all Cases, excepting Family-Government: They chuse first, eat first, drink first, go to Bed first, and have a peculiar Liberty in discovering their Affections, without incurring thereby the least Scandal or Reflexion'.[9] In France, Louis Rustaing de Saint-Jory's *Les femmes militaires* ('Militant women', 1736) discussed the rights of women in marriage. Writers like Delarivier Manley (*The New Atalantis*, 1709) and Eliza Haywood (*The British Recluse; or, The Secret History of Cleomira,* 1722) portrayed female friendship in a strongly idealized manner. Two notable British works, Sarah Scott's *Millennium Hall* (1762) and Mary Hamilton's *Munster Village* (1778), describe separatist retreats where women enjoy considerable educational opportunities and organize their lives largely without male assistance, with a resulting increase in altruism and cooperation.

Chapter 7

Revolution and Enlightenment

America, France and Worlds Remade

Utopia becomes practical when it ceases to dream, to hope and to speculate and demands that the world be remade in its own image. This moment, when the bounds of possibility are stretched far in the direction of the seemingly impossible, occurs most prominently in the modern era and is interwoven with the revolutionary impulse. From the English Revolution of the mid-17th century through to the American Revolution of 1776 to that of France in 1789 and beyond, vast numbers of people came to espouse fundamental social and political change. Not merely absolutist monarchy, but aristocracy, established religion and even patriarchy came to be challenged by a new egalitarianism, which was itself not a little indebted to the utopian tradition.[1] During this period millenarian fervour is still interwoven with constitutional proposals, the promotion of popular political sovereignty and the occasional revival of Morean communism. But, equally, what defines the modern political utopia is its secular character, its insistence on locating and promoting the good life in the here and now, rather than discovering or creating it imaginarily elsewhere. Increasingly, this secular idea became forward-looking, oriented towards progress, decreasingly nostalgic about the achievements of the ancients or primitives, sharply and often violently insistent on the novelty of institutions it sought to create and the types of human beings required to make them work. In proportion, perhaps, as they lose their faith in the eternal, the moderns become nervous, impatient and anxious about making the most of this life. As one heaven is abandoned for the image of another, they demand its immediate improvement.

The English Revolution made an immense contribution to this process. Classical republicanism was revived, as was Christian

Detail of an engraving showing the moment after the execution of King Louis XVI of France, 21 January 1793. The guillotining of Louis represents one of the most powerful symbols of the emergence of modern democratic revolutionism, and the reaction against monarchical absolutism.

enthusiasm for a purified, 'godly commonwealth'. The revolt against Charles I – which led to his execution in 1649 and to the creation of the English Republic, which lasted until 1660 – was essentially political. But it was often interpreted as possessing overtly religious overtones. Some Puritan sectarians assumed these events heralded the coming of the godly commonwealth and defeat of the Antichrist, if not the millennium itself. By far the most important political utopia of the period, James Harrington's *The Commonwealth of Oceana* (1656), was, as J. G. A. Pocock has most notably detailed, to have the most long-standing and pervasive influence throughout the French Revolution and beyond.[2] Harrington imagined a commonwealth based loosely on Venice, Italy, in which checks and balances, a secret ballot and a bicameral legislature (consisting of two chambers or Houses), and limits on landed property, were to ensure political stability. Such ideas were developed by writers such as Henry Neville, John Moyle, Algernon Sydney and John Toland. *The Free State of Noland* (1696) extended this literary tradition. Many of the literary utopias of the Restoration period, however, deferred to monarchy as their preferred

James Harrington (1611–77)

This English republican, soldier and politician was the author of *The Commonwealth of Oceana* (1656). Born in Northamptonshire on 3 January 1611, Harrington attended Trinity College, Oxford, but left without obtaining a degree. He travelled on the Continent for several years, served in the army, and despite his republican views was personally devoted to King Charles I. *Oceana* – dedicated to Oliver Cromwell, whom Harrington regarded as a legislator of the type of Moses or the Athenian statesman Solon – is perhaps the most loosely disguised, or alternatively one of the most 'realistic', of all utopias, being principally a set of constitutional proposals for replacing the monarchy by a more just and stable government. Freedom here rests on the due exercise of citizenship, which is based on independence and cannot therefore be enjoyed by dependants or servants. *Oceana* would later be of great influence on the American revolutionaries of the late 18th century. Harrington died on 7 September 1677 after a lengthy imprisonment.

form of government, and more radical political experimentation did not emerge again until after the so-called Glorious Revolution of 1688.

Two of the most important expressions of 18th-century utopianism were the Gulliverian satire and the Robinsonade island paradise (see p. 87). More overtly political literary works also emerged in this period. David Hume's essay, the 'Idea of a Perfect Commonwealth' (1752), placed no restraints on property but sought a political balance between mercantile and landed property in order to moderate political conflict. Other works rejected the existing constitution as overly chaotic; in *The Island of Content* (1709, author uncertain), for example, an unlimited hereditary monarchy is commended. But many utopian governmental proposals were indebted to some combination of the Platonic, Morean and Harringtonian traditions. In Britain most sought to demonstrate the possibility of virtuous independence in the face of executive corruption, and to resist the growing trend of the poor to imitate the luxurious lifestyle of the rich. The Harringtonian tradition is represented by frequent utopian injunctions to rotate offices, by proposals for an agrarian law to restrict landed property, and by suggestions that citizens' militias supplant standing armies that served corrupt monarchs. James Burgh's *An Account of the First Settlement, Laws, Form of Government, and Police, of the Cessares, A People of South America* (1764) clearly follows the Spartan and Morean traditions. Here the aim

BELOW Title page of James Harrington's *The Oceana* (1737 edition). Dedicated to Oliver Cromwell, *Oceana* was a loosely veiled plan for a model republic which regarded inequality of landed property as one of the most pressing social problems of the age.

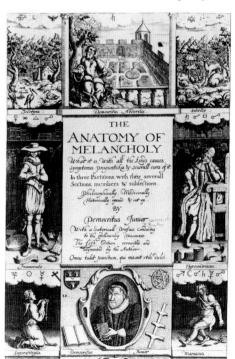

Frontispiece for the 1638 edition of Robert Burton's *The Anatomy of Melancholy*. Though notionally a medical treatise, Burton's work included an account of the full development of resources by the state, as well as a scheme for pensions, food production and employment.

was that 'every one should have an equal share, that so we might check every proud, ambitious, and destructive passion, and banish riches as well as poverty from us'.[3] Sumptuary and agrarian laws assist in maintaining this equality, the mining of gold and silver is prohibited and trade is restricted, luxury being regarded as the greatest social evil. But Burgh's regime is also intolerant towards Catholics, and bans gambling, lewd books and theatrical performances – as usual, the riotous and libertine suffer in utopia.

The Morean tradition is also represented in Gabriel-Etienne Morelly's famous *Le code de la nature* ('The law of nature', 1755), which enjoins community of goods and universal labour. Children are raised partly in common. All dress alike until the age of thirty, and all citizens over fifty are governors. By the end of the century the term 'utopian' was clearly identified with communal property-holding; enthusiasm for this was revived in various forms after the French Revolution – *An Essay on Civil Government* (1793, author unknown), based on William Godwin's ideas (see box, p. 96), commends such a system, as does the first utopia published in the United States, John Lithgow's *Equality – A Political Romance* (1802).

The 17th and early 18th centuries also produced a number of examples of what has been termed the 'full-employment utopia'. Here social organization, sometimes national, sometimes communal, was restructured to maximize economic productivity. The full utilization of resources was a key theme in the ideal society described in Robert Burton's *The Anatomy of Melancholy* (1621), which promoted old-age pensions, the draining of surplus land, the regulation of food prices and the state employment of physicians and lawyers, but suffered 'no beggars, rogues, vagabonds or idle persons'.[4] Later examples of the genre include Peter Chamberlen's *The Poore Man's Advocate* (1649), in which a state bank would centralize taxation and revenue in order to employ the poor in mining and agriculture; *A Way Propounded to Make the Poor Happy* (1659), by the Dutch Mennonite Pieter Plockhoy, which enjoined voluntary community of goods; and John Bellers's *Proposals for Raising a College of Industry* (1695), which suggested that workhouses for the poor could combine the advantages of 'college' life with devotion to useful labour. Two works printed at the end of the century, *An Essay Concerning Adepts* (1698) and *Annus Sophiae Jubilaeus, The Sophick Constitution: or, the Evil Customs of the World Reformed* (1700), also enjoin living in 'colleges', with uniformity of dress, goods shared in common and frivolous pursuits condemned; all are advised to be 'plainer than Quakers' and to embrace Christian and Spartan equality. These are among the last texts to feature alchemy as a key utopian focus (see pp. 152–53).

Feminist themes were also extended in the utopias of this period. By the early 18th-century an extraordinary discussion of the benefits of matriarchy and the evils of the existing European marriage system appeared in the form of James Lawrence's *Empire of the Nairs; or the Rights of Women, A Utopian Romance* (1811, second edition). Here 'matriotism' is seen as a leading virtue and the concept of fatherhood is unknown. By the end of the century marriage is generally portrayed in utopia as more voluntary, less tied to dowry, and more easily ending in divorce, than in the earlier period. Here, as often, utopia was in advance of the liberalization of public opinion. Lawrence's work was also a variation on the popular genre of the Eastern tale, in which oriental

Jean-Auguste-Dominique Ingres, *Odalisque with a Slave*, 1842. This painting was executed on the orders of King Wilhelm I of Württemberg, and shows an odalisque (female member of a Turkish harem) reclining and listening to lute music. Some suggest Ingres believed women belonged in the harem.

Hand-coloured etching, *c.* 1770–80, entitled 'The Destruction of the Royal Statue in New York'. It depicts the destruction of an equestrian statue of King George III of England on 9 July 1776 by a group of what appear to be slaves.

locations served to describe various depictions of life in the harem, of idealized Islamic commonwealths and similarly exotic phenomena.

The creation of the United States marks a definitive watershed in modern politics. But it is a moot point as to exactly what the utopic aspects of the American Revolution were. Revolts by colonists were nothing unusual; republics had existed on a small scale since antiquity. The political system of checks and balances eventually settled upon by the Americans imitated the British constitution to some degree and was designed to constrain the excesses of human nature, not to unleash a more benevolent strain thereof. Nor was revolutionary zeal intended to surpass the moment of rebellion. But what was utopic in the experience was the underlying investment of chiefly Protestant, partly millenarian zeal: when wedded to an image of bountiful, nearly free land and virtually unlimited opportunity, this would eventually define the destination of the United States for millions of emigrants. So, too, the relative egalitarianism of the American constitution –

LA DESTRUCTION DE LA STATUE ROYALE A NOUVELLE YORCK.

Die Zerstorung der Koniglichen Bild Saule zu Neu Yorck | La Destruction de la Statue royale a Nouvelle Yorck

New York. Ellis Island. reg. No. 3163 E

slaves, women and native Americans, and, for a time, many of the unpropertied, aside – owed much to Harringtonian concepts of the need to balance the influence of landed property ownership. The alluring 16th-century image of the 'new world' became transformed into a vision of America in which the streets were paved with gold – an image later assisted by real gold rushes – and the fields sprouted bountiful harvests. This is perhaps closer to the peasant image of the land of Cockaygne than to utopia (see p. 23). But the natives, once again, would pay much of the price for the abundance extended to immigrants.

The storming of the Bastille in Paris on 14 July 1789 marked an equally definitive moment (prior to the Bolshevik Revolution of 1917) in modern political utopianism. The distance separating the events that provoked the revolt of the American colonists and those that prompted the overthrow of France's *ancien régime* was considerable. The United States was a new country, with plentiful cheap land, invested with Protestant eschatological and millenarian expectation since its settlement in the 16th century. France was an old, corrupt country, and a far greater intellectual leap of faith was required to conceive fundamental reform. Such faith was, initially at least, often anti-religious, with some of the revolution's new festivals – including one that proclaimed worship of the goddess of Reason – mocking the formal ceremonies of earlier belief systems. A rigorous critique of the

Prise de la Bastille, a late 18th-century oil painting by an unknown artist depicting the storming of the Bastille on 14 July 1789 and the arrest of Governor de Launay – the events that marked the commencement of the French Revolution.

existing order was provided by leading Enlightenment figures such as Voltaire and Denis Diderot (see box, p. 95). To such writers, the progress of humanity entailed an assault on the mysticism fostered by Catholicism. Reason, unfettered, provided unto itself sufficient grounds to guide human conduct, if only meddlesome priests (the firmest allies of a corrupt monarchy and parasitic aristocracy) could be foiled. And writers such as Louis Sébastien Mercier imagined that if a 'loud voice' could 'rouse the multitude from their lethargy', monarchy would be no more.[5] Many believed that humankind was about to awaken, as from a coma: the people, feeling their sovereignty, would throw off their chains, never to be re-imprisoned. Wisdom and virtue would proceed from this catharsis. Small wonder that thereafter the concept of democracy would have many utopian, even millenarian overtones.

But was the revolution to be conceived as a movement forwards, perhaps in emulation of the new theories of commercial modernity being introduced by writers such as Adam Smith, or was it to aim at a return to a more pristine age of virtue? The most famous of all contributors to France's revolutionary impulse, Jean-Jacques Rousseau, the Lycurgus of his age, did not align himself with commercial progress. In his *Discourse on the Origins of Inequality* (1755) he recounted a secularized version of the Fall. Here an original condition of communal harmonious life, well advanced from the state of nature but prior to the institutionalization of the state and private property, had been rudely terminated by the imposition of a harsh social contract by the rich upon the poor, fettering them in perpetuity to a highly exploitative system of private property. In *The Social Contract* (1762) Rousseau proposed

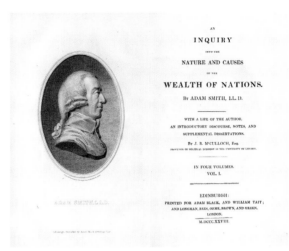

that the poor re-impose controls on the accumulation of property, luxury and political corruption. He asserted boldly that humankind was 'born free', in other words, originally innocent, but now found itself 'everywhere in chains',[6] ensuring an immediate identification with the Christian myth of Eden and the Fall, and more than a hint of Sparta. He prudently left open the vital question as to whether or how such a society might be created from the ruins of an imploding ancient monarchy like France, and in fact believed a return to virtuous purity to be impossible. But as both Hegel and Napoleon would later

ABOVE Frontispiece and title page of Adam Smith's *Wealth of Nations* (1776). Smith's text provided the paradigm of the liberal conception of unlimited free trade, increasing opulence and a relatively small sphere of state activity as the conditions of modern progress.

Jean-Jacques Rousseau (1712–78)

The French philosopher and political theorist was one of the dominant thinkers of his age, and his writings inspired the makers of the French Revolution. He was born in Geneva, then an independent city-state, on 28 June 1712, the son of a watchmaker. He became an apprentice engraver, then studied music. Moving to Paris, he was befriended by Diderot, Voltaire, d'Alembert and other leading Enlightenment thinkers. Rousseau's great fame was achieved through the publication of *The Social Contract* (1762), the work most often described as having provided the intellectual foundations of the French

Revolution. His link to utopianism comes chiefly through two earlier works, *Discourse on the Arts and Sciences* (1750) and *Discourse on the Origins of Inequality* (1755). The former, most notably, described a conjectural state of nature, milder than Thomas Hobbes's version, in which gradual development resulted in an enforcement of growing inequality by the rich upon the poor. Rousseau is often associated with the concept of the 'noble savage' and a glorification of the primitive, but he believed that any return to a more virtuous state would be extremely difficult.

French Revolution poster (1789) lauding the unity between the people and the army – Liberty, Equality, Fraternity or Death. The creation of a new popular army proved crucial to the life of the new republic after it was swiftly surrounded by hostile forces. But paranoia also militarized the regime and hastened the onset of the Terror.

acknowledge, he provided perhaps the most important impetus of all for the new doctrine of popular sovereignty, and for its association with a renewal of republican virtue. His hints at primitivism would be taken up by subsequent generations, in Britain most notably in William Godwin's *An Enquiry Concerning Political Justice* (1793), which would fuel the desire in his young followers – Samuel Taylor Coleridge, William Wordsworth and Robert Southey – to found a 'Pantisocratic' community in America (see box, p. 96). According to this system, labour was to be divided evenly, government shared equally and women released from drudgery.

The French Revolution would provide the template for much modern revolutionary utopianism, but it would also come to represent the mutation of utopia into dystopia. Originally modest in its aspirations, aiming to curb a corrupt monarchy, aristocracy and priesthood, the revolution lurched perilously into republicanism, emboldened with the ill-restrained excesses of popular enthusiasm.

Under the slogan of 'Liberty, Equality, Fraternity', it sought to export throughout the world an ideal of cosmopolitan republican brotherhood, which for some echoed the lost golden age or the principles of 'nature'. The suggestion has been made that those who most lusted after a return to such principles were also most susceptible to blood-letting.[7] Feudalism was abolished, slavery outlawed and oppression everywhere condemned.

However, by 1793 the tide had begun to turn. Surrounded by external enemies from the outset, the revolution, like the god Saturn, began to 'devour its own children'. In what is for many its most sinister turn, the desire to improve gave way to a desire to perfect. Virtue now required terror for its fulfilment and, increasingly, Monsieur Guillotine's 'holy' instrument became its assistant. Terror was 'the order of the day' on Jacobin command in late

August 1793. As expectation rose, feverishly fewer were inevitably capable of attaining its heights. The people, it was said, were 'sublime', incapable of error, but individuals were increasingly falling well short thereof. Failure (especially military inadequacy) indicated moral delinquency and was defined in terms of an absence of revolutionary zeal. General after general had brief and terminal meetings with the guillotine. The price of failure inflated like paper currency in the financial markets. The inability to attain virtue soon became equivalent to deserving nothing but death. All those not included in Rousseau's ideal of the general will, or in Louis de Saint-Just's term 'the sovereign' – that is, anyone opposed to the motions of the moment – became outsiders, the other, the enemy, traitors, fit only for disposal. What had formerly been heresy now became deviation from the party line. But in many respects the language of religion prevailed: the goal remained perfectibility. Some fifty-five thousand died in the Reign of Terror between 1793 and 1794, as the Committee of Public Safety threw judicial practice to the winds and began to execute on the basis of whether the supposedly guilty exhibited guilty faces, with no right to self-defence. Finally, the Terror's leaders – first Danton, then Robespierre – themselves fell victim and were executed without trial, and a sense of order was restored.

A faut esperer q'eu se jeu la finira bentot

To many later commentators this colossal eclipse of the promise of the revolution was an important turning point in the transformation of utopia into dystopia. Scholars such as Karl Popper would endeavour to extend the attack upon the ideal of the 'open society' as far back as Plato.[8] But few would dispute that the spirit of the mob, the revenge of the uneducated and unprivileged, was now unleashed and that its fury knew few bounds. It would thereafter often reappear, after 1917 in Russia, when some two million were executed, and again during the Chinese cultural revolution, when thousands of intellectuals were

Coloured etching (1789) of the populace oppressed by the wealthy. It plays upon popular resentment of the heavy burden of taxation imposed upon the poor under the *ancien régime*, and the inequality caused by exemptions from taxation enjoyed by the aristocracy.

killed or brutally persecuted, and yet again under Pol Pot following the Cambodian Revolution, to give only a few examples.

Yet the French Revolution was utopian in other, more positive ways. A new calendar was introduced to tame time and was constructed chiefly around the seasons (its originator was guillotined in year two of the revolution). The chaos of ancient and feudal territorial evolution was given order by a new system of communes. The new equality was celebrated in popular festivals, and through powerful symbols such as the tree of liberty and the Phrygian cap or *bonnet rouge*, the uniform of the *sans-culottes*, or artisans. Emblems of the old despotism, like the Bastille itself, were destroyed.

Despite its failings, the French Revolution provided the model for subsequent revolutions throughout the later modern period, most notably in Russia and China, then in many other countries. In its utopian aspect, in the writings of the Marquis de Condorcet, Godwin and others, it wedded a vision of scientific and moral progress to an ideal of political improvement. It gave rise to a variety of literary utopias, though perhaps fewer than expected: William Hodgson's *The Commonwealth of Reason* (1795) was a leading British example of the ideal polity underpinned by revolutionary principles, while the

Nicolas de Caritat, Marquis de Condorcet (1743–94)

This French philosopher is now regarded as one of the leading later Enlightenment figures. Associated with the Girondins during the early stages of the French Revolution, Condorcet opposed the execution of King Louis XVI and was imprisoned. After a period in which he lived as a fugitive, he died mysteriously, possibly by suicide. An opponent of slavery and a wide-ranging thinker, his chief contribution to the assessment of modernity came in his *Sketch for an Historical Picture of the Progress of the Human Mind* (1795), which traced in ten stages the evolution of social groups from tribal and pastoral peoples up to the founding of the French Republic. Condorcet believed that the progress of humanity rested on three suppositions: the abolition of inequality between nations; the advancement of equality within each nation; and the 'true perfection' of humankind. These themes, united as the most advanced 'state of civilization', he thought had already been reached by the French and Anglo-Americans. The key problem was thus extending them to barbarous or savage nations, without exacerbating the sense of racial contempt and the growing inequality between wealthy and poor that he condemned.

Godwinian vision outlined in *Memoirs of Planetes* (1795) described the coming utopian regime as established by a violent revolt. More importantly, the ideas of leading 18th-century utopians like Gabriel-Etienne Morelly were taken up by revolutionary conspirators such as François-Noël Babeuf and Philippe Buonarroti, two leading founders of the modern revolutionary communist tradition. We are here at the doorstep of socialism. Yet some remnants of republican utopianism would remain throughout the subsequent period: G. A. Ellis's *New Britain* (1820), for example, describes a large community settled in the interior of the United States. Money has been abolished, labour and trade are carefully regulated, property-holding is limited, public servants are unpaid, and the dominant religion is deism. As nearly as possible, the practice of philanthropy and abstemious conduct have brought the society to a condition in which virtually no laws are required.

François-Noël Babeuf (1760–97)

The French revolutionary was editor of *The Tribune of the People* (1794), which advocated an egalitarian communism. Influenced by Gabriel-Etienne Morelly's *Le code de la nature* ('The law of nature', 1755), among other works, Babeuf originated the conspiratorial tradition that would come to predominate in the 19th-century European and Russian revolutionary movements. Born to poor parents in Picardy on 23 November 1760, Babeuf became a labourer, then a clerk to a notary. By the time of the French Revolution he was already committed to some type of scheme for the redistribution of property. He became involved in a tax rebellion and advocated the leasing of confiscated Church lands to the peasantry. By 1791 he was interpreting natural law theory in terms of an 'agrarian law' that would permit the redistribution of common and wastelands to property-less peasants. From early 1793 he assumed the name of 'Gracchus' to identify himself with ancient Roman proponents of a similar scheme, and had begun to consider proposals for abolishing money and individual commerce as well as idleness, and the reduction if not abolition of foreign trade in luxury goods. Though he had been no friend to Jacobin dictatorship, he was guillotined under the Directory.

Chapter 8

Ideal Cities

Medieval to Modern

The quest for utopia can be seen in terms of two contrasting traditions, one essentially rural, the other urban. But utopia has often had a deeply ambiguous relationship with the city. Pastoral peoples who tend flocks have little need for towns. In regions where nature is abundant and the climate is kind, basic buildings ensure simple comforts. In the languid ambience of a tropical paradise, a grass shack, or at most a long hut for the extended family, is all that is needed to separate one set of satisfied sighs from another. For a small religious community, the simple elegance of a cluster of wooden dwellings, with some communal building, as in a Shaker village, is often adequate. But, as they increase in size and complexity, agricultural societies generate ever-larger urban centres. Industrialization then hastens this process greatly.

By the early modern period the promotion of city planning and the design of urban spaces became a means of creating and maintaining social control in utopian plans and fantasies. This resulted not merely from the increasing urbanization of the wider society but because of the specific function of utopian planning. Although social order in both rural and urban contexts relies on a blend of customs and manners, laws and constitutions, and the social regulation of potentially disruptive forms of behaviour (such as profligacy and sexual rivalry), rural images of the ideal society tend to rely less on formal embodiments of such restrictions. Social order is less worrisome when scarcity does not exist. The more urban the ideal, the more highly regulated its vision tends to be, though terror would be plentiful in the countryside under Marxist regimes.

With extreme urbanization the image of the city tends towards the dystopian. The most highly restrictive, totalitarian versions of this threatening image tend to compartmentalize human life into small, restrictive spaces of work and living – units organized to control

Tempera on panel work by Taddeo di Bartolo, showing the 4th-century bishop San Gimignano holding a model of his eponymous town, *c.* 1391. The city remains justly famous for its towers and the harmonious beauty of its setting.

Map of Aachen, from Franz Hogenberg's *Civitates orbis terrarum*, Volume 1, 1572. A hand-coloured copper engraving, it gives a good sense of the confined, compact scale of many medieval cities.

individual life to the maximum degree. These are juxtaposed with massive public spaces dominated by the regime's ideology. Some idealized urban spaces (including Francis Bacon's description of Bensalem in *New Atlantis*, *c.* 1624, Charles Fourier's *phalanstère* buildings and Robert Owen's proposed communities of the early 19th century) pay little or no attention to this concept of policing. In other urban utopian images, however, walls and the construction of buildings are integrated into surveillance systems that facilitate obedience. Thus architecture, urban planning and even the design of entire nations have always played a vital role in the utopian imagination.

The deliberate planning of towns and cities dates from the ancient world. Urban spaces tend to evolve around defensible sites, rivers, bridges and natural intersections of trade, or in proximity to agricultural land. Expanding populations, especially empires, have always generated new ideas of urban settlement. The Egyptian pyramids, though monuments to the dead, may be seen as the prototypical designs for urban spaces in which the functions of housing and propagandistic control – by their sheer impressiveness – were established. The Greeks built a number of grid-shaped cities to accommodate their needs, particularly in their colonies. To the Romans a viable city required a secure water supply, public baths, a good road system, as well as temples, administrative buildings, barracks, facilities for sports and, of course, housing. When Carthage was rebuilt after the Romans destroyed it, all these features were provided, and many Roman colonies and military camps were also grid-shaped. Great public spaces, such as the Forum in Rome, were designed to impress if not overwhelm, to wed religious, political and military symbols and, above all, to inspire patriotism. Apart from these practical concerns, cities have sometimes been planned in harmony with the supposed principles of nature or in accordance with mathematical principles, proportions of the human body or spiritual and religious conceptions. The City of God, the New Jerusalem, and the idea of heaven were interwoven with concepts of the ideal city from the early Christian era (see p. 33). Medieval Europe also produced a variety of urban mythical spaces. The legendary city of Camelot, based on the various descriptions of an English king, Arthur, dates from the 6th century and was reinvented in Sir Thomas Malory's *Le Morte d'Arthur* (1485) and again at various times, notably in Lord Alfred Tennyson's *Idylls of the King* (1891). Camelot is usually depicted as embodying a regime of peace and harmony following a lengthy period of Saxon civil war. Descriptions of the knights of the round table suggested a somewhat limited form of monarchy. Supposedly the capital of a southern English kingdom, Camelot progressed mythically from being a small-scale fortress to epitomizing the aspirations of medieval

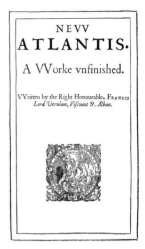

ABOVE Title page of Francis Bacon's *New Atlantis* (1628 edition). Bacon's was the prototypical text to portray a modern idea of indefinite scientific and technological progress.

BELOW Perspective view of Charles Fourier's 'phalanstère' (the rural areas and the gardens are not represented), from Victor Considérant's *Description du phalanstère et considérations sociales sur l'architectonique*, first half of the 19th century. Fourier regarded communal living and labour in a semi-rural setting as crucial to human happiness.

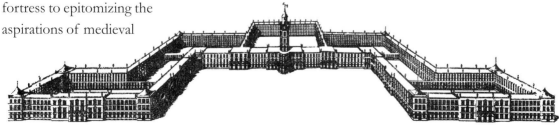

RIGHT Detail from Ambrogio Lorenzetti's *The Allegory of Good Government*, 14th century. This famous fresco, adorning the walls of the Palazzo Pubblico in Siena, shows the Virtues, Faith, Hope and Charity, surrounding the Good Governor.

BELOW Plan of the ideal city Sforzinda, 1457. The designer, Filarete, hoped his plan for an eight-pointed star with a circular moat would function like a 'communal organism'. It was intended to be contrasted to cramped and dirty medieval urban conditions, and was often imitated.

chivalry, including gallantry, bravery, justice and devotion to the common good. The virtues and wisdom of its court magician, Merlin, have frequently been retold and reembellished. Its idealized portrayal of courtly life is satirized in Mark Twain's *A Connecticut Yankee in King Arthur's Court* (1886), which pits the case for modern democracy against degenerate feudalism.

More fantastic still was the urban imagery in one of the most influential myths of the medieval period, that of the land of Cockaygne, the secular equivalent of pie in the sky, first described as early as the 13th century. Here, in some accounts, edible food grows wild, cooked animals present themselves for feasting, and on reaching the age of fifty people return to the age of ten, thus defying death. Houses are built of sugar and the streets are paved with pastry. In Cuccagna, the Italian version of this fantasy of gluttony or satiety, there are bridges made of salami, rivers of milk or wine, and mountains covered with cream cheese. Working is a punishable offence.

Medieval ideal cities often reflected some version of the concept of New Jerusalem, as this was regarded not only as the embodiment of the spiritually perfect City of God but also as the aesthetically ideal urban space (just as Babylon, and Rome after its fall, symbolized human degradation). Many circular or polygonal proposals – such as that described by Anton Francesco Doni in 1552 – were variations on fortress design, with the intention also of enhancing princely power, as in the great radial walled city of Palma Nova, built in 1593.

The idea that cities might promote order was evident by the 14th century, when allegories portraying good and bad governments were painted on the walls of some Italian towns, including Siena. Renaissance ideas of order, balance, harmony and beauty combined in a variety of 15th- and 16th-century models. Filarete's architectural plans for the ideal city of Sforzinda (1457–64) were probably the first such Italian proposals and included two great squares laid out within a circle, with sixteen radial spokes. Circular piazzas with radiating spokes, as at Siena, subsequently became popular. A plethora of towers, as at San Gimignano, symbolized upward mobility, civic wealth, competitiveness, and increasing property prices. In More's *Utopia* (1516) rational principles were applied to an island with fifty-four identical walled towns distributed 24 miles (38 kilometres) apart. Terraced streets, 20 feet (6 metres) wide, with large gardens at the rear and doors that open automatically to admit all, stress the public nature of property; fireproof roofs and glazed windows indicate technological innovation. A variety of planned cities in the colonized new world applied similarly rationalist principles. Some Inca cities, such as Cuzco, are equally imaginative.

Monasteries provided inspiration for other variations on the ideal city. As described by François Rabelais in *Gargantua and Pantagruel* (1532–69), the abbey of Thélème (from the Greek for 'will' or 'desire') is a subsidized retreat for the aristocracy founded by the giant Gargantua. Here well-heeled members reject the usual monastic constraints of poverty, chastity and obedience, and the pursuit of knowledge and spiritual enlightenment. Luxury, evident in the surroundings, is not renounced but made public for all to enjoy. Extensive gardens, ornate furniture and plentiful comforts encourage the indulgence of pleasure – this does not result in libertinage but in a regulated lifestyle,

Map of Cuzco, from Franz Hogenberg's *Civitates orbis terrarum*, Volume 1, 1572. This rare portrayal of the 'sacred city of the sun' in the new world shows the king being carried by bearers in the foreground, and the city, palace and temples in the centre, at the time of the Spanish conquest.

ABOVE Title page of Tommaso Campanella's 'The city of the sun' (1623 edition). The policing of the model city's inhabitants, the Solarians, included supervision of magnanimity, fortitude, chastity, liberality, truth, gratitude, cheerfulness, exercise and sobriety.

free of clerical interference. The central building of the abbey is a hexagonal, six-storey construction in the Loire Valley, surrounded by six towers. It contains over nine thousand elaborately decorated rooms, including a splendid library. Rabelais' text is considered a satire on religious hypocrisy. It identifies the monastic life with the splendour of aristocratic indulgence and also hints at the need to purify Christianity and to condemn money-grubbing, legal imposture and idleness.

Tommaso Campanella's *La città del sole* ('The city of the sun', 1602) recounts in dialogue form the existence of an ideal city in the southern hemisphere. Formed symmetrically of seven rings, the city epitomizes the relationship between utopian social engineering and urban spatial planning. Decorations on the walls inspire the love of nature, respect for the gods and pursuit of knowledge. Property is owned collectively; wives, in a Platonic system of regulated breeding aimed at fitness, are also common. A four-hour workday is the norm. Education for all in both natural science and agricultural skills helps to preserve social equality. Considerable attention is paid to regulating sexual intercourse by prohibiting promiscuity and promoting the cultivation of desirable physical traits. The powerful sentiment of patriotism – which for Campanella would ultimately assume the form of obedience to a new universal (Spanish) monarchy – is cemented by sun-worship, which is institutionalized through prayers four times daily. Simplicity of diet and rigorous exercise help to ensure longevity.

Tommaso Campanella (1568–1639)

The Italian philosopher and writer, born to a poor family in Calabria on 5 September 1568, is best known as the author of *La città del sole* ('The city of the sun', 1602). Trained as a Dominican monk, Campanella studied science and philosophy, as well as Kabbalism and Zoroastrianism. He wrote a critical account of the Spanish monarchy in 1602, and his interests in heretical ideas resulted in arrest by the Spanish Inquisition and trial in 1596. Released, he promoted a reformation movement based on an idealized religious and political authority – established if need be by violence. Arrested again in 1599, he was sentenced to life imprisonment and wrote his main work while manacled in prison. After almost thirty years in captivity, he enjoyed a brief period of freedom at the end of his life, eventually dying in Paris on 21 May 1639.

Johann Valentin Andreae (1586–1650)

The German Lutheran Humanist scholar and religious reformer, author of *Fama* (1614) and of *Christianopolis* (1619), perhaps the most famous proposal for the ideal Christian city, was born on 17 August 1586 near Tübingen in southern Germany. He studied literature, music, art, mathematics and astronomy at university, mastered seven languages and became a Lutheran chaplain. He travelled widely in central Europe, becoming increasingly interested in organizing workers' guilds and improving the educational system. At Calw he established a protective organization for workers in the cloth factories and dye works, which survived into the 20th century. He is also associated with the founding of the Rosicrucians, a secret brotherhood interested in alchemy, astrology and the occult. Set against the background of the Reformation and its subsequent upheavals, and modelled in part on the works of both More and Campanella, *Christianopolis* uses the narrative of a shipwrecked pilgrim to describe a society in which education has become universal and peace prevails, chiefly through the defeat of Catholicism; deviants from the official religion are expelled. Government is through a senate and triumvirate of princes, comprising a high priest, a judge and a scholar. An influence on Bacon's *New Atlantis* has been claimed.

Far more elaborate designs would soon follow. Johann Valentin Andreae's *Christianopolis* (1619) describes a capital city of some four hundred people built on a hill and arranged around a 700-foot (215-metre) square surrounded by four towers. There is one public street, and the city is divided into separate districts for food, exercise and military preparation, and beauty. The city is designed to ensure adequate food supplies, medicine, water and means of defence. Trade and commerce are organized by district on the medieval guild principle. Most skilled trades inhabit the city centre, which is dominated by a circular temple and large library. The population of Christianopolis participates communally in road construction, guard duty and agriculture, but each person also follows their own trade. Clothing, food and work tools are distributed by the civic authorities, who also assign housing to ensure rigorous equality, though meals are taken privately. Clothing and furniture are simple; 'vanity, extravagance' and the 'baggage of iniquity' are proscribed.[1] Children are separated from their parents after early youth, and although women enjoy the

BELOW The city of Christianopolis, from Johann Valentin Andreae's 'Reipublicae Christianopolitanae descriptio', 1619. Inspired by both More and Campanella, Andreae developed medieval guild ideas of craftsmanship and brotherhood, and also reflected his admiration for the city-state of Geneva.

same education as men, they are dedicated to domestic employment. The city excludes beggars and other ne'er-do-wells, but punishment aims at correction and is relatively mild. As in Bacon's *New Atlantis*, scientific research is undertaken in a laboratory.

The 18th century witnessed a variety of attempts at architectural innovation. The famous saltworks erected by Claude-Nicolas Ledoux in the 1770s comprised a large circular town entered by a gateway, with a central director's house and a church overlooking the production facilities. The workers' housing, illuminated at night, was adjoined by communal fruit and vegetable gardens. Beyond these were further administrative buildings. Other designs in the period indicate substantial variations on these themes, though geometric exactitude is evident in most. A few large cities, like St Petersburg, were planned in the period, and a variety of lesser ones.

The 19th century was the great age of European intentional socialist communities (see pp. 128–38). These were frequently parallelogram-style arrangements that housed large numbers in a central space, usually one building, to maximize the efficient use of resources (thus demonstrating the economic superiority of communal over private or individual living). Gardens and walkways were often planned around the central buildings, with factories and industrial facilities at some

RIGHT Claude-Nicolas Ledoux's plan for the royal saltworks at Arc-et-Senans in Franche-Comté. This plan, incorporated into proposals for an 'ideal city' named Chaux (1804), portrays industry as central to the good order of modern society.

OPPOSITE ABOVE The engraving shows the 'Familistère' of Guise in Normandy, built by the stove manufacturer and disciple of Charles Fourier, Jean-Baptiste André Godin, to house his workers and their families, 1859–80, and regarded as epitomizing the potential of such proposals.

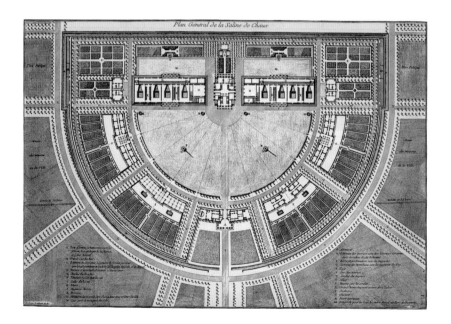

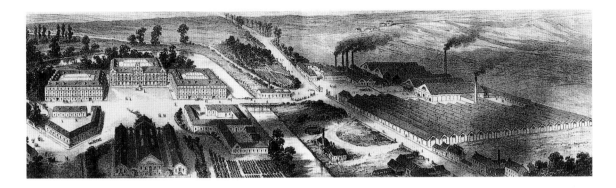

distance from living quarters. A design of this type was constructed at Guise in Normandy by Jean-Baptiste André Godin between 1859 and 1880. Here a system of internal galleries allowed movement around a courtyard, which provided an area for discussion and also ensured light, space and the circulation of fresh air.

A grid system was often suggested for larger colonies. In the capital city of Icaria in Etienne Cabet's *Travel in Icaria* (1840), for example, fifty boulevards intersect fifty avenues at right angles, while residential blocks each contain fifteen homes and gardens. Three civic centres, one in the middle and one at each end of the city, and the placement of all forms of noxious industry, such as abattoirs, on the perimeter of the city, assist the plan of urban order. Robert Owen's communities, as portrayed by Stedman Whitwell and others, and those of his associates, such as John Minter Morgan, usually followed a parallelogram design. Other designs for model towns based on socialist principles were proposed by James Silk Buckingham (for the town of 'Victoria', 1849) and by Robert Pemberton, among others, the latter for a colonial setting. Benjamin Ward Richardson's plan in *Hygeia* (1876) recognized the growing problem of sanitation.

Capitalists also designed and built various industrial cities and villages in this period. In Titus Salt's village of Saltaire, constructed in Yorkshire in the 1850s, a congregational church was placed at one end of the project and the entrance to Salt's textile mill at the other.

BELOW Plan of Etienne Cabet's Icarian settlement on a 39-acre site costing US$25,000 at Cheltenham, Missouri, which lasted from 1857 to 1864. Dining here was communal, and, unlike in the Nauvoo Icarian community, children remained with their parents.

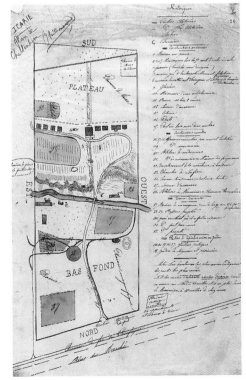

Other similar villages in England included Port Sunlight, begun in 1888 to house soap workers, and Bourneville, set up by the chocolate-maker George Cadbury in 1895. The United States saw the development of Pullman City in Chicago, and similar factory towns. It was not only in towns that the concept of social control was a crucial aspect of architectural design. Jeremy Bentham's famous model prison, the Panopticon, was constructed so that the inmates, who were housed in radial spokes, were permanently visible from a central observation hall.

As the century progressed, the United States produced a new capital city and a host of lesser variations on the theme, many of which were planned on the grid pattern, from the city of Savannah in Georgia in the 1730s onwards, though Washington, DC included a number of variations on circular themes. Haussmann's redesigned Paris, often thereafter considered the most beautiful modern city in Europe, also included many grand circles besides sweeping boulevards and plentiful greenery.

At the end of the 19th century the reaction to industrialization engendered a variety of proposals to reimagine a more rural version of urban life, most notably in fiction. These included William Morris's philo-medieval *News from Nowhere* (1890). The great overcrowded metropolis, it was asserted, fed the vicious cycle of poverty, drink and crime. A cleaner, more virtuous life for the poor could be attained by relocating them to colonies on the land, as General Booth's plans for the Salvation Army suggested. Or the city itself might be subject to a radical reconceptualization and, as visionaries like Patrick Geddes proposed, 'civicized' by being reduced in scale to manageable limits, enforcing the idea that any true utopia must start with the neighbourhood. Among the most important of these efforts was the 'garden city' movement. This was set in motion by the publication of Ebenezer Howard's *To-morrow: A Peaceful Path to Real Reform* (1898), which was an attempt to correct Edward Bellamy's excessive urban and technocratic emphasis, while hoping that landed property would eventually be abolished. The results of Howard's labours were the construction of Letchworth and several other garden cities, where a balance of housing, green space and scope for civic spirit was given priority. The moral dimension of promoting neighbourly cooperation through balanced urban design was later given support in Percival and

THIS IS THE PICTURE OF THE OLD HOUSE BY THE THAMES TO WHICH THE PEOPLE OF THIS STORY WENT. HEREAFTER FOLLOWS THE BOOK IT. SELF WHICH IS CALLED NEWS FROM NOWHERE OR AN EPOCH OF REST & IS WRITTEN BY WILLIAM MORRIS.

Paul Goodman's *Communitas* (1947), among other works. Such texts questioned whether cities should be designed for living or for promoting commerce. Nostalgia for the loss of village and small-town life is also common in this period, as in Sherwood Anderson's *Winesburg, Ohio: A Group of Tales of Ohio Small Town Life* (1919).

In the 19th century cities expanded outwards, but in the 20th century they grew massively upwards. The high-rise office and dwelling came to epitomize urban architectural aspiration in great cities such as Chicago and New York early in the century. Unlike later productions of glass and steel, these early examples were often highly refined, elaborated innovations based on Jugendstil design, among other styles. The 20th-century Modernist movement in architecture was led by Le Corbusier (the assumed name of Charles-Edouard Jeanneret, 1887–1965) and Tony Garnier. In Le Corbusier's plan 'Ville pour trois millions d'habitants' ('City for three million people', 1922) skyscrapers are set in parks, planned transportation and communication networks are prioritized and habitation is divided according to social class. In his 'Plan voisin' ('Neighbourhood plan', 1925) Le Corbusier proposed that the centre of Paris should be demolished to make way for skyscrapers, and in his later plans for the 'radiant city' he proposed that everyone should live in them. He provided impressive designs for cities like Rio de Janeiro,

William Morris (1834–96)

English designer, writer and socialist, Morris was a leading figure in the Arts and Crafts Movement, and author of late Victorian Britain's best-known utopia, *News from Nowhere* (1890). Born to a wealthy family on 24 March 1834, he studied at Oxford, where he consorted with Edward Burne-Jones and other artists, and came under the influence of John Ruskin. He formed a workshop, Morris and Company, to manufacture furniture and decorations, mostly in the medieval style. He also produced a variety of poetic works, notably *The Life and Death of Jason* (1867) and *The Earthly Paradise* (1868). Having begun life as a political conservative, in the late 1870s he became increasingly engaged with British imperial and then domestic policy, finally converting to socialism in the early 1880s. He lectured widely on the need to integrate creative art into the process of work, and to render the external surroundings of human life beautiful as a means of fostering humanity, themes central to the socialist vision of the future portrayed in *News from Nowhere*, which was written initially as a critique of Edward Bellamy's *Looking Backward*.

Ebenezer Howard (1850–1928)

This English urban planner was the author of *To-morrow: A Peaceful Path to Real Reform* (1898), reprinted as *Garden Cities of To-morrow* (1902), which established the idea of the 'garden city' as an ideal living arrangement. Born in London on 29 January 1850, Howard became a clerk, then in 1871 emigrated to the United States and spent time farming in Nebraska. Moving to Chicago, he encountered Benjamin Ward Richardson's *Hygeia, or, the City of Health* (1876), which persuaded him that 'a sort of marriage between town and country' would best define an intelligently designed urban space. Returning to London, he dabbled in spiritualism and fell under the influence of Peter Kropotkin and Henry George. The latter's conception of the 'unearned increment' collected by the landlord became central to Howard's economic ideas, as did the re-publication by H. M. Hyndman of a tract by Thomas Spence in 1882. He drew some inspiration from Edward Bellamy, too, though eventually came to sympathize more with William Morris. His firm belief became that a single, communally owned garden city, if successful, would provide inspiration for the rejuvenation of society as a whole. Two garden cities were built during his lifetime: Letchworth (1903) and Welwyn Garden City (1920).

BELOW Garden city concept by Ebenezer Howard, originally published in *Garden Cities of To-morrow*, 1902. Despite the plan's geometric appearance, it centred on balancing the best of urban and rural living by providing green belts and by attuning the needs of industry with ecology.

São Paulo, Montevideo and Algiers, and constructed vast buildings, notably in Marseilles (1947–52). But the beehive approach did not appeal to everyone. Writers like Ralph Borsodi urged decentralization of residence. Innovative individual housing was developed by, among others, the architects Frank Lloyd Wright and Hannes Meyer, a director of the Bauhaus school, which originated in Weimar following World War I. In a concept for Broadacre City, Lloyd Wright proposed repopulating the United States in thousands of decentralized homesteads, thus abolishing the distinction between rural and urban.

Some have found the movement upwards to be alienating, dehumanizing, ugly and impersonal; others insist that the logic of capitalistic development, and the subordination of all planning to commercial ends, especially the production of an efficient, controlled, cheaply amused working class, must be rejected. In the mid-20th century, experimental, human-centred architecture continued to be promoted by writers such as Buckminster Fuller, who sought to use mass-production methods to permit moveable, self-subsistent houses to be created that would maximize individual independence; and by

Lewis Mumford, disciple of Howard and determined enemy of Le Corbusier, who specifically linked urban redesign to utopian thought. Would humankind or machine prevail? Was the home to be the appendage of the workshop or factory, or vice versa? Would the nuclear family retreat to suburban fortresses or be reintegrated into more publicly defined spaces? Did standardization, as the philosopher Theodor W. Adorno insisted, always imply centralization? Did the urban, perhaps in part because of its carnivalesque possibilities, tend inevitably towards Babylon rather than the Heavenly City?

By the late 20th century, optimistic aspirations in many cities were beset by suburban flight, the growth of inner city ghettoes, rising crime rates and the deterioration of early tenement structures. As the suburb came to form the model township for the affluent, many cities deteriorated into wastelands, their downward spiral chronicled in Jane Jacobs's *The Life and Death of Great American Cities* (1961) and caricatured in theme parks such as Disneyland; some would later undergo urban regeneration. Sociologists like Richard Sennett have argued that a degree of urban chaos, disorder and anarchy might be more conducive to promoting human freedom.[2] Yet entire new cities of high-rises continued to be built. The tower block became the model of choice for postwar British planners; vertical ghettoes supplanted horizontal

R. Buckminster Fuller's pavilion for the New York World's Fair of 1964–65. The geodesic dome, which could also be mass-produced, was lightweight but strong, energy-efficient, and permitted a wide variety of internal design arrangements.

ghettoes. Cosmopolis seemed to be the ideal towards which the future tended. Among the world's first large-scale cities to be constructed in the modern style was Brasilia. Fuelled by such movements as Futurism and Cubism, the Soviet Union after 1917 produced an explosion of imaginative designs, including Konstantin Melnikov's 1929 'green city' plan, partly inspired by Fourier. But the Soviet style chiefly resulted in a distinctive form of apartment block, emulated in China and elsewhere, which often provided only cramped and uncomfortable living quarters. The redesigning of Moscow around a green belt and residential satellites, but centred on heavy industrial production, was one result of communist planning. The mercilessly complete destruction of old Beijing from the 1980s onwards was another.

The political uses of modern design were also evident in totalitarian planning and building. Totalitarian public architecture is usually imposing, intimidating, austere and militaristic. Large-scale meeting places, such as Nuremberg Stadium, Red Square or Tiananmen Square, function to focus both upon the cult of leadership and the overwhelming power of the anonymous but united crowds. Massive avenues permit the flow of crowds and their easy military control. Buildings may celebrate the heroic or mythic facets of the particular regime's ideology, as in Italy, and are often planned on a gargantuan scale – as was one of Hitler's favourite projects, Albert Speer's proposed new vision of Berlin, which was to be renamed Germania. Giant portraits, flags and other symbols reinforce the submission of the individual to the communal. Less thought was devoted to the design of concentration camps, which by

the 1940s held millions of individuals in the most dystopian of urban spaces. And in some instances, notably under the Khmer Rouge in Cambodia, the city itself came to symbolize degeneration and vice, and only small-scale village and country life, where the purity of the peasant ideal of 'real people' was maintained, was revered.

By the 21st century some reversal of the process of urban decay had become evident. Many innovative designs from the 1960s

Model for the Great Hall in what was to be Germania, capital of the National Socialist Third Reich, as designed by Adolf Hitler's chief architect and Minister of Armaments, Albert Speer, who had also designed the 'Deutsches Haus' pavilion at the 1937 Paris Exposition.

onwards, by architects like Paolo Soleri, incorporated ecological themes into their schemes. Designs such as Biosphere II, in Arizona, took sustainability as their central goal. Magnetic trains, wind farms and vast deserts generating solar energy are common images in contemporary portrayals of the sustainable future.

Great cities also require compelling buildings, like the Pantheons of Rome or Paris, the British Museum, the palaces of kings and aristocrats, such as Blenheim or Versailles, Warsaw's Palace of Culture, Hitler's Reichskanzlei, symbols of wealth and power, or places of entertainment, like opera houses and theatres. Great buildings are often small cities unto themselves and historically have often trumpeted supposedly classical or modern virtues, and been embellished with the symbols of military glory, religious pomp and civic authority. Such symbolically significant buildings, such as the new Bibliothèque Nationale de France at Tolbiac, continued to be built in the late 20th century. But far more common was the development of the mall, an import from the United States, where hundreds of shops provide wares in one gigantic space designed to furnish an all-encompassing, sanitized consumer experience.

Biosphere II in the Catalina Mountains near Oracle, Arizona. Columbia University aimed to permit scientists to live and work for extended periods in its enclosed 'biome'-based building in order to test the habitat's environmental principles.

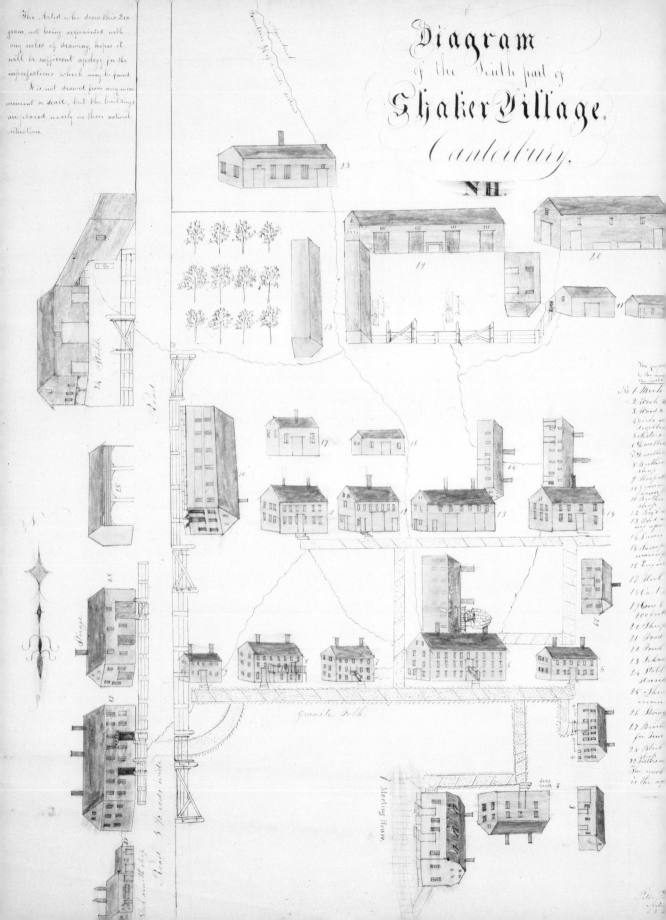

Chapter 9

Utopia as Community

From Shakers to Hippies

Utopianism may be seen, in part, as an attempt to recapture a lost sense of community or, in the face of social disintegration, to forge new bonds of collective purpose by laying down laws, constitutions and modes of organization that enforce a greater degree of social duty, order and often equality, than is provided in the wider society. Historians use the phrase 'intentional communities' to describe the formation of living and working arrangements by a group of usually unrelated persons united voluntarily by a sense of common purpose. Communities often view themselves as members of a larger family. The monastery is one such prototypical community, as are many forms of colonial experiment. Many have been small-scale and have failed fairly quickly but others have enjoyed considerable success. The modern communitarian movement is distinctive for its small-scale collectivist organization. Whether religious sectarianism or secular socialism provides an ideological link, most modern communities have shared the burden and produce of labour in common, often for many years.

The most important modern communitarian developments have taken place in the United States, often as part of a process of religious, and later political, settlement to escape persecution in Europe. About ninety communities were founded in the United States between 1780 and 1860. By 1914 at least two hundred more had been established, and many more were founded later in the 20th century. Such experiments have been regarded as an integral aspect of the development not only of the frontier of the United States, but of the society itself, particularly with respect to the waves of religious revivalism that have swept over the country from its foundation onwards, which have at times been integrally linked to the westward extension of the frontier.

Hand-drawn 'Diagram of the South part of Shaker Village', part of Canterbury, New Hampshire, by Peter Foster, 1849. The community, which Ralph Waldo Emerson described as an ideal 'protestant monastery', still had seven inhabitants, all women, in 2003.

American communitarianism commences in the 17th century with settlements in Delaware in 1663 by the Dutch Mennonite Peter Cornelius Plockhoy, and by the French Separatist Jean de Labadie, who established a monastic regime with enforced celibacy, equal labour and spartan living conditions. From the late 17th century a variety of German Pietists and sectarians made similar experiments, including the Dunkers, some of whom also practised celibacy and community of property, and whose best-known settlement was Ephrata in Pennsylvania.

Modern communitarianism dates from the late 18th century, and was initially largely sectarian and centred upon seeking religious freedom in the new world, much like the pilgrims a century earlier. One of the most successful early efforts of this type were the colonies of Shakers, some of which survive to this day. Led from the 1770s by the prophetess of the Second Coming, 'Mother' Ann Lee (1736–84), who stressed the centrality of female leadership, the Shakers emigrated from Britain and, beginning in Mount Lebanon, New York, in 1787, would eventually found over twenty settlements in Connecticut, Maine, Massachusetts and as far west as Indiana. Celibate, and thus able to expand only by attracting new members, the Shakers' vibrant religious culture, with its trance-like dancing, innovative music, powerful bonds of communal piety and economic prosperity – their furniture designs, in particular, continue to be produced to this day – proved a powerful recipe for success.

Like the Shakers, a variety of sectarian German Protestant sects also sought religious freedom in the United States. The best known of these were the Lutheran separatists known as Rappites, led by George Rapp (1757–1847), who began to share their goods in common on Christian conviction and in the face of grave economic challenges after emigration. They and their seceders founded a dozen communities between 1805 and 1862, one of which (Economy, Pennsylvania) had 1,200 members in 1847 and lasted until 1905. They also practised celibacy. The Rappites prospered through weaving, agriculture, saw-mills and other industrial ventures. Also of interest were the Zoarites, who emigrated to the United States in 1817 and settled in Ohio, where they

'Pennsylvania' by Katherine Milhous, 1894. This poster, promoting Lancaster County, depicts an Amish family. Milhous produced a series of colourful images of Amish life, demonstrating its distinctive dress, marriage rites, religion and culture.

soon abandoned celibacy and, after 1845, collective living arrangements for children. They cooked communally but ate in family units. Although they prospered greatly, they abandoned the communistic principle in the 1890s, whereupon the organization disintegrated. Another group of German Pietists founded various Amana colonies in the 1850s. Created initially on communal principles, the community was later reorganized into successful private but co-operative enterprises (based on agriculture and manufacture) and survives to this day.

The Amish and the Hutterite settlements are also examples of successful communitarianism. The Hutterites, whose origins date to early 16th-century Anabaptism, emigrated to North America from the 1870s onwards, and by 1991 had established more than three hundred communities in the United States and Canada, with over twenty thousand members. Like the Mennonites, both the Amish and the Hutterites are unified by distinctive modes of dress, forms of marriage and property-holding, as well as by strong religious beliefs enforced by daily congregational worship. Hutterite men are bearded and dress mainly in black. The Amish reject modern machinery as far as possible.

Even more successful in terms of its sheer scale has been Mormonism. Led by Joseph Smith (1805–44) and Brigham Young (1801–77), the movement originated in a supposed revelation to Smith, from the angel Moroni, of a supplement to the Bible, the Book of Mormon. Suffering constant persecution, and hounded from their New York origin, the Mormons moved westwards and founded a city at Nauvoo, Illinois, based on plots of 1 square mile (2.5 square km), with public buildings in the centre. Each plot was divided into half-acre (one-fifth of a hectare) lots that included a house. With twenty-five thousand inhabitants, at its peak it was the state's largest city, and there were plans to construct a central 'Jerusalem' with a temple and residence for a prophet. Eventually the Mormons were

Lithograph print of a Mormon family by Bernarda Bryson, c. 1930s. The husband, two wives and seven children appear in front of their dwelling, with several buildings in the community in the background. While not officially condoned, polygamy continues to be practised by some Mormons.

A MORMON FAMILY

The Great Mormon Tabernacle at Salt Lake City, Utah, photographed in 1868. Measuring 250 by 150 feet (75 × 45 m), its roof resting on forty-six stone columns and held up by wooden pegs and rawhide thongs, the building is the chief social and cultural centre of the Church of the Latter Day Saints.

driven still further westward into the desert regions of northwest America. From 1846 they moved to what became the state of Utah, with its capital at Salt Lake City. Today the Mormon church has over seven million followers, and is the fifth largest American religious denomination. Various types of communal organization and property-holding have been practised over the period of the history of the sect, and it retains a residual commitment to social equality and the relief of poverty. Some members still practise polygamy, though this is no longer officially condoned. Missionary work and the contribution of a tythe of income ensure the church's expansion and prosperity.

Both of the founders of British and French socialism, Robert Owen and Charles Fourier, set up communitarian experiments from the early 19th century onwards. Owen's factory village at New Lanark in Scotland was not strictly speaking such a community, as it was governed paternally by Owen himself as a manager and co-owner of the establishment and was not 'socialist' in the sense of sharing profits. However, Owen introduced certain features into the living arrangements of his workforce that indicate he intended to develop the village in this direction. Some two thousand people lived at New Lanark during the main period of Owen's stewardship over it, from 1800 to 1825. During this time he increased real wages, promoted infant education, discouraged illegitimacy, established a contributory sickness, injury and old age fund, policed pilfering and slackness, and organized the village into 'neighbourhood divisions' that elected members to hear disputes among residents. Sometimes referred to as 'happy valley', the model factory village was an immense success, drawing thousands of visitors from across the world, and providing proof that capitalist principles could be reconciled with workers' wellbeing. Today the village is a World Heritage site and a leading surviving example of 19th-century industrial communitarianism.

However, New Lanark simply marked the birth of Owen's vision. From 1817 onwards he increasingly dedicated himself to solving

Robert Owen (1771–1858)

This Welsh social reformer was the founder of British communitarian socialism. Born in Newtown, he was apprenticed to a sequence of textile merchants and became a factory manager in Manchester. In 1800 he assumed management of the New Lanark mills. Here he amassed a considerable fortune, and at the same time successfully improved working and living conditions. Less successful efforts to persuade fellow manufacturers to adopt a similar course coincided with a post-Napoleonic Wars economic depression, and Owen proposed rehousing the urban poor in 'parallelogram' communities on the land, where the benefits of labour could be shared in common. The resulting 'social system', termed 'socialism' by the mid-1820s, was contrasted to the 'individual system' of 'buying cheap and selling dear', or competition between individuals. Owen went on to become a leading trades union organizer in the mid-1830s, and to establish a substantial socialist movement in Britain in the later 1830s and early 1840s, when his Queenwood community absorbed considerable funding before finally failing in 1845.

poverty by relocating the poor in rural communities where goods would be shared in common and labour fairly distributed. As the Owenite movement developed from the 1820s to the 1840s, a number of attempts were made to replicate New Lanark's success. In 1824 Owen acquired the ready-made New Harmony community on the banks of the Wabash River in Indiana, then at the edge of the American frontier. Lured by newspaper advertisements, applicants flooded in. Few shared Owen's idealism but many more desired to share his fortune. Unruly, ill-equipped and badly organized, they

LEFT Model for a proposed community at New Harmony, designed by the architect Stedman Whitwell to be constructed by Robert Owen. The actual community was much less grandiose, being a set of farmhouses bought from a German Pietist sect. Note the industrial site in the background.

rebelled against his paternalism. Harmony was soon a scarce commodity and the experiment disintegrated within a few years. Nearly twenty other attempts were made to establish colonies on Owenite principles in the United States through the mid-1840s, including one in Kendall, Ohio (1826–29), and Equality in Wisconsin (1843–46), but few lasted more than a year.

In Britain, Owenite communities were started at Orbiston, south of Glasgow; at Ralahine in Ireland in the mid-1820s; and at Manea Fen, Cambridgeshire, and elsewhere, in the 1830s. A rival set of Chartist colonies also aiming to relocate the poor on the land was begun in the 1840s, notably at O'Connorville, Hertfordshire, named after the Irish Chartist leader, Feargus O'Connor. The most important Owenite effort was begun in the late 1830s at a site named Tytherly, also called Queenwood or Harmony, in Hampshire. Here Owen invested substantial funds drawn from a burgeoning movement of local branches in an effort to create a model institution. No expense was spared. Quality materials, including imported lumber, were used; a dumb-waiter system, which brought food to the dining room and removed dirty dishes, rivalled that of the best London hotels. Elaborate gardens were laid out and a fine, castle-like structure erected. But the land was of poor quality, and in the midst of a severe

Charles Fourier (1772–1837)

The French philosopher and communitarian socialist was born to a linen merchant in Besançon on 7 April 1772. He became a draper, lost his fortune during the French Revolution, and came to believe that the chief flaws of modern development could be solved by a system of community life revolving around a central building, the *phalanstère*, or phalanx. Besides the concoction of an elaborate metaphysics, Fourier's psychology centred on a description of the passions, the satisfaction of which was to be the chief goal of community life. Work, in particular, would be transformed into 'attractive labour', and performed in rotation, with many tasks undertaken during any one day, interspersed with elaborate meals and plentiful entertainment. Reward for labour would not be communistical, but shared between capital, labour and talent. Fourier's main works include *The Theory of the Four Movements* (1808) and *The New Industrial World* (1829). His daring paean to unrestricted sexuality, *The New Amorous World*, was not published until 1967. He died on 10 October 1837, having inspired a substantial following in France, the United States and elsewhere.

agricultural and industrial recession the colony collapsed. With it went the dreams of the communitarian socialists: a close observer of the failure was the young Friedrich Engels, who harboured a nostalgic affection for such efforts for a few years before conceding the need to found socialism on the scale of the nation-state, and by revolution rather than philanthropic example.

In France, Charles Fourier's followers were of some intellectual influence, but their attempts to found a *phalanstère*, or phalanx (commune), were less successful, though a variety of efforts was made, notably at Guise. Fourierism made a greater impact in the United States, where the publication of Albert Brisbane's *The Social Destiny of Man* (1840) coincided with an economic recession to induce a new wave of enthusiasm for community life. Some thirty colonies were established between 1841 and 1847, though most survived only a year or two. By 1850, by which time economic prosperity had returned, only one remained, the Wisconsin phalanx. The most famous community was Brook Farm (1841–47), originally founded by a group of Transcendentalists that included Ralph Waldo Emerson and Henry David Thoreau. Brook Farm was portrayed fictionally in Nathaniel Hawthorne's *Blithedale Romance* (1852). Some thirty members of the Brook Farm community at West Roxbury, near Boston, aspired to embrace practical Christianity. Voluntary rotation of labour was practised, though intellectuals soon shirked the harder tasks and financial problems resulted. Fourierist innovations were introduced in 1844, but without lasting success. Similar experiments were made at Fruitlands and Hopedale. Also of note was the North American phalanx in New Jersey, which lasted some thirteen years (1843–56). Here a 155-foot (45-metre) central building was constructed with family apartments and bachelors' quarters, as well as a dining room that seated two hundred. As in other Fourierist communities, women played an active role. Rotation of labour, perhaps Fourier's central economic idea, worked successfully most of the time.

French socialist communitarianism also included Etienne Cabet's attempt to implement the principles of his *Voyage en Icarie* ('Travel in Icaria', 1840) in the new world. Cabet led a group of followers to Texas in 1848, anticipating that a million acres (ninety-eight million hectares)

Etienne Cabet (1788–1856)

This French socialist was the author of *Voyage en Icarie* ('Travel in Icaria', 1840), which inspired a popular communitarian movement. Born in Dijon on 1 January 1788, he became a lawyer, and was attorney general of Corsica before attacking the institution of monarchy and retreating to exile in London. On returning to France in 1839, Cabet described in his chief utopian work an idealized community based partly on the ideas of Thomas More and Robert Owen. Here universal suffrage and direct democracy underpin government, labour is universal, goods and services are free and provided by the public, and equality is strictly mandated, down to the equal portions of food that are served at mealtimes. When his movement expanded to thousands of supporters, Cabet established a community in Red River, Texas, in 1848, and then at Nauvoo, Illinois. He finally moved to St Louis, Missouri, where he died. His ideals are defined by a rigid egalitarianism, the rejection of violent revolutionism, and considerable restrictions on individual freedom.

would be settled on democratic socialist principles. However, the first sixty-nine members were rapidly reduced by disease. Cabet himself arrived in 1849, acquired the vacated town of Nauvoo, Illinois, and ruled over two hundred members in an increasingly authoritarian fashion, banning both alcohol and tobacco, and setting spies among the inhabitants. The community eventually broke up.

The most famous later 19th-century commune in the United States was at Oneida, in upstate New York, led by the charismatic John Humphrey Noyes.[1] Prior to this, in 1831, Noyes underwent a religious conversion and came to believe in Christ's imminent return. More controversially, he concluded that if there was to be no marriage in the hereafter, sexual relations on Earth could be less restrained than they currently were. Gathering a small group of 'Perfectionists' around him, Noyes began to practise 'complex marriage' within the context of 'Bible Communism'. At the community he established in Vermont, group affection was permitted as long as no overly strong individual relationships developed; pregnancy was avoided by the practice of *coitus interruptus*. A process called 'mutual criticism' ensured publicity of all proceedings, although Noyes, who exercised authoritarian control, did not submit to it himself. After he was arrested for adultery, the group moved to Oneida, where some two hundred and fifty members lived in one building, the Mansion House. The community began experimentation with 'stirpiculture', breeding to achieve 'superior' or more perfect human beings. Several women chose Noyes himself to father their children; nine out of fifty-eight children born during this time were his offspring.

A few other communitarian experiments also merit mention. Colonies of freed black slaves existed in a variety of locations after the American Civil War (1861–65). Jewish agricultural settlements from the 1880s to the early 20th century were established in New Jersey, South Dakota, Oregon and elsewhere. Other groups were anarchist, Marxist or Positivist in inspiration. Of the anarchist communities that were set up in the United States in the later 19th century, perhaps the most famous was the colony at Modern Times, New York, inspired partly by the eccentric individualist economist Josiah Warren, and partly by the Positivism of Auguste Comte (see box, p. 144). Warren (1798–1874) began as a disciple of Robert Owen, but quickly became critical of New Harmony's organization and principles, and proposed instead

ABOVE 'The Children's Hour in the Upper Sitting Room', Oneida, New York, c. 1855. The system of 'complex marriage' or free love begun by John Humphrey Noyes and three associates in 1846 resulted in a growing population of children, whom Noyes attempted to raise as the collective property of the association.

John Humphrey Noyes (1811–86)

The flamboyant American communitarian socialist was founder of the Oneida Community in upstate New York and inventor of the system of 'complex marriage' practised there. Born on 11 September 1811 at Brattleboro, Vermont, he graduated from Dartmouth College, started studying law and then switched to theology. At Yale he underwent a religious conversion, and began to evolve the doctrines he termed 'Perfectionism'. By 1836 Noyes was practising his ideals in a small community in Putney, Vermont, but local hostility drove the group to Oneida, New York, in 1848, where they prospered for thirty years, manufacturing traps, bags and other articles, and preserving fruit. Several derivative communities were founded, which had more than 280 members by 1874. The Perfectionists proclaimed themselves to be utterly free from sin, which assisted in the practice of Noyes's system of sexual relations, one aim of which was the cultivation of more robust human beings. Variation in employment was also practised. The decline of Noyes's leadership and growing tensions resulted in a reversion to monogamy, and the community was dissolved in 1881. Noyes died in Canada, where he had fled in 1886 to avoid legal action.

A nursery school teacher with a group of children at a kibbutz in Yizreel Valley, Israel, 1936. In the early years of the movement children usually lived apart from their parents in communal quarters, but by the 1990s most remained with their own families.

that its core economic idea, 'equitable commerce', or trading labour at a fair rate to ensure a just wage, could be accomplished through 'Time Stores', which permitted producers to exchange their wares directly. Three communes based on these principles were started in Ohio and Indiana between 1827 and 1847, and Warren went on to propound the principle of the 'sovereignty of the individual' as the basis of his new system. Modern Times, founded in 1851, included such intellectual luminaries as Stephen Pearl Andrews among its members and is regarded as one of the earliest anarchist as well as free-love communes. Theosophists, spiritualists, vegetarians, feminists, 'General' William Booth's Salvation Army, the followers of John Ruskin, Henry George and other social prophets, and many minor sectaries, have also provided a sprinkling of other experiments in communal living. In the later 19th and early 20th centuries California and the Pacific Northwest became the sites of various experimental communities. Some of these were based on mystic principles (such as Thomas Lake Harris's Fountaingrove); some were later developments of earlier movements, such as Icaria Speranza; others were proto-ecological, such as Kaweah Cooperative Commonwealth, which aimed to protect the ancient Sequoia forests.

As far as community movements outside the United States are concerned, the most successful 20th-century initiative, inspired by the writings of Theodor Herzl and others, has been that of the kibbutz in Israel. The kibbutz ideal of collective labour, shared produce and economic self-sufficiency, wedded to Zionism, began with the

founding of Deganiah in 1909. It reached its peak in the 1950s and thereafter began a slow decline, accelerating in the 1980s as members found that the attractions of urban life outweighed the virtues of an abstemious communal existence. At its height the movement boasted some two hundred communities with around ninety thousand members. In Catholic countries convents and monasteries continue to provide a utopian space for believers, albeit in ever-declining numbers, to the present day.

Another wave of communitarian experimentation began with the social rebellions of the 1960s, resulting in the establishment of hundreds of colonies, urban and rural, in the US and elsewhere. To the slogan of 'Tune in, turn on, drop out', inspired by the reveries of gurus such as Timothy Leary, thousands of hippies and others rejected the conventionalism of middle-class, suburban consumer society in favour of an ideology of sensualism, free love and drug-taking. This was sometimes combined with various 'new age' philosophies, protests and anti-war politics, which were often linked to a plea for a return to nature. Although it was quickly commodified, its idealism diluted, its saleable produce integrated into mainstream culture, the movement generated an immense reservoir of social idealism and succeeded in eventually breaking many taboos on issues such as drug use and sex and pregnancy outside of marriage. Some ten thousand communities or more were established from the 1960s onwards, with as many as 750,000 members at their peak, some of which survive today.[2] Their aims were diverse, spanning a range of co-operative and living arrangements, varieties of property ownership and adherence to a common philosophy. A few, including the Diggers in the Haight-Ashbury district of San Francisco, were urban-based. Among the longest-lived are Twin Oaks, in Virginia, which currently has around one hundred members, and the Farm, in Tennessee. In the same period there emerged a number of cult-based communities centred on charismatic (often evangelical Christian) leaders but including scientologists (followers of the science-fiction writer L. Ron Hubbard) and various derivatives of Hinduism, notably the Rajneesh community in Oregon. Perhaps the best known of the modern cult-based communities were David Koresh's Branch Dravidian sect at Waco, Texas, which ended violently in 1993, and Jim Jones's 'Jonestown' cult in Guyana, where an infamous mass suicide took place in 1977.

Women's liberation demonstration in New York, 26 August 1970. Though feminism was an integral part of the radical social movements of the period, communes often retained a traditional division of labour. Sexual freedom also proved easier to achieve than equality of opportunity and reward in the wider society.

Chapter 10

The Second Age of Revolution

Socialism, Communism and Anarchism

It would be misleading to describe all forms of socialism as 'utopian'. Marx and Engels used the term to denigrate their political predecessors and to distinguish their 'scientific' doctrine from earlier forms of socialism. But such distinctions no longer hold. The thrust of the utopian argument, as discussed already, is that a better ordered society can be imagined if human failings are contained by a series of revisions to the law, the constitution, religion, social control, architecture and the environment, and so on. Socialism emerged in the early 19th century, in the immediate aftermath of the French Revolution. Its initial central premise was that the commercial system that was increasingly dominant in later 18th-century Europe had failed both to feed the poor and to hamper increasing selfishness and an obsessive desire for luxury. Socialism's response to these issues was varied and ranged from the provision of municipal milk supplies to the establishment of a centralized state economy based on Marxist principles. Not all forms of socialism in this period were communistical, and the degree to which the term 'utopian' can be applied to them depends on their adherence to a more rigorous egalitarianism, to the complete abolition of the market mechanism or to the insistence on perpetuating an ethos of self-sacrifice for the community.

Robert Owen (see box, p. 133) was a social reformer, the founder of British socialism and the successful manager of a cotton mill in Scotland. His mill became the site of the most famous experiment in behavioural engineering of its time. Owen was doubtless impressed by the potential power of the new steam engine and its capacity to reduce human labour. However, he was extraordinarily wary of the effects of cramming hundreds of workers into confined, overheated, dangerous conditions in order to generate high profits. He opposed the idea that

Edouard Manet, *Commune de 1871: la barricade*, 1871. This watercolour depicts the execution of Communards by Versailles troops after the failure of their uprising. Marx regarded the Commune, and particularly the principle of electing working-class political leaders, as the most successful demonstration of the viability of his socialist theories.

the capitalist rightly possessed unlimited power to exploit the workforce and he succeeded in improving the lives of his workers.

When the Napoleonic Wars came to a close in 1815, and with unemployment mounting, Owen proposed the construction of communities of 'mutual co-operation', which, by 1817, were to include forms of labour that ensured self-subsistence and profit-sharing. He termed this the 'social system'. By the mid-1820s the word 'socialism' was being used to describe this 'new system'. In the late 1830s it was being noted that socialists would 'be struck with the resemblance in many important particulars' between More's *Utopia* and 'the system they are endeavouring to establish'.[1]

Owen began a series of communitarian experiments (see pp. 132–35), which, among other things, promoted a more radical approach to family and marriage, making divorce more readily available. By the mid-1830s he was insisting that democratic-style elections should be supplanted by a system of social organization and government in which all passed successively through eight age groups that were designed to replace the existing class system. These stages included being educated, labouring, supervising others, governing the community and overseeing the community's relations with other communities. This 'anti-political' scheme, rooted in the preceding utopian tradition, would also be mirrored in later Marxist efforts to suppress partisan divisions.[2] Economically, Owen's communities were designed to organize production for use in the first instance, though any surplus could be traded with other communities. The desire for luxuries would be offset by the provision of greater free time for leisure. Eventually all great cities would be supplanted by such co-operative villages. Owenism spawned some literary utopias, notably John Minter Morgan's *The Revolt of the Bees* (1826) and John Francis Bray's *A Voyage to Utopia* (1842).

The other leading early 19th-century communitarian socialist, Charles Fourier (see box, p. 134) was, like Owen, a vigorous opponent of the effects of the commercial system on individual character. Unlike Owen, he did not believe that a fully communistical scheme of distribution could address the needs of human nature. Instead, Fourier proposed a three-fold division of profits in his *phalanstères*, or communes, with capital receiving a third, labour five-twelfths, and talent a quarter of the aggregate reward. But in other respects Fourier's scheme was more fantastic than Owen's. Phalansterean life was to be guided by a principle of 'passionate attraction', whereby individuals would indulge their pursuit of pleasure to as great a degree as possible, without stigma or fear of sin. 'Sexual courts' would ensure a minimum of carnal gratification and regulate congresses so that personal jealousies could be avoided and erotic experimentation encouraged. Like Owen's communities, Fourier's plans centred on one grand central structure, several of which were built in France and the United States. Among the other early communitarian socialists was Etienne Cabet, whose *Voyage en Icarie* ('Travel in Icaria', 1840) inspired an impressive communistical movement in France. The novel describes a fictional Mediterranean republic divided into one hundred provinces and led by Icar, who ensures a strict egalitarianism, with the regulation of diet, clothing and age of marriage, and the organization of labour.

The last of the early leading pre-Marxian socialists was Henri de Saint-Simon, who analysed the newly emerging 'industrial society'. He proposed replacing feudalism with a pacific, federative European state.

Henri de Saint-Simon (1760–1825)

This French nobleman assisted the American revolutionaries in their struggle against Britain, renounced his title, and went on to become a leading social theorist in early 19th-century France. Speculating in canal and land development after the revolution of 1789, he lost his fortune. His most important writing concerned the emergence of the new form of society that he termed (claiming to have coined the word) 'industrialism', about which he began to write from 1802 onwards. His influences included the Marquis de Condorcet and Jean-Baptiste Say. His *On the Reorganization of European Society* (1814) proposed a European parliament to ensure universal peace by arbitration of disputes. From

1816 to 1818 he published a journal, *L'Industrie*, and further pamphlets followed over the next few years. His central theses in these works focused on the need to empower productive labourers, including both capitalists and workers, to ensure a smooth transition from feudalism, or the militarist stage of society, towards a peaceful system oriented towards maximizing productivity. In his *Nouveau Christianisme* ('New Christianity', 1825) he argued for a purified variant of Christianity to assist the process of social transformation. Many of Saint-Simon's ideas were developed by a series of followers, including Auguste Comte, Barthélemy-Prosper Enfantin and Pierre Leroux.

According to his vision, scientists and administrators would assume most of the functions traditionally ascribed to government, with promotion based on merit, and the 'administration of things' supplanting politics as such (an idea that Marx found appealing). The Saint-Simonians, who achieved considerable influence in mid-19th century France, gave emphasis to feminism and to providing a new religion that wedded spiritual authority to the secular state. Saint-Simon's secretary, Auguste Comte, extended these themes further to describe a new 'religion of humanity', and designed his own decentralized version of a European utopia of the future. He became one of the fiercest critics of France's and Britain's expanding empires in the mid-19th century.

The degree to which Marx's and Engels's brand of socialism can be termed 'utopian' is contentious. The definition of utopianism given here is that of an imaginative projection of a better ordered society (not a perfectionist 'dream') that offers a solution to grievous social and political problems. And according to this definition Marx can be seen as the greatest of all modern utopian writers, in the sense of both having been far and away the most influential figure and of projecting the utopian scheme – community of property – onto a far larger population than ever envisioned before. Marx's starting-point, like

Auguste Comte (1798–1857)

A French philosopher, disciple and student of the Marquis de Condorcet and Henri de Saint-Simon, Comte was a key founder of the social science he first named 'sociology' in 1830. Born in Montpellier, and expelled from the École Polytechnique in Paris in 1816 for leading a student rebellion, Comte was intrigued by Saint-Simon's account of industrial society, and by the process of the secularization of knowledge. He famously classified the latter in terms of three stages – religious, metaphysical and positive – loosely terming his own system 'Positivism' to distinguish its scientific character. His six-volume *Course of Positive Philosophy* (1830–42) attracted a variety of disciples, including, briefly, John Stuart Mill. Comte's utopianism was defined in part by his proposals to break up all larger states into smaller entities, in which civic identity could flourish more actively. He also proposed an idealized government of scientists and industrialists, which would compose the temporal authority, and a priesthood centred in Paris, which would furnish spiritual authority through promoting the 'religion of humanity'. His four-volume *System of Positive Polity* (1851–54) outlined the main features of his system. He was also a leading anti-imperialist. His influence was considerable in Britain and in South America.

Owen's, was an appraisal of the deleterious effects of a narrow division of labour on the working classes, and of the increasing tendency of the capitalist commercial system to engender growing poverty on the part of the many and a concentration of riches in the hands of the few. In *The Communist Manifesto*, Marx and his associate Friedrich Engels (1820–95) proposed a highly centralized system of economic administration in which credit, transportation and the method of production generally were to be managed by the state and distributed on a communist basis. Engels, in particular, flirted briefly with communitarianism in his youth, having been much influenced by Owenism. Marx, famously, in 1845 described the ideal human life as one in which it would be possible to hunt in the morning, fish in the afternoon, rear cattle in the evening and engage in criticism after dinner, without being narrowly defined by any of these activities. Such essentially Fourierist aspirations, however, disappear from the more mature works of both authors, though a willingness to entertain federalist rather than more centralist schemes of organization is evident in Marx's writings on the Paris Commune (1871) in particular. Another utopian theory was that nationalism would generally disappear once a cosmopolitanism based on a sense of common

Karl Marx (1818–83)

This German political philosopher and economist, founder (with Engels) of modern communism, is the most important of the modern socialist writers and the most influential secular writer of all time. Born in Trier on 5 May 1818, Marx attended university at Bonn and then Berlin, where he was introduced to the philosophy of Georg Wilhelm Friedrich Hegel and became involved in radical journalism. In Paris, he met Friedrich Engels, the communist son of a German merchant, with whom he formed an intellectual partnership. After the failed revolutions of 1848, Marx, expelled from Paris, moved to London, where he would devote his life to the study of political economy. During his life, *The Communist Manifesto* (1848) and *Das Kapital* (1867) were his best-known works, but subsequently published studies include the so-called 'Paris Manuscripts' of 1844, which explore the possibility of creating an unalienated communist society, and 'The German Ideology' of 1845–46, which takes up Fourierist ideals of the rotation of labour. Marx's leading critic during his lifetime was the Russian anarchist Bakunin. By his own self-definition, Marx is not regarded as a 'utopian' socialist, that label being reserved chiefly for his socialist predecessors, including Robert Owen, Charles Fourier and Henri de Saint-Simon.

workers' identity, or proletarian consciousness, was established. Marx's language in his early works, however, notably in his aspiration for the 'complete redemption of humanity', bears parallels to millenarian traditions of earlier ages. Various writers have thus assumed that Marx inherited a millenarian set of assumptions from Judeo-Christianity recast as a determinist theory of history.[3]

The utopian quality of Marx's and Engels's thought lies also in its assumptions about the more robust sociability and continuing sense of self-sacrifice of the working classes, about the ability of centralized economies to produce and distribute as efficiently as the market, about its reliance on the historical inevitability of a successful proletarian revolution, and about the tendency of a supposedly interim 'dictatorship of the proletariat' to instigate an eventual 'withering away' of a coercive state apparatus and its replacement by a fully democratic regime. Marx and Engels also usually conceived the overthrow of capitalism to be necessarily violent and to have a cleansing effect on its perpetrators; some later Marxists would assume the possibility of a parliamentary road to socialism.

These ideals became perverted into totalitarianism following the Bolshevik Revolution of 1917. Marx renounced, however, the tradition of a moralizing, Spartan attitude towards luxury and proposed instead an expanding system of production to meet increasing human needs. The arcadian and pastoral motifs in communitarian socialism are largely lacking in Marx's and Engels's later vision. But these ideas were taken up by, among others, Thomas Carlyle (1795–1881), whose *Past and Present* (1843) presented an idealized version of feudal paternalism wedded to a Saint-Simonian industrial strategy, and William Morris (see box, p. 123), whose famous 'utopian romance' *News from Nowhere* (1890) described a London purged of noxious industries, reduced in size and population, and defined by the encouragement of creative labour and the management of society at the local level. Morris also, unusually for a utopian writer, described a revolutionary path to the ideal future, with the capitalist system being violently overthrown, as he hoped it would, as a prelude to the introduction of the new society. Morris's poem *The Earthly Paradise* (1868–70) also indicates Victorian linkages to earlier forms of millenarianism.

Soldiers and workers, Bolshevik Revolution, Petrograd, 1917. The overthrow of the Tsar following the collapse of Russia's war effort against Germany resulted in the ultimate victory of the small Russian Marxist party led by Lenin in November 1917. After years of tumultuous civil war and economic turmoil, Stalin would emerge as Lenin's successor, unleashing his own Terror to destroy his remaining opponents in 1937–38.

Anarchism is often regarded as part of the utopian tradition. Modern anarchism began with William Godwin (see box, p. 96), adviser to Owen, but, as with socialism, anarchist ideas gave rise to a spectrum of positions and considerable internal disagreement. Most anarchists have aspired to the creation of a non-coercive 'stateless society' in which leadership is absent or minimized, production is geared towards use rather than profit, and society is decentralized in small communes. Some of the more extreme individualist forms of anarchism, such as that associated with Max Stirner's *The Ego and Its Own* (1845), seemingly indicate no real alternative vision of society, but merely indulge a fantasy of individual egotism. In some later forms this is often rights-based, as in Robert Nozick's *Anarchy, State and Utopia* (1974). Some anarchists engaged in communitarian experiments. Others, such as Benjamin Heywood, Lysander Spooner and Emma Goldman, made substantial contributions to anarchist theory in the United States.

In Europe the leading schools of 19th-century anarchism, associated with Pierre-Joseph Proudhon, Mikhail Bakunin and Peter Kropotkin, all provided long-lasting and powerful visions of alternate social organization. Proudhon (1809–65), who was the first writer to promote himself as an anarchist, contended that mental independence was one of the greatest goods the individual could possess. His ideal society was defined by a 'mutualist', co-operative structure in which power was decentralized as much as possible. Proudhonism remained a powerful trend in French socialism through the last decades of the 19th century.

Bakunin, unlike Marx, aspired to see revolution emerge from the peasantry rather than the proletariat. Believing that humankind was essentially sociable, and possessed of an instinct for freedom, he posited a future society defined by egalitarianism, common property and a federative communal system of organization. In *Statism and Anarchy* (1879) he famously predicted that Marx's political ideal would result in a dictatorship over, rather than by, the working classes.

Kropotkin (1842–1921) also insisted on collective property, maximum decentralization and voluntary co-operation in the system of production. Leo Tolstoy and Mohandas Gandhi (see box, p. 57) can be included among the most famous representatives of the anarchist tradition in the following century, while anarchist collectivist communes were a notable feature of republican organization during the Spanish Civil War (1936–39), and were also erected in Italy, Argentina, France and elsewhere.

Mikhail Bakunin (1814–76)

This Russian anarchist and political writer was the most famous critic of Marxian communism during Marx's lifetime. Raised in a privileged milieu on an estate near Moscow, Bakunin served in the Imperial Guard but rejected Russia's treatment of the Poles. Moving to Berlin in 1840, then to Paris, he participated in the European revolutions of 1848, and wrote *An Appeal to the Slavs* (1848) proposing an independent federation of Slav republics. He was subsequently imprisoned and exiled to Siberia, then escaped to the United States. In Switzerland in the 1860s he emerged as one of the leading anarchist thinkers and activists, first describing himself in these terms in 1867. Joining the International Working Men's Association (or First International), he became Marx's leading opponent in the organization: Marx eventually engineered the removal of its General Council to New York in 1872 to avoid it falling entirely into the hands of Bakunin and his associates. Bakunin participated briefly in the uprising in Lyons in 1870–71 and was a supporter of the Paris Commune of 1871, writing *The Paris Commune and the Idea of the State*. Many of his better-known works, such as *God and the State*, were published only after his death.

Although some anarchists were pacifists, others, particularly in Russia, also became associated with terrorist tactics, notably the use of dynamite, to overthrow the tsar. Here the classic problem of how to establish the ideal society became interwoven with a complex argument about the relationship between means and ends, whether violence would beget further violence or was justified by the violence used to maintain existing exploitative and oppressive regimes. These arguments would in turn become integrated into anti-colonial and anti-imperialist movements from the later 19th century onwards.

The 19th century witnessed the most substantial outpouring of practical utopian experimentation, both at the communal and state levels, of any period in human history prior to the creation of communist systems in Russia and China in the following century, when at one point more than half the world's population notionally subscribed to the 'utopian' programme of communal property-holding. It is no exaggeration, either, to describe this period as witnessing the culmination of the Western ideal of scientific and technical progress that had been emerging since the 17th century. Now, however, it was increasingly assumed that the regulation of human behaviour in new forms of society could counteract the increasing tendency towards selfishness and inequality, which later 19th-century capitalism seemed to assume as the norm. But the ideal society, as conceived by socialists of this period was a realizable aspiration defined by greater equality, social justice, a more harmonious attitude towards the environment, and a more satisfactory balance of work and pleasure. As these ideals echoed the earlier concerns of Thomas More, so too would they be taken up again in a variety of forms in the following century.

Chapter 11

Inventing Progress

Rationalism, Technology and Modernity as Utopia

The wedding of science to utopian aspiration is largely a product of the 17th century. Prior to this virtually all utopias assumed a static or ideal state of affairs, in which forward movement through scientific investigation and technological discovery was unimportant and even potentially counterproductive. Since then, apart from a stiffly fought primitivist resistance movement, utopia has come increasingly to rely on science, to the extent that the two are inextricably intertwined and scientific progress has emerged as the quintessential ideology of modernity.[1] As early as the 16th century, the French historian Jean Bodin rejected the ancient positing of an original golden age, suggesting instead that inventions would unfold future progress. In the early 17th century scientific themes were taken up in Johann Valentin Andreae's utopia, *Christianopolis* (see p. 119). In this ideal city, money was abolished, wealth was created by use of the philosopher's stone, and science was given a central role in social life by establishing the laboratory, pharmacy and anatomical theatre as state institutions.

But the text that let the genie out of the bottle was Francis Bacon's *New Atlantis*, written around 1624 and published posthumously in 1627. This became the prototype for all subsequent utopias based on scientific and technological foundations. The self-sufficient island of Bensalem portrayed by Bacon is a well-ordered patriarchy in which property is distributed to mitigate poverty. Crucial to the narrative, and to the success of the society described, is Salomon's House, a centre for scientific research. Here the experimental method is given maximum encouragement, with the aim of establishing 'the knowledge of causes and secret motions of things, and the enlarging of the bounds of human empire, the effecting of all things possible'.[2] In principle this involved experimentation to improve the quality of

Postcard of 'The city of Skyscrapers', New York, *c.* 1913, published by Moses King. The first edifice to be regarded as a skyscraper was the Tower Building at 50 Broadway, a ten-storey construction 129 feet (40 m) high. By 1913 a thousand such buildings had been erected, with the Woolworth Tower reaching 790 feet (240 m).

Francis Bacon (1561–1626)

The English statesman, scientist and scholar is best known in this context as the author of *New Atlantis* (*c.* 1624), which remains the prototype of the utopia based on progressive scientific improvement. Bacon grew up around the court of Elizabeth I and was educated at Trinity College, Cambridge. He studied law at Gray's Inn, and became a barrister in 1582. A member of parliament from 1584, he was knighted, and rose under King James I to become successively solicitor-general, keeper of the royal seal, and in 1618 lord chancellor. He was made Viscount St Albans in 1621, but that year he was also convicted of taking a bribe and fined £40,000; the fine was remitted but the scandal nonetheless signalled the end of his public career. The author of *The Advancement of Learning* (1605) and *Novum Organum* (1620), two of the best-known philosophical works of the epoch, Bacon was a dedicated empiricist and a leading literary figure of the Renaissance.

foods, medicines, manufacture and the study of science. Crucially, it is a paternalist state, acting in the public interest, which promotes such research. Yet in practice it may have implied an invitation to open a Pandora's box of ghastly secrets, to tinker with nature for the sheer sake of dominating it. 'I understand how,' Winston Smith would reflect in George Orwell's *Nineteen Eighty-Four* (1949). 'I do not understand why.' Bacon might already have told him.

In Bacon's time the new science had not yet severed its links from Renaissance alchemy and the utopian search for the legendary

RIGHT Engraving of Pieter Bruegel the Elder's *The Alchemist*, 1558. The illustration portrays a poor alchemist who has ruined his family. A pun in Bruegel's inscription (not shown here) uses 'al gemist' to indicate 'all is ruined'.

philosopher's stone that would convert base metals to gold, and for an original 'elixir of life' that would ensure immortality. Into the early decades of the 17th century utopias still portrayed 'adepts' beavering away in secret, sometimes in imitation of obscure sects like the Rosicrucians, leading abstemious, monastic lives while delving into the deeper mysteries of the natural world. Many utopian writers of this period, such as Johann Amos Comenius, Tommaso Campanella and the physician Peter Chamberlen, were interested in prolonging longevity through medical reform, the alteration of diet and the improvement of the lives of the poor. Secret societies such as the Freemasons were also thought to harbour utopian ambitions, while the Hermetic philosophers – followers of Hermes Trismegistus, the legendary Egyptian author of magical and alchemical works – were believed to have transmitted the sacred wisdom of the East to Europe. The Rosicrucians were also rumoured to have had political aims, such as substituting rule by a philosophic elite for monarchy. Similar themes would later emerge in the accusation that the French Revolution had resulted from a conspiracy by a philosophical sect, the Illuminati, to upset all the monarchies of Europe.

One well-known text to emerge from these concerns was Gabriel Plattes's *A Description of the Famous Kingdome of Macaria* (1641), which was heavily indebted to the scientific thought of the Prussian émigré Samuel Hartlib and aimed to organize the economy under the supervision of five parliamentary councils, with science helping to boost output and employment. A 'College of Experience' would centralize and superintend scientific research (including alchemy), aiming at 'the establishment of a millennial Kingdom of God on earth'.[3] This probably inspired another well-known Puritan utopia, Samuel Gott's *Nova Solyma, The Ideal City; or Jerusalem Regained* (1648).

In the wake of the English Revolution, many of the leading themes of medieval and renaissance utopianism respecting science, notably alchemy, began to give way to more modern conceptions of scientific experimentation and consequent social engineering. Their leading result was the creation of the modern ideal of progress. One of the great mid-17th-century fantasies of scientific endeavour was Margaret Cavendish's *The Blazing World* (1666), which contains extensive intellectual speculations on the great scientific questions of the day and an engaging series of elaborate speculations on their possible outcome.

However, scientific themes do not figure centrally in most 18th-century utopias. In such texts as *The Island of Content* (1709) due reverence is paid to physicians on account of the fact that 'the Dread of Melancholy, and the Fear of Death, makes them adore their Physicians as their Life's Safe-guard'.[4] Hospitals are often commended in similar works but a suspicion of quack doctors and apothecaries appears in others (for example, 'A Description of New Athens in Terra Australis Incognita', 1720).[5] A deeper ambiguity respecting the results of scientific investigation would soon appear. The 19th century was a period of almost unbridled optimism, in which an increasing sense of the mastery of nature through the discovery of radiation, electricity and refrigeration, and growing advances in medicine, food cultivation and birth control, seemed to promise universal affluence and increasing longevity. The quintessentially modern utopia – urban or suburban, replete with labour-saving devices, dedicated to maximizing pleasure and minimizing pain – would flower most fully in the middle of the 20th century. Well before this, however, science increasingly seemed to promise anything and everything: in *Cromwell the Third: Or, the Jubilee of Liberty* (1886, author unknown), electricity is used to raise the dead. Yet we glimpse suspicions of the darker side of science, the concern that not all research was unself-interested, or that evil motives might lurk beneath the surface of apparent public-mindedness.

More than any other text, it was Mary Shelley's *Frankenstein* (1818) that would reawaken the theme of the quest for immortality, coincidentally creating a sub-genre of science fiction that has remained immensely popular to the present day. Rich in Faustian irony, *Frankenstein* almost singlehandedly flips the optimistic, Enlightenment ideal of progress and discovery to reveal a far darker underside. The 19th century's many advantageous discoveries would eventually have to be weighed against more dubious inventions, such as the Gatling or Maxim machine guns, poison gas and, by 1914, aerial bombardment. Contrasted with the weapons of mass destruction, the lessons of mass instruction seemed pitifully inadequate. The scientific utopia and the scientific dystopia were to march firmly forward, hand in hand, into an increasingly uncertain future. By the mid-20th century few literary portrayals of scientific aspiration could appear anything but schizophrenic.

Of all the later 19th-century texts to express the burgeoning optimism of the period, it was Edward Bellamy's *Looking Backward: 2000–1887* (1888) that would have the greatest influence, becoming the best-known American utopian text, with sales of over four hundred thousand in the United States alone by 1897. In 1864 Bellamy underwent religious conversion. When his beliefs failed, he remained convinced both that a 'religion of solidarity' of a Comtean type might be created and that a great social association might be constructed that would ensure justice, employment, industrial progress and stability. In *Looking Backward* a rich young Bostonian, Julian West, awakens from a dream to find himself in an ideal world, in which the evils of 'excessive individualism' have been eradicated. The previous system of anarchic competition and private property has gradually been supplanted by a harmonious, co-operative state in which all are shareholders. Production and distribution are organized centrally, though there is a wide range of trades and professions. Most people serve twenty-four years in the industrial army; shirkers are jailed and subsist on bread and water. Women may take up duties in the industrial army or become mothers. Money has been replaced by a system of non-transferable credits paid into a national bank and withdrawn by a credit card-like device, with

Edward Bellamy (1850–98)

This American writer is famous for *Looking Backward: 2000–1887* (1888), the most influential work of utopian literature to appear in the 19th century. The son of a Baptist minister, Bellamy studied law, economics and other subjects, and travelled in Europe before becoming a journalist, chiefly for the *Springfield Union* in Massachusetts. He wrote several other novels, including *Six to One: A Nantucket Idyll* (1878), *The Duke of Stockbridge* (1879) and *Dr Heidenhoff's Process* (1880). The success of *Looking Backward*, however, gave him cult status and resulted in the foundation of dozens of Bellamy clubs, as well as in the creation of a socialist-style movement that Bellamy termed 'nationalism', which promoted economic justice, technological innovation, universal labour and social equality at the expense of capitalist exploitation and competitive individualism. The novel's sequel, *Equality* (1897), was less successful, and Bellamy was attacked by William Morris in *News from Nowhere* as being overly reliant on technology to provide an ideal human life.

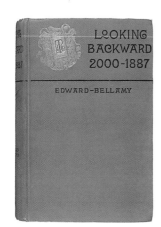

equal pay for work of equal difficulty. Among the many labour-saving devices are cars that fly. City-dwellers are protected from the elements by canopies over exterior walkways. Television and radio exist but there is considerable expenditure on art galleries and other public sources of culture. Public and private are delicately balanced; meals are in communal dining rooms but with seating according to family groups. There is little crime, few disputes and no army.

Based on the principles outlined in Bellamy's text, societies were founded throughout Europe and in South Africa, Indonesia and New Zealand; the work was also translated into Chinese in 1893. Such immense appeal bears witness to the fact that *Looking Backward* offered a compelling image of the future of modernity. (Today the book is virtually unread.) Various other late 19th-century utopias were also principally aimed at social and political justice through the organization of labour, democratic control over economic institutions and the suppression of capitalist monopoly. Among the more interesting are Theodor Herzka's *Freiland: A Social Anticipation* (1890); a sequel is *A Visit to Freiland, or the New Paradise Regained* (1894). The more technological, urban-oriented utopias include Chauncey Thomas's *The Crystal Button* (1891). Bellamy also spawned a range of satires, including *Looking Further Backward* (1890) and *Looking Within* (1893), as well as a few worthy imitations, such as Ignatius Donnelly's *Caesar's Column* (1890). This moment also gave rise to the expansion of feminist utopianism, notably in Mary H. Lane's *Mizora: A Prophecy* (1889).

The utopian embrace of science in the later 19th century led to an increasing fascination with machines, particularly those used in travel, exploration and warfare. Here the works of the great French writer Jules Verne (see box, p. 167) were immensely influential. Verne wedded two leading utopian themes: the epic voyage and the use of technological innovation to push back the frontiers of human knowledge. Deep in the oceans, high in the air, far beneath the Earth, his heroes worked tirelessly to subdue nature in the service of humankind. But as the century progressed, the threat of ever more destructive wars also loomed, and the future war novel, such as Admiral Columb's *The Great War of 189–* (1892), gained in popularity. Clouds began to gather over the facile optimism of earlier decades.

Cover of Edward Bellamy's *Looking Backward: 2000–1887* (1888). This was the first book to sell over a million copies, and it resulted in the foundation of the Nationalist political party, whose views were advertised in Bellamy's paper, the *New Nation*, established in 1891.

These clouds also began to grow darker. Late 19th-century utopianism took up the Darwinian theory of evolution and reiterated both the promise and the threat suggested by the idea of 'natural selection'. Control of the birthrate and regulation of the quality of offspring had been utopian themes since the age of Lycurgus and Plato, and it is therefore no surprise that utopian authors took up such concepts once again. By the late 1880s, eugenics, or selective breeding, attracted a host of supporters. Eugenics was largely the invention of Charles Darwin's cousin, Francis Galton, who sought to demonstrate in *Hereditary Genius* (1869) that human ability and genius are hereditary, and that if such characteristics are cultivated they can be utilized to improve the species-quality of humankind. This argument inspired an extensive literary discussion in utopian form. It would be tempting to dismiss all such speculation as tilting in a genocidal direction, but this would be muddled. Eugenic themes were portrayed positively in this era in much the same way as genetic engineering is today. And indeed from Plato onwards they can be seen as an integral component in utopianism, particularly with respect to the desire to extend physical health.

What was often termed 'negative' eugenics, including euthanasia and the killing of unhealthy children, was then, as it is today, far more controversial. Ellis James Davis's *Pyrna: A Commune; or, Under the Ice* (1875) describes a society living beneath a Swiss glacier that is defined by equality, mutual love and community of property. But unhealthy children are not permitted to live, as is also the case in Grant Allen's short story, 'The Child of the Phalanstery'.[6] In John Petzler's *Life in Utopia* (1890) those with diseases such as cancer are not permitted to marry. In W. J. Saunders's *Kalomera: The Story of a Remarkable Community* (1911) those with defective sight and hearing, and even poor teeth, are prohibited from marrying; in William Herbert's *The World Grown Young* (1892) it is professional criminals who are excluded. Sometimes the poor are merely separated from the general population, as in the anonymous *In the Future: A Sketch in Ten Chapters* (1875), where they inhabit 'new Laboratories, each a combination of asylum

Caricature of Charles Darwin from the *London Sketch-Book* (1874), entitled 'Scientific Breakthrough Darwin'. Darwin's conception of natural selection was seen by many as consistent with traditional utopian emphases upon birth and population control, and efforts to create a more physically perfect human species.

and manufactory'; elsewhere 'Street Arabs' are raised in separate institutions and educated to become 'a kind of superior race' (in *A Thousand Years Hence: Being Personal Reminiscences as Narrated by Nunsowe Green*, 1882).[7]

The positive portrayal of eugenic ideas, such as the reduction of family size and the attempt to eliminate harmful diseases, tends to obscure an increasing focus on eugenics as indicating a turn towards 'dystopia', and as pointing solely towards the later tradition defined by Aldous Huxley's *Brave New World*. In Henry Wright's *Mental Travel in Imagined Lands* (1878), for example, science promotes the best qualities in humanity, notably generosity and nobility. Other works took up the regulation of marriage by the state (G. Read Murphy, *Beyond the Ice*, 1894), the restriction of family size (Andrew Acworth, *A New Eden*, 1896) and the state promotion of hygiene (*Quintura: Its Singular People and Remarkable Customs*, 1886). Kenneth Follingsby's *Meda* (1892) addresses the theme of world overpopulation as a consequence of indiscriminate births, as does William Hay's *Three Hundred Years Hence* (1881), which assumes that colossal race wars would result from overpopulation. (Other race fantasies envisioned the decline of the white races in face of the superiority of black races – for example, *The Reign of the Saints*, 1911, by 'John Travena', the pseudonym of Ernest George Henham). Satires of such themes included *Red England: A Tale of the Socialist Horror* (1900, author unknown), in which three doctors approve all marriages, and children are removed from their parents for state education from the age of three months. Eugen Richter's *Pictures of a Socialistic Future* (1893) satirized the idea of state-care for children. And writers such as Walter Besant lampooned the proclamation of the complete 'Triumph of Science'.[8]

Representations of progress in the 19th century were also intimately linked to European imperial

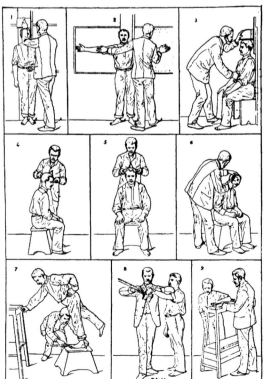

RELEVÉ
DU
SIGNALEMENT ANTHROPOMÉTRIQUE

expansion. The faster European technology evolved, the more apparent it seemed to be that Europeans were superior as a race or people. Many utopias, particularly in Britain, were set in the new colonies, such as Australia and New Zealand, and often commend proto-socialist solutions to colonial problems.[9] By the mid-19th century, however, satires on the civilizing mission of the great European colonizing states began to emerge. In *The History of Bullanbee and Clinkataboo: Two Recently Discovered Islands in the Pacific* (1828, author unknown), for example, a tropical paradise is ruined by the introduction of a corrupt and superstitious form of Catholicism. Benjamin Disraeli's *The Voyage of Captain Popanilla* (1827) also portrays a land in which the detrimental effects of the introduction of European civilization are evident.

A utopian reaction against 'progress' thus emerges as a central theme in this period. By the early 19th century a number of critics of urbanization and industrialization had begun to express their opposition to modernity in utopian literary form. Among them were Thomas Carlyle, John Ruskin and William Morris. The reaction to technological utopianism marks a number of other later 19th-century texts. In William Dean Howells's *Traveler from Altruria* (1894) a benevolent socialist regime uses technology – in the form of a system

John Glover's painting *Mr Robinson's House on the Derwent, Van Diemen's Land*, c. 1838, depicts a typical colonial house in Hobart, Tasmania. The idyllic rural setting is achieved in part because the natives were systematically exterminated during this period.

WALDEN.

By HENRY D. THOREAU,
AUTHOR OF "A WEEK ON THE CONCORD AND MERRIMACK RIVERS."

ABOVE Frontispiece of Henry David Thoreau's *Walden* (1854), showing the 10 by 15 foot (3 × 4.5 m) one-room cabin on Walden Pond, near Concord, Massachusetts, in which the author spent two years ruminating on the various spiritual and intellectual problems he later discussed in his book.

of transport – to unite its population, but the inhabitants live relatively simply in cottage-like structures and eat plain food in communal dining rooms. Morris's *News from Nowhere* (1890), although set in London, portrays a retreat from the over-urbanization of later Victorian England and gives a positive image of the nation as a garden 'where nothing is wasted and nothing is spoilt, with the necessary dwellings, sheds, and workshops scattered up and down the country, all trim and neat and pretty'.[10] In W. H. Hudson's *A Crystal Age* (1887) the setting for the matriarchal society is bucolic and pastoral, and the life led is an ascetic retreat from a corrupt and degenerate past; Hudson's *Green Mansions* (1904) is located in a South American rainforest. Samuel Butler's *Erewhon* (1872) also has a pastoral setting and satirizes both technologically based ideals of progress and social Darwinism. In the United States, Henry David Thoreau's *Walden, or Life in the Woods* (1854) contrasts a peaceful life of rural solitude, in harmony with the natural world, with the complexity, hypocrisy and materialism of modern urban existence. *Walden* became a cult classic in the 1960s and '70s. Two well-known South Sea Islands utopias by Herman Melville, *Typee* (1846) and *Omoo* (1847), were based on the author's own voyages in the region. They helped to cement the islands' reputation as idyllic tropical paradises *par excellence*, depicting the eventual destruction of the

Henry David Thoreau (1817–62)

The American practical philosopher, naturalist and author was a leading member of the Transcendentalist movement. Born on 12 July 1817 in Concord, Massachusetts, he was early interested in botany and zoology, as well as literature and many other subjects. He graduated from Harvard University in 1837 and initially became a teacher; later he worked in the family pencil-making business. In July 1845 Thoreau began his experiment in simple living, building a hut by the edge of Walden Pond, where he would live for two years. *Walden, or Life in the Woods* (1854) describes a life of simplicity, lived in harmony with nature, with restricted needs and conducive to philosophic concentration. The experience made him neither a primitivist nor an anti-capitalist, but did help commit him to an ideal of moral and social reform. This resulted famously in his essay on 'Civil Disobedience', after his refusal to pay a poll tax. He wrote a variety of anti-slavery tracts and defended the anti-slavery agitator John Brown. No anarchist, he was nonetheless a key source for later advocates of non-violent resistance, including Emma Goldman, Gandhi and Martin Luther King.

Paul Gauguin, *Delightful Land (Te nave nave fenua)*, 1892. To escape the 'artificial and conventional', Gauguin spent his old age in Tahiti, and explored the motif of the female Tahitian body as epitomizing the exotic, primitive and desirable, akin to the idea of the Christian Eve figure.

indigenous culture by interfering Christian missionaries. *Typee* bluntly juxtaposes the 'pure and natural enjoyment' of primitive society with the 'swelling aggregate of human misery' evident in 'civilized' life, though women still bore the brunt of domestic labour while men lolled in indolence.[11] (The Typees, moreover, are said to be cannibals.) Gauguin's paintings of Tahitian women would come to epitomize the artistic expression of this romanticized image of a primitive idyll. As the century came to a close, a sense of looming despair, decadence and impending conflict became increasingly widespread in Europe. The lure of the primitive could not but continue to appeal.

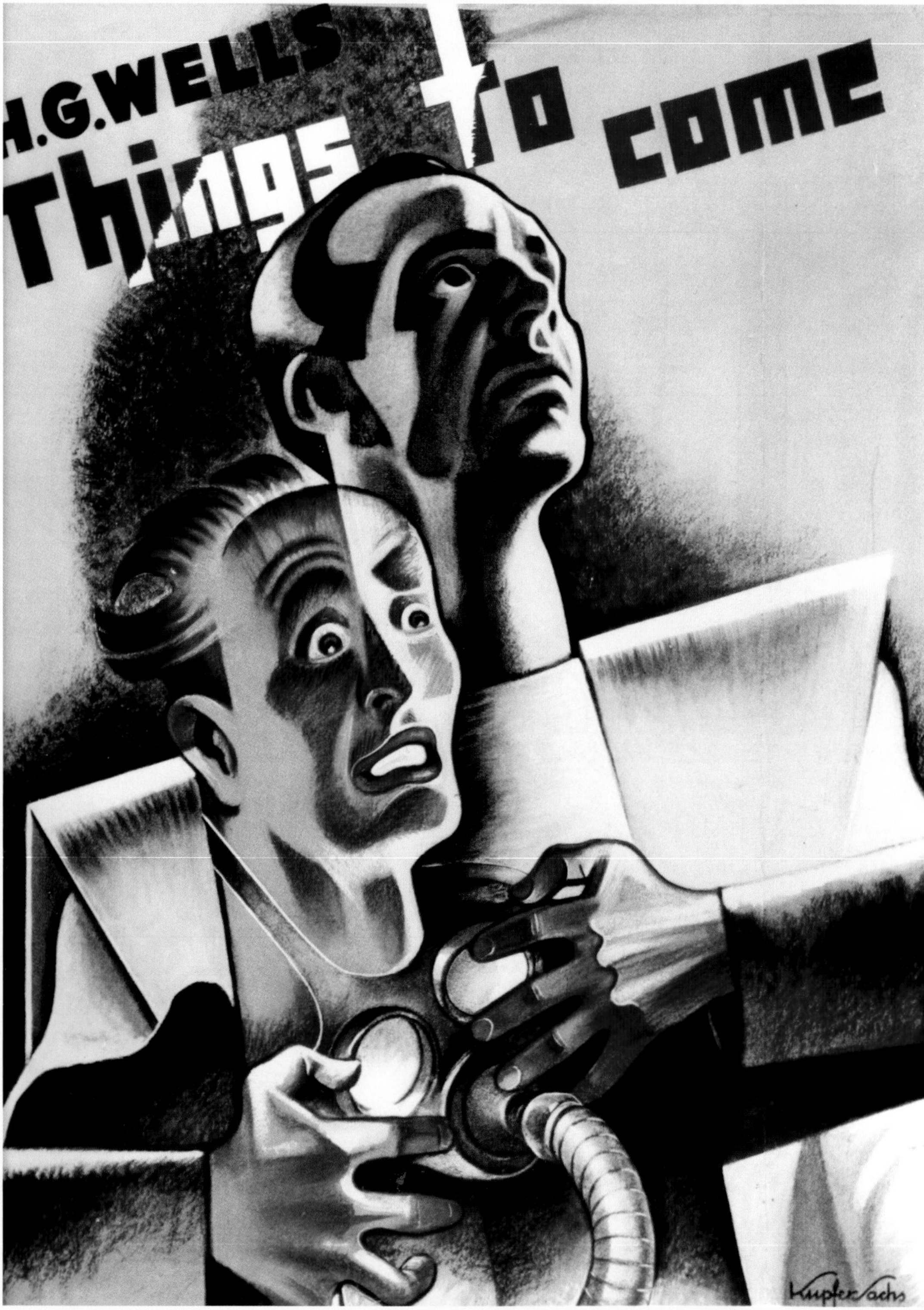
H.G.WELLS
Things to come
Kupfer-Sachs

Chapter 12

The Emergence of Science Fiction

New Worlds Above and Beyond

Whether science fiction is strictly speaking a part of utopia – or indeed whether utopia is merely a branch of science fiction – has been hotly debated. The term 'science fiction' was only invented in 1929 by Hugo Gernsback. Given the definition offered here, in which utopia narrowly construed is centrally a formal representation of one strand of the tradition of the ideal commonwealth or city-state, science fiction is a sub-genre in which science and technology predominate thematically – utopically, when expressed positively, or dystopically, when used negatively. (Some writers additionally use 'sf' to mean 'speculative fiction', which invites a much broader definition and is much closer to the wider domain of 'utopian fiction'.) In the narrower version, science and technology are central to the vision of the future: the focus is not upon constitutional, institutional, communal or other means of improving human order, maintaining greater security, harmony, happiness or anything else. Sci-fi works can, however, still function primarily as social criticism or satire.

The genre of science fiction has captured the popular imagination in a manner never achieved by utopian fiction. Modern film and television are pervaded by science fiction, and from the turn of the 20th century magazines and novels that focused on science fiction have had immense popular appeal, and major popular cults, such as Scientology, have even emerged out of the fascination with outer space and UFOs. Indeed, outer space is humanity's final frontier, the last conquerable domain (and possibly even the last domain by which to be conquered). In the modern world theological speculation has, by and large, been displaced by speculation concerning science and technology.

The daring relocation of the fantastic voyage from Earth to outer space marks for many the origins of modern science fiction. This

Poster for the 1936 film production of H. G. Wells's novel *Things To Come*. Set in a British 'Everytown', the film envisions a century of plague and war from 1936 to 2036, after which survivors dwell in underground cities after the environment has been destroyed.

imaginative leap eventually exceeded the bounds of utopian possibility
by suspending any restraints of realism or plausibility and focusing on
conjecture concerning a plurality of worlds. The genuine possibility
of space travel would, of course, not be proposed seriously until the
end of the 19th century, when engine-powered flight was projected by
H. G. Wells, among others. Before this – and following the Montgolfier
brothers' successful launch of a hot-air balloon in 1783 – balloon
exploration opened up the possibility of aerial movement. Prior to this,
the idea of flight was merely fantastic and the doomed Icarus rather
than the inventive Da Vinci remained perhaps the best-known symbol
of the human aspiration to take to the air. Yet the ancients, notably the
Pythagoreans, also sometimes speculated on a plurality of worlds in
both time and space.

Although the satirical lunar flight dates from Lucian's playful
speculations in *The True History* (*c.* AD 125), and imaginary islands
floating in the air occur in a similar period, the 17th century witnessed
the emergence of the voyage to the Moon as a sub-genre of utopia.
Ancient lunar myths now came to be displaced by the scientific truths
that were revealed by the development of the telescope, challenging

the Aristotelian view that the Earth was the only possible existent world. Among the best-known texts of this early period were Cyrano de Bergerac's *Histoire comique: voyage dans la lune* (1657). Apart from its speculation on a multiplicity of worlds, the text is a satirical portrayal of an inverted society in which, among other things, virginity is criminalized and money has been replaced by poetry; John Wilkins's *The Discovery of a New World in the Moone* (1638) posits 'Selenites' inhabiting the Moon; Francis Godwin's *The Man in the Moone* (1638) describes a flying machine propelled by geese that discovers a prelapsarian paradise defined by virtue and harmony, ruled by an absolute monarch, and where food grows without labour; and Bernard Fontenelle's *Conversations on the Plurality of Worlds* (1686) speculates at length on the planetary system.

By end of the 17th century, then, scientific speculation had been imaginatively wedded to Christian ideals of harmony and utopian visions of social order. Christian authors could plausibly suggest – as did David Russen, author of *Iter Lunare: or, A Voyage to the Moon* (1703) – that a plurality of worlds was consistent with orthodox

Frontispiece and title page of the English translation of Cyrano de Bergerac's posthumously published satire, 1687. Bergerac is usually credited with first introducing the idea of a rocket as a vehicle for space travel. He had studied physics and was influenced, in particular, by Pierre Gassendi.

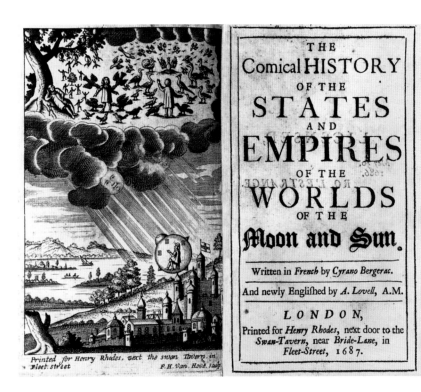

THE Comical HISTORY OF THE STATES AND EMPIRES OF THE WORLDS OF THE 𝕸𝖔𝖔𝖓 𝖆𝖓𝖉 𝕾𝖚𝖓.

Written in *French* by *Cyrano Bergerac*.

And newly Englished by *A. Lovell*, A.M.

LONDON,

Printed for *Henry Rhodes*, next door to the *Swan-Tavern*, near *Bride-Lane*, in *Fleet-Street*, 1687.

Jean-Baptiste Morret, *Fontenelle Meditating on the Plurality of Worlds*, 1791. The scientist and man of letters Bernard Fontenelle is portrayed with his dog, contemplating the possibility of life on the moon and other planets.

Christian doctrine. Enlightenment thinkers (including Immanuel Kant, Louis-Sébastien Mercier and Johann Gottfried Herder) also subscribed to the idea that the soul might transmigrate to other planets after death. The first utopias set specifically in the future also emerge in this period: among the earliest is Mercier's extremely popular *Memoirs of the Year Two Thousand Five Hundred* (1771). The text describes a Paris of the future in which luxury has been renounced and life is more austere than it was in the past. Constitutional monarchies prevail, and justice between classes and nations ensures world peace. Mercier's vision not only introduced progress towards a greatly improved future; it did so on a world-scale. A spate of imitations in Dutch, German and other languages ensued.

Like other utopias of the period, the cosmic literary voyages of the 18th century tend more towards satire and less towards serious scientific speculation; an example was Murtagh McDermot's *A Trip to the Moon* (1728). One extremely popular text was Robert Paltock's *The Life and Adventures of Peter Wilkins* (1750), which weds the Robinsonade to speculative flight. The lunar and planetary romance, then, did not initially add much of substance to the utopian search for harmony and justice in the world. It tended to focus more on space exploration or the speculation surrounding it – a subject that was once minor and merely entertaining but was eventually to assume central importance in the human imagination. In the 19th century Verne, Wells and others would become immensely popular by exploiting the appeal of this vision. By the end of the 20th century men had landed on the Moon, only to discover that what they had glimpsed distantly through a lens centuries earlier was not utopia but, yet again, a refracted image of their own hopes and wishes. But there were also worlds to be discovered below. Apart from voyages to the Moon, the prehistory of science fiction also includes imaginary explorations of the interior of the Earth, such as Ludwig Holberg's *Journey of Niels Klim to the World Underground* (1741).[1]

Modern science fiction emerged in the mid-19th century with the work of the French writer Jules Verne, beginning with the short story 'A Voyage in a Balloon' (1851) and moving to *Voyage to the Centre of the Earth* (1863), *From the Earth to the Moon* (1865) and *Twenty Thousand Leagues Under the Sea* (1870). Albert Robida, another immensely skilful French writer, also provided a variety of compelling images of a future life, especially of warfare. In England, the most influential utopist of his

ABOVE Frontispiece of Robert Paltock's *The Life and Adventures of Peter Wilkins*, 1750. The novel portrays a shipwrecked sailor's encounter with a flying people, one of whom he marries, and his efforts to extend them the benefits of Christianity and modern technology.

Jules Verne (1828–1905)

The French speculative author was the most famous science-fiction writer of his era and a pioneer of the genre. Born in Nantes on 18 February 1828, he was educated to his father's calling, the law, but became a stockbroker, then produced a series of plays, operas and music-hall sketches. He then became fascinated with futuristic forms of transportation. Generally optimistic about the ability of humankind to utilize technology in order to master nature, he wrote dozens of novels and short stories with scientific themes, crafting them to keep up with scientific developments as closely as possible. Verne epitomizes the obsession with machinery and technological innovation that dominated much of his age. His best-known works include *Voyage to the Centre of the Earth* (1863), *Five Weeks in a Balloon* (1863), *From the Earth to the Moon* (1865), *Twenty Thousand Leagues Under the Sea* (1870) and *Around the World in Eighty Days* (1873).

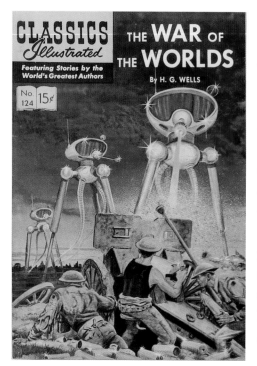

generation was H. G. Wells, author of a series of best-selling dystopian satires. In *The First Men in the Moon* (1901) he began to explore the possibility of evolutionary mechanisms that produce widely variant species outside the Earth. *The Time Machine* (1895) recounts the discovery of a world eight thousand years ahead of the present, where the population is divided into the diminutive Eloi, a bland, subject population incapable of advanced organization, and the Morlocks, an aggressive, cave-dwelling group of predators. *The War of the Worlds* (1898) was one of the first novels to portray humans as inferior to their alien rivals. However, at the turn of the century Wells had a moral and intellectual change of heart and began to conceive of his role as essentially utopian. *Anticipations of the Reaction of Mechanical and Scientific Progress upon Human Life and Thought* (1901) was the first of his efforts to formulate a positive utopian vision. In *A Modern Utopia* (1905) a comprehensive model of the ideal world-state is described. Here Wells not only outlined an evolving, 'kinetic', rather than static form of utopia; he also provided a key agency, the 'voluntary nobility', or Samurai class, united by a system of group marriage, whose keen sense of public duty would maintain the future society and assist in the promotion of 'better' and restriction of 'inferior' types. Although most property is collectively owned, labourers are not enslaved to the state. The majority of the population lives in cities. Wells also offered proposals for the creation of new communities along the lines of those suggested by Robert Owen (see box, p. 133). Similar plans appeared in William Thomson's *A Prospectus of Socialism, or A Glimpse of the Coming Millenium* (1894), where the working classes are rehoused in grand hotels.

The development of science fiction in the early 20th century followed actual events quite closely: where science proceeded, so science fiction often followed. The discovery of radium and its application to the X-ray provoked, among other things, the invention of a fictional ray gun. The use of poison gas in World War I was mirrored in its widespread fictional application. Manned flight began

Front cover of a 1955 edition of H. G. Wells's *The War of the Worlds*, with artwork by Lou Cameron. The novel's portrayal of a Martian invasion near London caused panic when broadcast by Orson Welles as a radio drama in 1938. Its film setting was transferred to the United States.

with the Wright brothers' experiment in North Carolina in 1903. The idea of aerial warfare was explored in works such as Wells's *The War in the Air* (1908). But it was the invention of rocket technology in the 1940s that made the possibility of space flight a reality, and by the end of the decade flying-saucer mania had seized the popular imagination. The line between fiction and reality was increasingly blurred as millions became convinced that UFOs existed. Many believed that confirmation of their existence, the greatest secret of modernity, was withheld to avoid public panic. Other major developments included the discovery of nuclear power and the invention of nuclear weapons, which changed forever the vision of how science might direct or dictate the future, and how human beings might become dependent on, or prisoners of, their scientific creations. By the 1950s, in the wake of atomic warfare, post-apocalyptic visions began to appear, including Wilson Tucker's *The Long Loud Silence* (1952). Within twenty years the spectre of eco-catastrophe would also begin to assume fictional form. More traditional images of the apocalypse appeared in novels about comets colliding with Earth or galactic explosions; an early example is *When Worlds Collide* (1931) by Edwin Balmer and Philip Wylie.

The degeneration of science had been explored in Mary Shelley's *Frankenstein; or, The Modern Prometheus* (1818), which provided two powerful images that would play key roles in 20th-century science fiction: the scientist-gone-mad (which formed the subtitle and the subject of one of Percy Shelley's poems) and the monster created by the mad scientist. Here, as in utopia, what is perhaps most compelling is the ambiguity of the concept: science may bring health and wealth but it also has the potential to unleash dark, destructive powers, just as utopia may bring security and plenty, but at the cost of liberty and spontaneity. (A later popular example of this idea was Robert Louis Stevenson's *Strange Case of Dr. Jekyll and Mr. Hyde*, 1886.) Overlapping this concept was an enduring fascination with the undead or partially dead, which lent popularity to various works on vampires (reawakened in Bram Stoker's *Dracula*, 1897), mummies and other

Il mondo del futuro, an album for collecting figurines, was designed by A. Martin, *c.* 1959. By the end of the 1950s the possibility of space travel had become a reality, with the Soviet launch of the satellite Sputnik 1 in 1957, quickly followed by the launch of an American satellite. The phrase the 'Space Age' came to epitomize the dramatic new achievement.

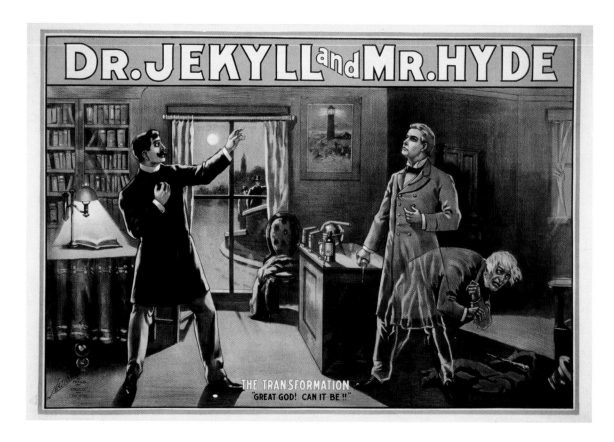

Mary Wollstonecraft Shelley (1797–1851)

The English author of *Frankenstein; or, The Modern Prometheus* (1818, revised 1831) was the daughter of the philosopher William Godwin, the founder (under the name of Mary Wollstonecraft) of modern feminism, and the wife of the poet Percy Shelley. Born in London on 30 August 1797, Mary Shelley was raised in financial difficulty, her mother having died in childbirth. She eloped to the Continent with Percy Shelley in 1814, marrying in late 1816. *Frankenstein* was composed in Switzerland in the company of Byron, with Shelley providing a preface. The work is usually held to have commenced the modern genre of science fiction through its wedding of the Faustian myth to Gothic themes, with echoes of French revolutionary ideas associated with her father's political writings. Mary Shelley focused on the idea of the scientist overextending his mortal brief by attempting to create life itself, and the work also dwells on such Godwinian themes as the innocence of humankind, or 'natural' humanity, and the process of corruption by the system of dominant values of the period. Mary Shelley's other published works included *Valperga* (1823) and *The Last Man* (1826).

ghoulish themes. And it shares features with works that portray superhuman beings, such as Edward Bulwer-Lytton's *The Coming Race, or the New Utopia* (1871), often claimed as a science-fiction novel. The distance between such works and the monsters of ancient and medieval lore is not as great as we might imagine.

But if the trope of the monster was old, what was new was the idea that humans were capable of creating monsters. The first fictional monster was the result of experiments on human beings; by the early 20th century, in works such as Hugo Gernsback's *Ralph 124C 41+* (1925), mechanical beings, or robots, were increasingly displacing their more fallible human predecessors. Artificial intelligence began to emerge as a viable concept just as, in the wake of World War I, the limitations of human intelligence were becoming more obvious than ever. (The search for intelligent life on other planets also invited the retort that it had yet to be discovered on Earth.) Monsters could also be discovered lurking in far-flung quarters of the Earth, as the 'lost world' motif – itself an offshoot of the earlier literature of the fantastic voyage – seized the popular imagination around the dawn of the 20th century. Works such as H. Rider Haggard's *King Solomon's Mines* (1885), Edgar Rice Burroughs's *Tarzan* series and Sir Arthur Conan Doyle's *The Lost World* (1912) wedded the romance of discovery to the

OPPOSITE Poster for Robert Louis Stevenson's *Dr. Jekyll and Mr. Hyde*, published in 1886. The story relates the discovery by Dr Henry Jekyll of a drug that releases his baser nature (the Hyde personality). The story dwells on the dual nature of mankind, and epitomizes anxiety about the 'scientist gone mad'.

Edward Bulwer-Lytton (1803–73)

This English politician and writer was the author of *The Coming Race, or the New Utopia* (1871), one of the best known late-Victorian British utopias. Born in London, the youngest son of a general, Bulwer-Lytton graduated from Trinity College, Cambridge, in 1826 and achieved success with his novel *Pelham* in 1828. His other publications include *The Last Days of Pompeii* (1834), a popular historical work, and *Rienzi* (1835). His fictional output eventually extended to some forty-three volumes, excluding plays. Editor for a time of the *New Monthly Magazine* and *Monthly Chronicle,* Bulwer began his political career as a Liberal Benthamite, and was a member of parliament from 1831 to 1839. He re-entered politics in 1852 as a Conservative, serving as colonial secretary from 1858 to 1859. He retired in 1866, when he was elevated to the peerage as Baron Lytton. *The Coming Race* satirized middle-class, particularly American, values, as well as Darwinian evolutionary theory and a fascination with scientific and technological power. It focuses in particular on the evolution of the Vril-ya, a superior race living underground, who possess an electromagnetic power that enables the abolition of poverty and toil.

lure of lost riches and the appeal of the primitive and monstrous. Darwinism provoked a new scrutiny of primitive peoples as well as a new contempt for 'inferior races', which were now portrayed as doomed to perish in the evolutionary struggle, and whose treasures might therefore as well be looted before their inevitable downfall. Non-human creatures have often been portrayed as possessing larger heads and hence greater intelligence, though not necessarily a more profound moral outlook, than human beings. The more humanoid they are in appearance, the more friendly they generally turn out to be. But more often than not they are portrayed as aggressive and bent on domination, in an interesting inversion of human imperial adventurism in the early-modern and modern periods. For the most part, however, they are overcome – often by space pioneers from the United States; an early example is *Edison's Conquest of Mars* (1909).

Eugenics provided fertile material for dozens of utopian/dystopian works in the late 19th and early 20th centuries, and a new mechanical-human hybrid, the cyborg, emerged. By the 1980s cyberpunk, another sub-genre or hybrid of science fiction, appeared. The best-known early example of this is William Gibson's *Neuromancer* (1983), in which the themes of dominating information systems and urban alienation are wedded. The millenarian racist utopia/dystopia would emerge again most infamously in Adolf Hitler's *Mein Kampf* (1925), in which the extermination of world Jewry and conquest of the USSR are hinted at. The perspective provided by evolutionary theory also meant that by the early 1930s science-fiction authors were beginning to envision extremely long-term futures. Writers such as Stephen Baxter (*Manifold: Time*, 1999), Olaf Stapledon (*Last and First Men*, 1930) and Robert Heinlein (*Stranger in a Strange Land*, 1961) would become famous for projecting human evolution millions of years hence. Perhaps the most popular science-fiction series ever was Isaac Asimov's *Foundation* trilogy, which began publication in the early 1940s, and which also dwelt on the theme of the long-term decline of civilization and how it might be rescued.

Science fiction engaged with politics in a number of ways. The future war novel gained in popularity from the late 19th century as Britain's imperial position came to be challenged by Germany.

Ursula Le Guin (born 1929)

The most renowned works of this American science-fiction, fantasy, dystopian and feminist writer include *The Left Hand of Darkness* (1969), *The Dispossessed: An Ambiguous Utopia* (1974) and *Always Coming Home* (1985). The daughter of an anthropologist and a writer, Le Guin was born and raised in Berkeley, California, and educated at Radcliffe College and Columbia University. She began writing for publication at the age of eleven and published her first science-fiction novels, *Rocannon's World* and *Planet of Exile* in 1966. These were the start of the Hainish Cycle novels, which include *The Left Hand of Darkness* and *The Dispossessed*, as well as *The Word for World is Forest* (1976) and other works. A more pessimistic example of her dystopian writing is *The Eye of the Heron* (1983). Le Guin's output also includes many short stories, as well as poetry collections, children's stories and non-fiction works. Besides feminism and science fiction, her works address non-Western religious themes and anthropological, psychological and sociological issues, as well as anarchism and environmental questions and the problem of ageing.

Beginning with George Tomkyns Chesney's *The Battle of Dorking* (1871), the publication of works such as William Le Queux's *The Invasion of 1910* (1906) aroused immense anxiety. Inter-racial wars were commonly portrayed, with a variety of victors: in Standish James O'Grady's *The Queen of the World, or Under the Tyranny* (1900), the great struggle of the 21st century is between the English and the Chinese. Dictatorships of various kinds were imagined. In Alexander Bogdanov's *Red Star* (1908), a Bolshevik-style society is described as existing on Mars. Science fiction also engaged with religion on a number of levels. In Louis Pope Gratacap's *The Certainty of a Future Life on Mars* (1903) spirits reside on the red planet and communicate with their earthly offspring via occultism and electricity. Mars is also the setting for one of the best-known postwar science-fiction works, Kim Stanley Robinson's trilogy, *Red Mars*, *Green Mars* and *Blue Mars* (1992–96), in which the prospect of real settlement on the planet is broached in extravagant detail. Gender politics loomed large in science-fiction works published from the late 1960s onwards, most famously in Ursula Le Guin's *The Left Hand of Darkness* (1969), which explores gender roles through the portrayal of a planet inhabited by hermaphrodites.

Chapter 13

Varieties of Dystopia

Totalitarianism and After in Satire and Reality

The historical emergence of fascist and communist dictatorships in the 20th century, often referred to as totalitarianism, was mirrored by a focus on dystopianism in some literary texts of the period. The idea that utopianism contained within it the seeds of totalitarianism had been implicit from Aristotle's critique of Plato's *Republic* onwards (see p. 26). According to Karl Popper, several aspects of Marx's theories can be traced back to Plato.[1] Their hopes for a better society involved a desire for perfectibility. And both believed that the population should be forced, by whatever means necessary, to submit to the pursuit of this ideal. The Reign of Terror at the end of the eighteenth century gave this theory a definitive modern focal point: it is a period that has been seen as the ultimate manifestation of political arrogance.

Parodies of political and human aspiration appeared as early as Swift's *Gulliver's Travels* (1726). These were sustained and reinterpreted with the emergence of new trends in science-fiction writing that are often associated with the publication of Mary Shelley's *Frankenstein* (1818). Warnings of the inevitable collapse of all forms of grand-scale, idealistic social engineering were, from the French Revolution (1789) onwards, often derived from T. R. Malthus's *An Essay on Population* (1798). His central proposition was that no matter how ideal any society was, it would inevitably result in overpopulation, which would lead to poverty, hunger, disease and war. From this time onwards many versions of the secularized coming Apocalypse began to appear; utopias that were set in the past declined in number.

However, dystopias (negative or anti-utopias) did not begin to appear as a definitive sub-genre until the later 19th century. They generally arose in response to the burgeoning socialist movement

Communist-era Chairman Mao souvenir statues found at the Hollywood Road Antiques Market in Hong Kong. 'Emperor' Mao – mummified, like Lenin before him – remains exhibited at Tiananmen Square in Beijing. He led the most important communist revolution of the 20th century, and produced a long-lasting personality cult.

from the mid-1880s onwards, but also adopted themes from Social Darwinism, particularly the implications of eugenics. Before the Russian Revolution of 1917 such works frequently portrayed revolutions gone astray, collapsing into dictatorship, drenched in blood and often resulting in a restoration of capitalism (as in Charles Fairchild's *The Socialist Revolution of 1888* [1884]). H. G. Wells (see p. 168) experimented with a variety of dystopian forms in his early years as a novelist, satirizing both communism and eugenics in *The Time Machine* (1895), eugenics again in *The Island of Doctor Moreau* (1896) and oligarchical enslavement in *When the Sleeper Awakes* (1899). Fantasies of race wars, such as Robert William Cole's *The Struggle for Empire: A Story of the Year 2236* (1900), were also common in this period. Some capitalist dystopias appeared before World War I, notably Jack London's *The Iron Heel* (1908), a revolutionary socialist novel that portrays an oligarchical dictatorship (based loosely on the American trusts, or industrial monopolies), run from Wall Street, that is intent on suppressing workers' rights. Feminist dystopias also made an appearance with Charlotte Perkins Gilman's *With Her in Ourland* (1916) and other works. The advent of fascism spawned a few anti-fascist dystopias, notably Katherine Burdekin's *Swastika Night* (1937), which portrays the triumph of brutality over Christian mercy.

Charlotte Perkins Gilman (1860–1935)

The American economist, feminist, teacher and author is best known for *Women and Economics* (1898) and the novel *Herland* (1915), often regarded as the most important early 20th-century feminist utopia. Born into a poor family in Hartford, Connecticut, Gilman had an irregular education, and married an artist. Politically active, she was a member of the Fabian Society as well as Edward Bellamy's Nationalist movement. First published in the journal *The Forerunner*, which Gilman herself produced and edited, *Herland* depicts the discovery of a lost civilization in Africa where women play the leading role in society, religion centres on a scheme of maternal pantheism, reproduction is by parthenogenesis and population is strictly controlled. From 1904 to 1928 Gilman promoted the cause of female suffrage and women's rights more widely, as well as urban regeneration, rural resettlement and world peace. She was also the author of *The Home* (1903), *Human Work* (1904), *Moving the Mountain* (1911) and *Man-Made World* (1911). Gilman's initially unpublished works include 'A Woman's Utopia' (written 1907; printed 1995). A sequel to *Herland*, entitled *With Her in Ourland*, was published by *The Forerunner* in 1916.

IMPERIAL FEDERATION—MAP OF THE WORLD SHOWING THE EXTENT OF THE BRITISH EMPIRE IN 1886.

The new sub-genre of the communist dystopia appears seminally with the publication of Yevgeny Zamyatin's *We* (1924), the most important early satire on Bolshevism and a powerful indictment of state centralization and the suppression of individuality. Following a lengthy war in which much of the population has died, a 'Benefactor' and Platonic-style 'guardians' supervise a highly regimented society, the One State, in which individuals are numbered, live in cubicles in glass houses and are subject to constant behavioural rectification in order to suppress dissident thoughts. Daily life is closely regulated – deviation from proscribed activities is permitted only in the 'Personal Hour'. Sexual relations are arranged through an application and rationing system. In contrast to this bleak, oppressive atmosphere the text describes a land lying beyond the boundaries of the state, where primitive people reside. The hero, D-503, becomes disillusioned with the uniformity of the system and succeeds both in passing beyond this

Map of the British Empire, 1886. Embracing a quarter of the world's population at its peak, with India as the 'jewel' in its crown, the British empire was the largest attempt ever undertaken to impose alien rule over subject peoples. Its motives, cost and legacy all remain highly controversial.

border and in engaging in illicit sexual relations. He engages in a minor
act of political rebellion but is captured and killed. Much of the
structure of the novel was reworked in George Orwell's *Nineteen
Eighty-Four* (1949). Similar themes were developed in Joseph O'Neill's
Land Under England (1935), where mind-control is a central motif.

The most important inter-war satire focused not on totalitarianism
as such but on behavioural manipulation within capitalism. Aldous
Huxley's *Brave New World* (1932) describes a rigidly stratified society
in which eugenic selection and social engineering secure a privileged
ruling class and a vast reservoir of willing labour. The elite alphas are
distracted by frequent sex and drug-taking rituals, with the famous
drink *soma* temporarily banishing all worldly concerns. Huxley provides
a contrast to the brainwashed elite in the figure of the uncorrupted,
aboriginal character, John. But his innocence and subsequent rejection
of the traditions of the dominant civilization are ultimately of little
relevance – his suicide is a confirmation of the impossibility of life in
Huxley's new world. The mindless uniformity portrayed in the novel
is presented as a real danger lurking within the capitalist system, where
a shallow egotism has become increasingly dominant. Huxley felt, like
Orwell, that hedonistic materialism and godlessness were responsible
for many of modernity's key problems, but was unable to offer any

Aldous Huxley (1894–1963)

This English writer and critic was the
author of *Brave New World* (1932), the
most important 20th-century dystopian
satire to centre on the theme of
eugenics. Born on 26 July 1894, in
Godalming, Surrey, to a family of
famous scientists and philosophers
(his grandfather was Thomas Henry
Huxley, 'Darwin's bulldog'), Huxley
was educated at Eton and Oxford
University. In the 1920s he became a
successful novelist, writing, among
other works, *Antic Hay* (1923), *Point
Counter Point* (1928) and *Eyeless in Gaza*
(1936). In 1937 he moved to the United
States, where he would live, mainly in
California, until he died of cancer in
1963. He treated dystopian themes in
both his major work and its sequel, *Brave
New World Revisited* (1958), and provided
his own utopian vision in *Island* (1962),
which was much influenced by his
interest in Buddhism, mysticism and
experimentation with mind-expanding
drugs such as LSD. *Brave New World* is
often viewed as a satire on behavioural
manipulation by the mass media,
particularly in the modern United States,
as well as a warning about the hubris of
scientists and the dangers of eugenics.

George Orwell (1903–50)

This English novelist and journalist was the author of *Nineteen Eighty-Four*, the most famous modern dystopian novel. Born in Bengal as Eric Blair on 25 June 1903 into a family of imperial civil servants, Orwell was educated at Eton (on a scholarship), then from 1922 to 1927 served in Burma in the Indian Imperial Police. Radicalized by this experience, on returning to England he started to write both novels and reportage, including *Down and Out in Paris and London* (1933), *Burmese Days* (1934), *A Clergyman's Daughter* (1935) and *Keep the Aspidistra Flying* (1936). A sense of his new-found socialist faith was conveyed in *The Road to Wigan Pier* (1937). Orwell was in Spain from 1936 to 1937, having joined the republican resistance to Franco's coup, an experience he would recount in *Homage to Catalonia* (1938). *Coming Up for Air* (1939) established him as a critic of commercial capitalism, but in his wartime tract *The Lion and the Unicorn* (1941) Orwell insisted that the virtues of British toleration and individualism needed to be wedded to socialism if the latter was to succeed. Orwell's wartime and postwar journalism as well as his two great political satires, *Animal Farm* (1945) and *Nineteen Eighty-Four* (1949), indicate a disillusionment with communism, and in particular a disgust with the power-worship that he believed had infected socialist intellectuals everywhere. Orwell died of tuberculosis in 1950.

viable philosophical solutions, beyond the anodyne spiritualism hinted at in his later novel, *Island* (1962). Similar themes were taken up in Ayn Rand's *Anthem* (1938), where the dehumanized protagonist, Equality 7–2521, is the product of a state eugenics programme. He regains a sense of individuality by rebelling against the system (symbolized by his diary-keeping and rediscovery of classical literature). Rand became a spokesperson for right-wing libertarianism in the United States.

By contrast, the best-known of all modern dystopias, George Orwell's *Nineteen Eighty-Four* (1949), resulted from the author's political engagement as a socialist during the Spanish Civil War and his subsequent disillusionment with the Soviet Union's manipulation of the republican cause. The world described by Orwell is sombre, grey and depressing. It is defined by the omnipresence of the leader, Big Brother (a messianic Hitler- or Stalin-like figure), and

King Leopold's rubber slaves. The Belgian king owned the Congo as a personal fiefdom, and his functionaries extracted cruel punishments on those unable to deliver their imposed quota of rubber. Some ten million natives are estimated to have died in the colony.

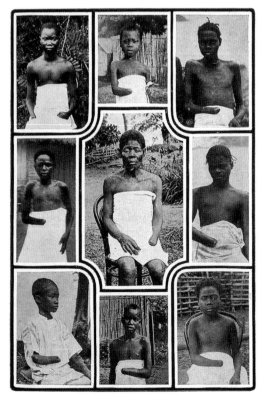

by constant ritual submission and slavish devotion to the state. Telescreens permit constant surveillance, and the ubiquitous Thought Police ensure deviance is controlled. Children betray their parents, party members denounce each other and an atmosphere of mutual distrust pervades the ruling strata. The system is designed to fulfil the aims of the 'Inner Party', which seeks power and views it as an end in itself. Manipulation of the past and denial of the concept of objective truth serve to confuse the educated minority. The 'proles', or working people, however, are left largely to their own devices, entertained by a diet of hard labour, gambling and cheap amusements. Individuality in the form of 'ownlife' is ruthlessly suppressed, and the hapless rebellion by Orwell's anti-hero, Winston Smith, is easily uncovered. Torture and subsequent rehabilitation follow an inevitable course and, by the conclusion of the text, Smith himself comes to love Big Brother. Orwell was concerned that the great dangers facing modernity would emerge as much from capitalism as from communism. *Nineteen Eighty-Four* undoubtedly satirized aspects of Hitler's fascism and Stalin's communism, but it was not an anti-socialist tract as such: its warning focuses more on the effects of power-worship on intellectuals within the socialist movement and the effects of the pursuit of unbridled hedonism on the masses. Orwell, like Huxley, had a premonition that modern society might literally amuse itself to death.

Among later 20th-century utopias that include a dystopian element is B. F. Skinner's *Walden Two* (1948), which develops the theme of behavioural engineering, or the scientific regulation and even eradication of spontaneity and individuality with the aim of promoting pleasure and profit. The novel focuses on state-run nurseries where children are conditioned to embrace love and social virtues and to avoid anti-social behaviour. More overtly dystopian are Doris Lessing's *Memoirs of a Survivor* (1974), whose feminist appeal is balanced by its despairing portrayal of a violent, gang-ridden city; and Marge Piercy's

Woman on the Edge of Time (1976), which chronicles feminist resistance in a psychiatric institution and contrasts it to an idealized commune in a 22nd-century setting. Ursula Le Guin's *The Dispossessed: An Ambiguous Utopia* (1974) occupies the grey area between dystopia and utopia (see box, p. 173).

The ill-documented prehistory of actual totalitarianism occurred during the second half of the 19th century under the despotic colonial regimes of the great European imperial powers. Concentration camps that had herded large numbers of the civilian population were used in Cuba and South Africa in the last years of the century. Large-scale executions and the cutting off of hands were routine punishments, integral to the operations of King Leopold's Congolese rubber slave state. Beatings, imprisonment and denial of basic civil rights were common throughout the colonial world. Racism was an important tool in imposing a sense of inferiority on conquered peoples everywhere. The ideal 'super-states' of the great European empires of Britain, France, Germany, Italy, Spain and Portugal thus imposed a vast dystopian experience on hundreds of millions of non-whites.

In the 20th century, dictatorships were established in most countries in which a Marxist-inspired revolution had taken place: legality either became meaningless or was subordinated to the will of the party. From 1917 onwards numerous efforts were made to create new images of

Soviet *Proletkult* poster designed by Ivan Vasilyevich Simakov and dedicated to the fifth anniversary of the October Revolution and the fourth Congress of the Communist International, 1922. After the Bolshevik Revolution, priority was given to those of working-class origins, who were regarded as epitomizing the communist ideal.

BELOW Members of Fidel
Castro's militia in the Escambry
Mountain area of Cuba, January
1961. President Kennedy's
abortive attempt that year to
deploy some 1,300 exiles in
anticipation of an uprising
against Castro formed the
backdrop to the United States'
main anti-communist efforts
in this decade, in Vietnam.

OPPOSITE ABOVE Poster
for a sporting event to be held
in Fuhlsbüttel, Germany, on
10 August 1930. The National
Socialist regime cultivated an
ideal of Aryan racial purity
as part of its campaign of
suppressing other races. The
mentally feeble were used for
the first euthanasia experiments,
which later formed the basis for
the 'Final Solution'.

OPPOSITE BELOW
Propaganda poster for the
National Socialist Party, 1932,
reading 'Our Last Hope: Hitler'
and playing on the mass
unemployment in Germany
following the Wall Street crash,
which assisted Adolf Hitler's
rise to power in 1933.

the socialist man and woman who would selflessly cultivate, create and produce the goods required by the new society. *Proletkult* – proletarian culture that rejected bourgeois influence – inspired an art form that dominated Soviet propaganda from the early 1920s onwards, providing a constant succession of images of heroic tractor drivers, engineers, peasants and soldiers. This was the largest attempt ever made to remould human nature and to subordinate the individual to the community. In every communist nation that had been created by an anti-imperialist revolution, cults emerged that were centred around heroic events and heroic individuals: in Cuba, for example, Che Guevara became perhaps the most universally known symbol of the revolutionary ethos, while the abortive counter-coup attempted by the United States at the Bay of Pigs (Playa Giron) in 1961 provided plentiful images of the Cuban David pitted against the American Goliath. In Vietnam, one particularly powerful symbol was of a young girl dragging a tail-piece from a downed US aircraft.

There were, of course, important differences between fascist and communist ideals of the nation. National Socialism, or Nazism, promoted a concept of racial superiority in which the blond Aryan symbolized the Nietzschean ideal of the Superman. Eugenic

engineering designed to hinder miscegenation and prevent the procreation of individuals with grave hereditary ailments echoed the literary projection of such experiments a generation earlier. Jews became the particular target of propagandistic hatred; later gypsies, homosexuals and others would share a similar fate. National Socialism also celebrated the German nation as such; Soviet communism in principle promoted an internationalist ideal in which the export of socialism, particularly in the form of anti-imperialism, was extended to China, Korea, Vietnam, Cuba and elsewhere. Through much of the mid-20th century the United States was the particular target of such anti-imperialist propaganda, though France and Britain were similarly disgraced.

One of the most effective tools of the fascist and communist regimes was the mass rally, which functioned as a celebration and demonstration of power. The first rally of note was attempted by the Nazis at Nuremberg; the USSR routinely institutionalized such rallies at Mayday and the celebration of the 'Great October Revolution'. A cult of health, athleticism, virility and manliness pervaded Nazi propaganda. Motherhood was celebrated to some degree, at least insofar as the promotion of large families was an aim of the regime; childhood was a focal point to the extent that the youth of revolutionary regimes were considered uncontaminated by the decadence of past societies. Harmony with nature was also a leading theme in some National Socialist propaganda. In fascist Italy, Mussolini attempted to invoke the spirit of the Roman empire as he moved to extend Italy's African colonies. Japanese imperialist militarism focused on a cult of the emperor and of self-sacrifice, epitomized in the use of suicide kamikaze techniques in the closing months of World War II.

Cultural Revolution, *c.* 1966. This rare photograph shows the ritualized public humiliation of a 'rich peasant' or landowner, of the type that occurred thousands of times during the period. Mao's regime was endeavouring to recapture and extend the original egalitarian aims of the 1949 revolution.

In other regimes, however, notably in China, the past was simply regarded as an alien symbol of the *ancien régime*, to be ruthlessly eradicated as a means of assisting the creation of a new 'red' identity. During the Cultural Revolution, Ming emperors were disentombed and unceremoniously dumped into rivers, while countless temples, ancient books and other vestiges of the past were destroyed. In various countries, notably Germany and the USSR, new styles of architecture also emerged to replace the old, with an emphasis on the statuesque, imposing, overawing style.

Much of the imagery of modern totalitarianism and modern dystopia is dominated by the omnipresent figures of its great dictators, from Lenin to Stalin, Adolf Hitler and Mao Zedong, to Kim Il-sung and Fidel Castro at the end of the period. Most communist societies produced innumerable portraits and statues of their leaders; lesser luminaries often appeared on posters, mugs, clocks and other everyday furnishings. These latter-day saints and prophets indicate the central role played by charismatic leadership in the history of utopianism, and the inadequate accounting of this role, which can be linked to the heroes of ancient lore as well as to those of modern comic books and science fiction, in much of the theoretical literature. In many 20th-century totalitarian societies large-scale portraits of key revolutionary events commonly decorated public spaces, with the aim and effect of politicizing daily life to the maximum degree. The 1933 projected

model of the Palace of the Soviets in Moscow was to have included a giant statue of Lenin, an image curiously reminiscent of an advertising poster for the film *King Kong*, which had opened two months earlier. After their deaths many leaders, notably Lenin, Ho Chi Minh and Mao, were mummified in an effort to fix their status in time. Communist societies quickly became, and often remained, highly militarized and increasingly paranoid. Denunciations for treachery, thinking unacceptable thoughts, or simply

for being different from the majority, characterized many 20th-century
communist regimes. Xenophobia and paranoia became ubiquitous.
The last remaining vestige of this extreme militarization to survive into
the 21st century is the regime in North Korea.

It transpires, we now know, that life excels art in the totalitarian
experience. The representation of savage oppression in works such
as Orwell's *Nineteen Eighty-Four* pales in comparison with the rampant
brutality of everyday life in such regimes. In Orwell's text, for example,

the proles, or mass of working people, are largely untouched by the cruelty used by the party to control its members. But peasants made up the majority of the inmates of Stalin's gulags. And in Mao's China, thousands were clubbed, stabbed and kicked to death in public with a savagery that is barely imaginable. Elsewhere millions of ordinary workers were killed, enslaved and starved to death under communism: the process of demonization, denunciation and dehumanization extended to the entire population. The scale of mass deaths, however, owes as much to enforced but grossly inefficient industrialization – which produced widespread famine in the USSR, China, Vietnam, Cambodia and elsewhere – as it does to the anti-humanist ideology of the ruling regimes.

Perhaps the most significant expression of the blood-letting inspired by communism was the 'Killing Fields' established by the Khmer Rouge after the Cambodian revolution of 1975, when around two million people were murdered or starved to death out of a total population of some six million. 'Re-education' was the notional aim of incarceration, but in fact large-scale slave labour was the reality faced by millions. Here knowledge of a foreign language could entail certain death, and the only 'real' Khmer were the least educated peasants. This was noble savagery with a vengeance, and the result was no Garden of Eden. The 'other' – Jew, foreigner, heretic – has often had a difficult

Skulls of victims of the Khmer Rouge at the 'Killing Fields' memorial at Choeung Ek, outside of Pnomh Penh, Cambodia. Among other victims, prisoners from the infamous Tuol Sleng prison were brought here after torture to be executed and buried in mass graves.

time in utopia. Communist Man, like Millennial Man, was expected to be a pure type, and washing in blood was expected if no other cleanser was available. Here, perhaps, the humans can truly be said to have become monsters: we finally meet Satan and, as Ludwig Feuerbach, who described God as a projection of human wishes, might have surmised, he is us.

With the collapse of both the Nazi and Soviet systems, the predominant image of these regimes remains that of oppression, enslavement and mass death. From the discovery of Nazi concentration camps, most notably Auschwitz-Birkenau, and the account given of the Soviet gulag system by Alexander Solzhenitsyn and others, it has become abundantly clear that modern totalitarianism was characteristically a system of mass extermination and mass slavery. The 'Hall of Hair' in the museum of Auschwitz, which contains a mountain of now almost entirely grey, shaven, human hair, some ten metres long and several metres high, intended for use in uniforms, as boot-liners and so on, stands as perhaps the most chilling single symbol of the wedding of the mundane and utilitarian to the ethos of mass murder. The collapse of the Soviet Union in the early 1990s left few such regimes intact. But dystopia would not only return to more traditional themes, such as the threat of nuclear war and environmental destruction, but would also move further into space and onwards in time as the imaginative boundaries of science fiction were pushed ever outwards.

The 'Hall of Hair' at Auschwitz-Birkenau, Poland. Prisoners sent to what became the most infamous death camp in the Nazi system had all their possessions confiscated by the camp administration and were shaven before entering the gas chambers.

Chapter 14

Utopia, Science Fiction and Film

The Final Frontier

The genre of science fiction and the making of films flourished around the same time, at the turn of the 20th century. Both share a fascination with technology. One of the earliest films, *À la conquête de l'air* ('The conquest of the air', 1901), directed by Ferdinand Zecca, first used the split-screen technique to superimpose an image of a flying machine over Paris. From the 1980s onwards, computer-generated graphics rendered large-screen cinema viewing more impressive than ever before. Utopias, virtually by definition, possess little action and minimal plot development or drama. Many of the best-known literary utopias have never been filmed. Among the few exceptions is *Lost Horizon* (1937), directed by Frank Capra, set in the mythical valley of Shangri-La high in the Himalayas. The film portrays a mystic community where ascetic exercise, self-renunciation and the religious secrets of Tibetan Buddhism promote long life and virtue. Film adaptations of the book were also made in 1972 and 1979, but the original is usually considered the most successful. Far more common has been the adaptation of dystopias, which are often full of action and adventure, and have therefore attracted filmmakers for decades.

The translation of science fiction into cinema begins with such films as *Le Voyage dans la Lune* ('A trip to the Moon'), directed by Georges Méliès in 1902, a reworking of Jules Verne's *From the Earth to the Moon*, which used special effects on a grand scale. Méliès also made *Deux cent milles lieues sous les mers* ('Twenty thousand leagues under the sea', 1907), again based on Verne's text of the same name; a Hollywood version of this was made in 1916. The first Tarzan film appeared the following year. Thereafter a variety of sub-genres would provide many of the best-loved films of all time, covering and embellishing a wide spectrum of science-fiction themes. Fascination with the monstrous is one of

The set of Steven Spielberg's *Close Encounters of the Third Kind*, 1977. The film played upon both popular fascination with the existence (and threat) of aliens as well as supposed government conspiracies to deny real-life contacts with other-worldly beings.

ABOVE LEFT Ferdinand
Zecca's *À la conquête de l'air*,
1901. The flying machine,
named Fend L'air, is depicted in
one of the first films to portray
the possibility of air travel.

ABOVE RIGHT Film poster for
Merian C. Cooper and Ernest
B. Schoedsack's *King Kong*, 1933.
The 'lost world' genre is here
represented via some scientists'
discovery of a giant gorilla.

OPPOSITE ABOVE Film poster
for the *Flash Gordon* serial, 1938.
Depression-era comic-book
heroes, such as Flash, Batman
and Superman, contrast deep
villainy and super-heroic virtue.

OPPOSITE BELOW Film poster
for Harry Horner's *Red Planet
Mars*, 1952. Produced at the
height of McCarthyism, the
film portrays Mars as a utopia,
and indicates that mankind can
be saved by religion (i.e. by
controverting communist values).

the most enduring. The Frankenstein genre was established in 1910
with a sixteen-minute film of the same name directed by J. Searle
Dawley. Dozens of similar films followed in subsequent decades: in
a 1931 adaptation, often considered the best of its kind, the monster
was played by Boris Karloff. Derivatives include the much-praised
The Bride of Frankenstein (1935) and *Frankenstein Meets the Wolf Man*
(1943). Variations on the mad scientist theme would, of course,
reappear in many other types of film. In *Dr Cyclops* (1940) an evil
genius miniaturizes his captives for fun. In *The Fly* (1958; remade in
1986), a scientist succeeds in substituting a fly's head for his own. In
The Island of Terror (1966) mutant viruses suck the marrow from their
victims' bones.

The lost island motif was defined by a variety of early films,
including *Die Herrin von Atlantis* ('The Mistress of Atlantis', 1932),
a German film that locates the mythical space beneath the sands of
the Sahara. Later incarnations of the idea include *The Lost World*
(1925; remade in 1960), where dinosaurs appear in Marion Fairfax's
production of Arthur Conan Doyle's novel of the same name. *The
Land That Time Forgot* (1975) explores similar themes, as do various films
associated with exotic monsters, such as *King Kong* (first filmed in 1933).

The science-fiction genre as a whole developed substantially through the use of special effects, particularly with the introduction of computer-generated images (GGI) at the end of the 20th century. Steven Spielberg's *Jurassic Park* (1993), and its sequels, as well as the Indiana Jones series, are evidence of the continuing popularity of the genre.

The science-fiction equivalent of utopianism's legislators and communitarianism's charismatic founders is the superhero. Linked to ancient myths in which the offspring of gods and humans possess divine powers, the superhero genre, most often associated with Batman and Superman, emerged from American comic strips in the 1930s. The first film of this type was *Flash Gordon* (1936), followed shortly by *Flash Gordon's Trip to Mars* (1938) and *Buck Rogers* (1939). *Superman* appeared in 1948 and *Batman* in 1966; both were subsequently remade. The simplistic contrast of good and evil in these films alleviates a growing sense of urban decay, criminality and disintegration in the fabric of postwar society.

Non-human heroes and villains have also had a part to play. The robot genre was first used to effect in Fritz Lang's *Metropolis* (1927). This film is often cited as an example of imaginative, futuristic cinema, and features a (wooden) robot in a central role and a plot that draws on Marxian theories of the class struggle. The robotic theme was continued in such successful productions as *Westworld* (1973), *Futureworld* (1976), *Robocop* (1987) and *I, Robot* (2004).

Perhaps the most famous of all science-fiction themes to be adapted to film is that of the flying saucer/alien invasion. This came of age, with the rocket, in the early 1950s, when genuine invasion scares and the lurking suspicion of government cover-ups, gripped the imagination of young and old alike. In the paranoid Cold War era some films, such as *Red Planet Mars* (1952),

H. G. Wells (1866–1946)

This English writer is best known for his science fiction. Author of *The Time Machine* (1895), *The Island of Doctor Moreau* (1896), *The War of the Worlds* (1898), *The First Men in the Moon* (1901), *A Modern Utopia* (1905) and many other works, Wells unusually began his career as a dystopian satirist and then spent most of his long life writing variations on the theme of utopia. Born in Bromley, Kent, the son of a shopkeeper, he became a draper's assistant, then studied biology under Thomas Henry Huxley. Largely self-educated, he achieved early fame as a novelist and enjoyed a long and successful career before falling into obscurity. From *A Modern Utopia* onwards, he tirelessly advocated some form of world-state, though he fell out with the Fabian Society, to which he belonged for a time, and was also disappointed by the League of Nations. Wells's chief utopian themes include the need to resuscitate a strong sense of civic or republican responsibility, to cultivate a ruling elite, and to harness technology to serve human ends. His *Experiment in Autobiography* (1934) provides a compelling account of much of his life.

combine the genres of alien scare and red/communist scare. The decade began with *Rocketship X-M* and *Destination Moon*, both made in 1950. Far better known were *The Thing from Another World* (1951), *The Day the Earth Stood Still* (1951), *It Came From Outer Space* (1953) and *Invasion of the Saucermen* (1957). A recent example of the theme of the alien invasion of Earth is *Independence Day* (1996). H. G. Wells's *War of the Worlds* was first filmed, rather clumsily, in 1953 but was remade far more successfully by Steven Spielberg and, appropriately enough, starred the world's most famous Scientologist, Tom Cruise.[1] The special effects were way in advance of the first film.[2] Still more successful was Spielberg's *Close Encounters of the Third Kind* (1977) and *E.T.: The Extra-Terrestrial* (1982). Both heralded the landing of benevolent forms of extra-terrestrial intelligence on Earth and are generally regarded as two of the most crafted Hollywood approaches to the subject. Even more influential has been the series of *Star Wars* films directed by George Lucas, which began in 1977, where special

effects are deployed on a grand scale; and also the television series and the films associated with *Star Trek* (first filmed in 1979), which are often seen as vehicles for extending the American way of life onwards into a grateful universe, though they have also been noted for giving greater prominence to roles for women and minorities.

A variation on the alien invasion genre was space travel and encounters with aliens in space. Perhaps the best-known example of this was Arthur C. Clarke's pioneering *2001: A Space Odyssey* (1968), directed by Stanley Kubrick, which became the definitive science-fiction film of its epoch in terms of special effects and of intellectual and moral ambiguity and sophistication. Dr Who first appeared on the big screen as *Doctor Who and the Daleks* (1965). The theme of the alien invasion of spaceships was also taken up in various versions of Stanislaw Lem's *Solaris* (1972). *Alien* (1979) is another well-known example of this type.

Several science-fiction classics have been adapted to the screen. Jules Verne's *Twenty Thousand Leagues under the Sea* (1870) has many film versions. A number of Wells's utopian and dystopian novels have been filmed, often several times: *The Time Machine* (1895) was adapted in 1960, and again in 2002, by which time the narrative device of time

Film poster for George Lucas's *Star Wars*, 1977. Innovative in its portrayals of robots, aliens and women in positions of power, the film and its sequels wedded stunning computer-generated graphics with simple plot-lines exploring the contest of good and evil.

travel had reappeared in many other well-known films, such as *The Time Travellers* (1964), *Back to the Future* (1985) and the *Terminator* series, which commenced in 1984 and made a star of Arnold Schwarzenegger. *The Invisible Man* was first filmed in 1933, again in 1940, 1944 and 1951, and has been filmed since then. *The First Men in the Moon* was filmed in 1953 and again in 1964, though both had poor reviews. *The Island of Dr Moreau* was adapted as *The Island of Lost Souls* in 1932, but the eugenic elements that are central to the novel's plot were removed in the film.

The eugenic dystopia is represented in literature primarily by Aldous Huxley's *Brave New World*, which was filmed in 1980. The theme was also taken up in a variety of later films, such as *The Boys from Brazil* (1978), where clones of Hitler are manufactured in South America, and *The Island* (2006). A variation on the theme is presented in *Planet of the Apes* (filmed in 1968 and remade in 1969, 1971, 1972, 1973, and again by Tim Burton in 2001) and portrays an inverted Darwinian (or Swiftian) world discovered by three astronauts, where intelligent apes have subjugated brutish humans.

Among the more successful literary dystopias brought to the big screen have been Anthony Burgess's *A Clockwork Orange* (1962), which portrays a sadistic dystopia dominated by mindless teenage violence, gang warfare, the disintegration of morals and the collapse of the nuclear family. The novel's limited political content is defined by the

Film still from Stanley Kubrick's *2001: A Space Odyssey*, 1968. The most important space-oriented film of its period, it explores themes of both evolution and contact with alien species, and exhibits a complexity and moral ambiguity rarely exhibited in the genre.

Film still from Stanley Kubrick's *A Clockwork Orange* (1971), adapted from Anthony Burgess's novel. Viewers were disturbed by the vision of an apparently mindlessly violent society, in an epoch when rising crime rates and urban decay were becoming increasingly prevalent.

government's attempts to impose behavioural modification methods and by the subsequent rebellion against this. The book was filmed in 1971, with Stanley Kubrick as director, and became one of the most influential late 20th-century dystopian films. William Golding's *Lord of the Flies* (1954) – filmed in 1963, and again in 1990 – also explores the effect on children of a life of lawlessness, devoid of adult order and discipline. Although cast initially as a potential utopia (by means of a plane crash that lands the group of schoolboys on a deserted Pacific island), the narrative shifts rapidly into a nightmarish dystopian vision. Innocence and goodness disintegrate in the face of a wanton propensity to evil. Despite the idyllic setting, and the presence of adequate food and shelter, sadism and cruelty predominate over more noble human qualities.

Dystopia also proved popular in a number of other genres. Following World War II, the post-nuclear holocaust was the setting for a variety of films, including *On the Beach* (1959), *The War Game* (1965) and *The Day After* (1983). Two decades later, the ecological disaster gained in popularity, notably through *The Day After Tomorrow* (2004). Worlds decimated by disease have often been portrayed in film. Futuristic urban decay has also been projected, as in Ridley Scott's *Blade Runner* (1982). Ray Bradbury's *Fahrenheit 451* (1953), filmed in 1966, also pits attempts at totalitarian control against individual efforts to escape behavioural manipulation. Set against an apocalyptic background of nuclear war, the book recounts a 24th-century book-burner's revolt against the suppression of the past by attempting to recreate a classical canon. The protagonist, Guy, is discovered, but escapes in search of like-minded rebels, leaving a glimmer of hope for the viewer.

One of the most important later dystopian films to feature feminist themes is Margaret Atwood's *The Handmaid's Tale* (1985; filmed in 1990, with a screenplay by Harold Pinter, and starring Faye Dunaway and Robert Duvall). Set in the late 20th-century fictional republic of Gilead, following a nuclear war, the film explores a decaying fundamentalist Christian theocracy in which women, non-whites, homosexuals and others regarded as deviant are suppressed. Sexual intercourse is highly regulated and 'handmaids' function as breeding-machines for the elite.

Finally, mention should be made of one further aspect of the utopian/dystopian tradition – children's literature. An animated version of *Gulliver's Travels* appeared in 1939. Here, the voyage to Lilliput becomes a pretext for a Hollywood romance. The film was remade in 2010. Far more popular was L. Frank Baum's *The Wonderful Wizard of Oz* (1939), which updates Bunyan's *Pilgrim's Progress* by retelling the children's tale of the adventures of the Cowardly Lion, the Tin Man and the Scarecrow in Oz. By their heroic deeds each recaptures, respectively, their lost courage, heart and intellect, while the central narrative figure, the Depression-ridden girl Dorothy, comes

Roland Emmerich's film *The Day After Tomorrow* (2004), having portrayed the deluge of New York City by the ocean and extreme cold in the wake of radical climate change, then showed the destruction of Los Angeles by tornadoes. The film also focused on the value of international co-operation in addressing ecological catastrophe.

Margaret Atwood (born 1939)

This Canadian novelist, poet and critic is best known in the utopian context for her feminist dystopia *The Handmaid's Tale* (1985). Born in Ottawa on 18 November 1939, the daughter of an entomologist, Atwood did not attend school regularly until the age of eleven. Later educated at the University of Toronto and Radcliffe College, she went on to publish many novels, including *The Edible Woman* (1969), *Surfacing* (1972), *Cat's Eye* (1988),

Alias Grace (1996) and *The Blind Assassin* (2000), as well as numerous other works of poetry and prose. Her 2003 novel *Oryx and Crake* is a work of dystopian science fiction, though Atwood sometimes refers to it, along with *The Handmaid's Tale*, as 'speculative fiction'. In 2009 she published a follow-up to *Oryx and Crake* called *The Year of the Flood*. She is also well known for her work on Canadian identity.

BELOW Film still from Volker Schlondorff's *The Handmaid's Tale* (1990), adapted from Margaret Atwood's novel. The film depicts a right-wing religious tyranny which emerges after a nuclear war, when 'handmaids' are forced to cater to the sexual needs of the elite.

to appreciate the spartan but innocent virtues of her rural Kansas homestead. Utopia is represented by the Emerald City, wherein dwells the wizard, who turns out to be a charlatan manipulating his audience with mere trickery; the forces of evil are represented by the presence of a powerful wicked witch. One of the most beloved of children's tales, Lewis Carroll's *Alice in Wonderland* (1865), recounts Alice's pursuit of a talking rabbit down a hole into Wonderland, which is inhabited by a variety of strange animals and people. *Through the Looking Glass* (1872) is also, at one level, a satire on existing mores and manners. Both of these texts have been adapted for screen many times. Richard Adams's *Watership Down* (1972) recounts the fleeing of a colony of rabbits from a life of misery in search of improvement. An animated version was

produced in 1978. Equally popular has been J. M. Barrie's play *Peter Pan* (1904), which describes the adventures of three children who are propelled through the air from London to Neverland, an imaginary place inhabited by lost boys and their guests, and a variety of Indians, pirates and curious animals, not to mention the fairy Tinker Bell, the Indian princess Tiger Lily and the evil Captain Hook. First staged in the year of its appearance, and reprinted as a novel,

Film still from Victor Fleming's *The Wizard of Oz* (1939), adapted from L. Frank Baum's novel *The Wonderful Wizard of Oz*. Here Dorothy and her friends, the Scarecrow, Tinman and Lion, walk along the Yellow Brick Road to Emerald City.

Peter and Wendy, in 1911, the work has been almost continuously in the public eye ever since.

Among other works adapted for children, George Orwell's brief but cutting satire of revolution, *Animal Farm* (1945), has also been reproduced in animated form. The narrative describes the overthrow of Farmer Jones (epitomizing feudal and capitalist exploitation) by a group of animals bent on founding an equal society. Soon, however, three ambitious pigs, Snowball (representing Trotsky), Napoleon (representing Stalin) and Squealer, begin to subvert the original principles of the Farm, infamously establishing the precept that some animals are more equal than others, and eventually usurping power and re-establishing the privileges formerly possessed by humans. Orwell's *Nineteen Eighty-Four* (1949) has been filmed twice: the first version starred Edmond O'Brien in Michael Anderson's 1956 production; the second version was in 1984 and starred John Hurt. The first adaptation, somewhat stark and bleak, partly as a result of being shot in black and white, is more amateurish and less impressive than the second, in which Richard Burton gives a powerful performance as O'Brien, the villainous inner-party leader.

Paradise Lost?

'Your system is very good for the people of Utopia;
it is worthless for the children of Adam.'
JEAN-JACQUES ROUSSEAU, 1767.[1]

U topia has been pronounced dead and buried so often, generally
by its detractors, that its continual reappearance to frustrate its
obituary writers may almost seem to indicate a miraculous Second
Coming.[2] Undoubtedly, at least in more developed countries, some
aspects of the traditional impulses fuelling utopia have declined. By
the early 20th century, the conquest and exploration of most of the
Earth eliminated the possibility of discovering a pristine state of
human development to which we might return. The lure of the
primitive, never entirely lost, declined sharply. Speculation in utopian
stock, which had reached an all-time high a few years earlier, began
to recede as the Bolshevik experiment degenerated under Stalin.
As Judith Shklar suggests, the price of enforced unity in terms of
individual liberty was perceived to be far too high.[3] With the collapse
of Soviet communism following the revolutions of 1989, and the
conversion of China, in particular, to a free-market hybrid of
capitalism and socialism, the appeal of the command-economy
brand of communism waned. Finally, symbolized perhaps most
clearly by the fall of the Berlin Wall in 1989, the utopian bubble burst.

Utopia came widely to be perceived as possessing too much Sparta
and too little carnival, too much celibacy and too little celebration,
too much work and too little play. For many the ideal became tawdry,
grim and humourless. Revolution has not instilled greater virtue, at
least not for long, but it has invited greater cruelty and, accordingly,

Increasing numbers of natural
disasters in the early 21st
century have been linked
to global warming and its
concomitant effects.
Thousands, for example,
were displaced in Shyamnagar
Upazila, Satkhira District,
Bangladesh, after a cyclone
in May 2009.

utopianism can be seen as fuelling modern barbarism.[4] Its vaunted equality dissipates quickly. Newly privileged elites soon possess special compounds, designer stores and extravagant lifestyles. They devour all the eggs not broken in the making of the revolution. Most members of modernized societies no longer hearken back to a golden age. We do not want to be shepherds any longer, whatever suspicions may still linger – they are few – as to whether our predecessors were 'better' than we are. We would rather shop. There is nowhere to shop in Arcadia, and there was nothing worth buying in communist Moscow. The golden allure of utopia first appeared gilded, and then was proclaimed fool's gold, iron pyrate, about as useful as Spartan money. Give us – or so the late 20th century seemed to say – suburbia, luxury, celebrity culture, telegenic amusement, constant, compelling novelty, and a sop for our unlimited cravings. Our wealth is real, our golden age is the present, progressively more glittering, more digitally precise, and miniaturized. Adam Smith has seemingly delivered us the culture of choice. So we continue, in Thomas More's phrase, to pay divine honours to its prophets and heroes, the mega-rich, to pray for their blessings and to worship in their reliquaries. The mall is our temple, and hallowed are the names of Gates and Buffett. All hail the silicon age!

And yet at this exact moment, in many developed societies, a simple faith in free-market 'growth' and progress – as if resources and population could expand indefinitely – also began to wane. In the late 20th century the spectre of ecological catastrophe came increasingly to displace totalitarianism as the dystopia of choice. The chief concrete utopia of the past two centuries, the United States, now faces stark economic and political decline. Only in fantasy does even outer space seem to offer a ray of hope, but here a blast of the death-ray seems as likely. Amid widespread denials, and a

The Berlin Wall, erected in 1961 to prevent East Germans from fleeing their communist regime, came to symbolize the differences between liberal and totalitarian governments generally. The destruction of the Wall in 1989 is captured in the 'Walls are not everlasting' slogan portrayed here.

decadence dented only by financial crisis, doom-mongers and cults of the apocalypse began to emerge, to tell us 'the end is nigh'. We shop more resolutely, more desperately, and embrace narcissism more obsessively, for few of us look forward to certain salvation. We retreat into the interiority of our music-players, emerging occasionally for social moments such as music festivals. But this temporary utopian space belies the fact that we are well aware of our generally decaying sense of community. There is no point in embracing gluttony once again when we know we are reaching our natural limits. If our choice, to follow Buckminster Fuller, is 'utopia or oblivion', it is an obvious one.[5] We must choose nowhere, for here and now is a dead end. We have seen 'I-wanna' land and it will not do. Nowhere must become somewhere, become here. There is a clear danger that the silicon age will give way to a very crowded final age of water, and we are wary that few of us can swim well enough.

Such a perspective provides us with brief and fragile glimpses of optimism, albeit mixed with desperation. Growing individualism, the fragmentation of family and community life, is met occasionally by the call to reaffirm stronger communitarian bonds. Anomie, isolation, moral and intellectual confusion are for some mitigated or offset by a reaffirmation of 'traditional', often religious values, sometimes wedded to 'identity politics'. Nostalgia for some form of past moral ideal is particularly acute in societies undergoing rapid modernization. Yet the central value of market society – secular, hedonistic consumption – is often difficult to offset by recourse to nostalgia for disappearing worlds.

And do such longings for past certainties conform to what we have identified as a 'utopian' tradition? Not, it seems, if we continue to confuse utopia with religion. As with many journeys of spiritual discovery, we may well ask – after returning from the long voyage in search of utopia – whether we knew clearly what we were in search of at the outset, or merely wanted to project our own illusions upon another, more convenient, pliable space. At the psychological level this quest resembles the search for enlightenment: we desire great answers to grand, persistent questions. Grasping at every intellectual straw that floats our way, we become ever more extravagant and ever less concrete in our demands for salvation. Indeed, we hope mostly for hope itself. And yet we may wonder, gazing up at *swamis* in obscure foreign climes, whether the answer did not lie within, or at least within reach, to start with. Mystic journeys to the East may not have been necessary. But we may then throw our crutches aside, and still find there is nowhere to walk. We will probably beg, once again, for heroes and saints to save us: making the effort to save ourselves has become too much.

If we regard utopia as neither religion nor an inner psychic state, but a discourse about voluntary sociability, we may reach a different conclusion. It is possible to create utopic spaces or periods of time without reimagining an entire society recast as utopia. The festivals of Saturnalia and carnival are evidence of this, as are religious institutions like churches, where the greater pretence of equality and the reinforcement of communal bonds remind us, momentarily, of the advantages of obligation and faith. Intentional communities are utopian niches in an alien space. And More's island of Utopia itself is, of course, an oasis in an un-utopian desert, even though it may have been intended to represent a real space. Is it possible, then, that we might still conceive of a vision of mutual, even global, assistance that does not make the mistakes that define dystopia?

In this book a distinction has been made between a tradition of imagining final, paradisical, or sometimes apocalyptic visions of the ultimate destination of humanity, and a tradition in which human nature, while improved, bears sufficient resemblance to actual human behaviour that its idealized depiction remains plausible. The second domain, which lies between the possible and the impossible, is utopia: it is not perfectibility, neither is it flawless, complete, final, total or ultimate; it does not demand unceasing and undiluted virtue; it heralds neither salvation nor some form of ultimate 'emancipation' or 'end of history'. When utopia aspires to such goals, it becomes increasingly intolerant and compulsory and mutates into dystopia. For then it demands salvation rather than improvement, and striving for salvation in this life leads inevitably to impatience, and thereafter to violence against heretics and failures. In such a vision the refugees from utopia soon outnumber its inhabitants.

This process is often said to emerge from modern revolutionism. Having dispensed with Revelation, we have also lost our appetite for Revolution. We have glimpsed this version of the secular millennium and realize we have been gulled. The monster, we discover with horror, lay within, and could all too easily burst forth. Its external projection – as a Frankenstein creation, a Wolfman, an alien – simply mirrored our inner nature. Generations of hostile scholars have also identified this calamity with socialism and particularly with schemes of centralized economic planning. Yet a sense of proportion is necessary here. We lament the fifty-five thousand dead of the Reign of Terror in France, the twenty million or so killed by Stalin, and the estimated seventy million victims of Mao. But we more rarely recall the one hundred million or so who died under European imperialism in the 19th century alone, and the similar numbers that died during the conquest of the Americas. The great European empires were 'utopias' to their designers – extravagant dreams of national and personal glory, imposing order on vast populations of unwashed, heathen savages, but they were also dystopias to those who had no wish to be 'civilized' so violently and rapidly. Mass killing and extreme cruelty have assumed many forms and not all can be traced to the abuse of the socialist 'utopia' as such. Nor is there much pity today for millions blighted by semi-enslavement at starvation wages. The 'open society' has rested at times upon slavery, serfdom and a mass of impoverished wage-labour. Its freedoms have to some extent been paid for by this bondage.

The quest for utopia has involved the effort to contain if not eliminate vice and to limit disruptive human impulses in order to secure a measure of order and certainty, and a greater degree of altruism in society. Ambition, or the desire for power, rank and influence; sexual desire; the wish to accumulate property in order to gain distinction, maximize inequality and satisfy the

The utopia of universal Western affluence is undermined by its dependence upon cheap produce manufactured under appalling conditions in poorer parts of the world. Here, a young girl works in a brick-crushing factory in Dhaka, Bangladesh, earning perhaps US$10 per month.

demands of pride – all have been the most common enemies of the ideal society, whether writ large as the nation or small as the intentional community. Regulation has often been the utopian response to such impulses. Uniformity of clothing, the suppression of luxury and the embracing of patriarchalism have commonly been proposed as a means of containing the urge to uniqueness. Order takes precedence over enjoyment, and equality over liberty. Utopia is usually – Charles Fourier's model being a conspicuous exception – the enemy of unbridled hedonism.

Yet it would be mistaken to describe utopia as the enemy of pleasure. In utopia pleasure is often conceived of as something to be enjoyed by all. Gluttony may not occur but neither, generally, does austerity – one person's indulgence is not usually purchased at the cost of another's pain. And virtue is acquired by not over-indulging the pursuit of pleasure, or of any other of the stronger desires, especially pride. What makes this work in the ideal society is an instilled sense of shared purpose – whether love of country, religion, or of the community or leader – and a sense of living in the public eye. The physical scale of utopia, crucially, functions to encourage systems of mutual observation. Public spaces frame public behaviour: familial and private life is often diminished accordingly, to a degree that we would find unacceptable today.

The ownership of property and the social inequality that results from this have been regarded as the most important problems addressed by utopianism. The utopian tradition that followed the publication of *Utopia* in 1516 was identified with communal ownership in some form. To discover simplicity on a South Sea isle, where nature is bountiful, offered an easy solution to the problem. To instigate revolution among millions of people in an ancient, highly corrupt, complex and embittered society poses a far different and vastly more complicated problem. If utopias are imagined communities, they are specifically *more equal* imaginary communities: the differentiation imposed by luxury has proven the single greatest enemy to utopia across the ages. Recent assessments suggest that equality is a key factor in contributing to greater contentment in society.[6] The utopians, then, have often been correct in their central assumption. Where they may have erred, many would claim, is in being unable to define a form of equality that is compatible with freedom.

ECOLOGY, UTOPIA AND DYSTOPIA

It is reasonable to suggest that the age of the unrestrained pursuit of happiness, defined in terms of egotistical consumption, has now passed. In the early 21st century many of our concerns with both utopia and dystopia are shifting in an increasingly ecological direction, as evidence mounts swiftly of the potential catastrophe facing the planet. By the late 19th century it had become evident that industrialization was causing widespread pollution, and the degradation of the urban life of the poor in particular. One response was the revival of apocalyptic imagery that was formerly associated almost exclusively with religion, particularly Christianity. The fantasy of immense, and increasing, scientific and technological power – which runs steadily on as the chief theme of modern science fiction, the leading sub-genre of utopianism – gives rise from the mid-19th century onwards to a despairing sense of inability to restrain the excesses of invention. Machines become more complex, but with their fiendish application wars become more destructive. Utopia and dystopia march ever more closely hand in hand, until for many they seem finally to merge indistinguishably.

Africa has been particularly badly affected by cyclical droughts and floods. Here, in Niger, Oussenyi Moussa contemplates the loss of his herds, weakened by drought, then wiped out by catastrophic rains.

There are, however, moments of brightness here, too. In the late 20th century a number of proto-ecological utopias were published: both Ernest Callenbach's *Ecotopia* (1975)[7] and Marge Piercy's *Woman on the Edge of Time* (1976) portray societies that strive towards ecological balance, greater self-sufficiency and a more acute sense of social and environmental responsibility. Concretizing such reveries, however, implies the coordination of world powers on a scale hitherto conceivable only…in utopia, or on an even wider planetary scale, in cosmopolis. The ideal of world government, as conceived by H. G. Wells and others, permits an image of mutual assistance that in the modern period has been identified mainly with communism. Yet the latter represents dystopian modernity *par excellence*. How can these contradictions be reconciled? Can the quest for utopia be salvaged, or is the very proposition not merely futile but doomed to repeat the atrocious follies of the 20th century? Why bother to try to save utopia if the secular religion of modernity has proven so utterly, monstrously destructive?

THE POLITICS OF REALISTIC UTOPIANISM

There are, perhaps, two main types of answer to these questions, both of which hinge on the definition of utopia. On the one hand, utopia represents a fantasy of escapism, the rejection of an unpleasant reality and substitution of an inverted or dream-like opposite, polar set of pleasures, sometimes portrayed realistically, sometimes indirectly or satirically. Many utopias involve fleeing (by ship, rocket, time-machine, or even dream) from the woes of the present. Psychological interpretations of utopianism focus on this tendency towards wish-fulfilment and stress the naïve and infantile qualities of the utopic impulse. In *Peter Pan* and *Alice in Wonderland*, for example, and even in the retelling of such utopian classics as *Robinson Crusoe* and *Gulliver's Travels* as children's stories, we encounter the meeting of the juvenilia

Smokestacks in Pittsburgh, Pennsylvania, blacken the skies in the 1890s. Having promised affluence in the 19th century, heavy industry by the early 21st century came to symbolize environmental devastation and urban decline.

of the human species – real myths – with entertainment of children. Even after the world became almost entirely demythologized, a persistent fascination with, and often genuine belief in, magic continues, as evident in the enormous success of the fantasy novels of J. K. Rowling (the *Harry Potter* series) and J. R. R. Tolkien (*The Hobbit*, *The Lord of the Rings*). These works, too, form part of the discourse of utopia insofar as they feed our sense of fantasy, expand the boundaries of possible realities, and promote hope, illusion and sometimes a passion for change. They may also, however, reinforce our infantilism and our desire for instant gratification. Fascination with the unknown continues to dwell on outer space – geographical distance helps to lend credibility to the incredible. But such inclinations may also feed our propensity for unreason and the irrational, sap our faith in empiricism and the scientific method, and leave us prey to conjurors, conmen and charismatic manipulators who are keen to disguise their own ambitions with claims of spiritual and supernatural powers. We have exchanged old-time lying travellers for new-age lying storytellers. To some degree they also displace our anxieties and give focus to our fantastic projections. But they do so at a considerable price. Utopia may be in retreat, but gullibility certainly is not. We agree with the emperor – please do not tell us we have no clothes on. In the silicon age we almost beg to be misled.

This view of utopia, then, essentially addresses the domain of fantasy. It corresponds to psychological needs or desires, to expectations or hopes, as well as to fear of the unknown, wonderment at the vastness of infinity and the apparent unknowability of so much. Echoes still remain in the present of the search for the Fountain of Life or of Youth. Myth and religion do not disappear, are not succeeded by secular ideals and aspirations, by positive science dispersing ignorance. All come to coexist in an indigestible confusion of expectation, superstition and half-baked secularity.

The most powerful symbol of mankind's destructive capabilities, atomic weapons were used twice against Japan at the end of the Second World War. Here, following an attack on Hiroshima on 6 August, the second bomb explodes above Nagasaki on 9 August 1945, killing some 80,000 people.

The prophets of progress were mistaken. We are not becoming more hard-headed, empirical, scientific. We think, relativistically, that one brand of nonsense that whitens our intellectual teeth will serve as well as another brand of sense, which might cost more in intellectual effort to grasp. 'Postmodernism', indeed, asserts as much. And, if the truth be told, we like being gulled, flattered and entertained more than being informed and instructed. It makes us feel good, and for many that is the point of the experience, indeed, of all experience.

But, on the other hand, are we capable of using the idea of utopia in a more constructive way to deal with the problems of the present? And can we avoid reducing utopia to a psychological impulse, as tends to be the case with Ernst Bloch's famous interpretative work, *The Principle of Hope* (1959)? The answer, of course, is yes. For 'hope' is merely a vapour, a chimera, capable of being instantaneously dispelled in the glare of day. 'Utopia', by contrast, is a moment in human existence, sometimes real, sometimes reimagined, often mistaken for something else, but no mere dream. And if we need large-scale – what used to be called, negatively, *utopian* – social planning to deal with the problems of the future, then we also need an image of the future that accounts for long-term problems and offers long-term solutions on a global scale. This, then, is utopia in a positive sense.

Two variations on the more concrete or plausible, less fantastic, incarnation of utopia have been explored in this book. One of these addresses the fragmentation of existing communities and proposes their reconstruction on the basis of more traditional values. Here patriarchal rule by elders and priests, or charismatic leaders, and severe and often religious injunctions against immorality, are regarded as antidotes to the intoxication induced by the idea of rapid or extensive betterment. The spirit of revolution is here chiefly reactionary; we grasp out to retain what we have lost or are losing, for it is more certain than any future we can contemplate. The old books, the old ways, the old prophets, hold out more hope than any of their modern counterparts. We *had* order; we can regain it by moving backwards in time. Out of degeneracy will come regeneracy. The floodgates from which modernity pours will be closed, or the flow at least reduced to a trickle.

The other variation, more liberal and forward-looking, assumes that greater but quite different planning and collective organization to avert an apocalyptic global catastrophe must emerge from our present condition. Its orientation, more scientific and academic, is towards practical problem-solving. It acknowledges the anxieties of individual isolation and family and community breakdown consequent on modernization. But it rarely suggests reimposing more traditional forms of authority as a response to such issues. It proposes no new committees of public safety, and has little faith in philosopher-kings or prophets. Inheriting many of the concerns of the liberal gender- and identity politics of the past half-century, it envisions no re-enslavement, no reinforced intolerance of minorities, no rejection of individuation in principle. The legacy of modern socialism encourages it to retain a commitment to reducing if not eliminating poverty while addressing environmental catastrophe by restraining needs and population growth. Imaginative architects propose cities that are both sustainable and habitable, in which neighbourhood life is revivified, and neither rich nor poor are ghettoized. Political theorists advise the extension of democratic control, not its limitation by plutocratic or partisan dictatorship. One part of this version of the modern utopia also focuses on physical perfectibility, that age-old utopian theme, and the promise of modern science to prolong our individual lives indefinitely. Plastic surgery, the elimination of many diseases, cloning, cyber-replacement and a hundred other developments herald greater longevity and enhanced life-experience; here is not one philosopher's stone, but a mound of geneticists' pebbles. Both individual life, then, and our collective existence can hold out significant promise. We can reconstruct order by slowing time down and managing 'progress' rather than being driven by it. We can embrace a new form of austerity and achieve a degree of sobriety after the inebriety of the self-indulgent consumerist culture. The transition from our obsession with luxury will be painful, though it

By the early 21st century fantastic projections of mankind's ability to create life became increasingly realistic as cloning, genetic modification and the creation of artificial living matter all advanced dramatically. Here the image of 'test tube babies' hints at the possibility of interfering with natural procreation in order to improve human stock.

need not be suicidal. But we will not achieve moral redemption, emancipation, enlightenment or salvation. We may, however, still be promised something like it. Quacks, medicine-men (and women) and social-spiritual healers will come out of the woodwork, as in a burning fire. When the messiahs arrive – and there will be plenty – we had better check their credentials carefully.

Can we, then, still think in terms of utopia? Guardedly, yes. Its anticipation is not predicated upon merely 'realistic' premises, for its breadth of vision easily exceeds these. It heralds no mere improvements in *Gemeinschaft*, the more emotionally satisfying form of community described by sociologists such as Ferdinand Tönnies, for the same reason. It is not an act of faith, certainly not merely an expression of hope, not an acknowledgment of some fundamental, underlying need for a religion of some type. It may or may not be indebted to some form of 'enlightenment project', though certainly we will need reason aplenty to make it a workable vision. It cannot solely be a novel form of nostalgia, however, and the less wrapped in myth the better – for of lies, noble and otherwise, we have had enough to last. Yet it will be utopia nonetheless.

The historical retelling of the utopian tale recounted in this book is therefore only part of the story, for utopia is interwoven with humanity's fate at every level, and is as immediate and meaningful to our lives today as at any point in the past. Indeed, it is manifestly more necessary than ever. For at the end of the day, utopia is chiefly about prophecy, or imagining, though not necessarily foretelling, the future. Non-believers will always view creation myths allegorically, as attempts to provide meaning by accounting for origins, and to satisfy the desire for harmony, and even eternal life, and to overcome the fear of death. Seen from this perspective, the natural or organic history of utopianism recounts the emergence from primitive myth of more elaborate forms of theology and their subsequent gradual, if uneven, replacement by secular attempts to reorder society. Here Thomas More plays a pivotal role in providing us with a serious alternative to an increasingly exploitative class system. But as we have seen, each of these modes – myth, religion, secular utopian social theory – have co-existed in parallel forms for the past five hundred years and more.

Prophets, saints, charlatans and rogues brush shoulders and elbow ribs along the massed volumes of utopian and dystopian writings on library shelves. At one level religion is nearly inseparable from utopia because virtually no utopia, at least none of note, has imagined a society held together solely by individuals striving for self-satisfaction, without the bonds provided by faith in gods, or an ideology of common sacrifice, unless such a vision is based on fear and submission to violence. Many 19th-century utopians, including Robert Owen, Henri de Saint-Simon and Auguste Comte, felt compelled to invent a new religion to fulfil the functions played by the old. Their 20th-century successors often used the cult of personality to perform the same role. Utopia cannot function without authority, leadership and a common sense of purpose, regardless of whether it proposes to return to a lost state of past virtue or to create something entirely novel. We gasp out, desperately, for statesmen, and are given politicians.

However, our future is necessarily composed of two parts: the brief span of earthly existence and the rather longer span of eternity. We would like each of these to be as satisfactory as possible. But the two paths of the pilgrim's search for a lost paradise – for redemption, salvation and the promise of eternal life, and the quest for utopia, for a good life in real time – are not the same, despite their manifold intersections. The first is primordially a religious discourse, and its needs are satisfied ultimately only through faith. The second is a secular discourse about the good ordering of society, in which both saints and sinners will have to be accommodated. We may have sought streets of gold in El Dorado, as in John Bunyan's heaven, but we do not require a new religion today to cement the plausible utopia, or any reconstruction of older forms of spiritual identity. *Our* ideal world cannot be the New Jerusalem or the Sparta of Lycurgus. It cannot be defined by the reveries of Karl Marx, but will it match the dreams of Adam Smith? The old ideal worlds can lend us hope, inspiration, a sense of what to aspire for as well as what to avoid. But *our* ideal world must be very much our own creation, and a serious reckoning with the fate we face if we fail to create it.

Notes

Full bibliographic information for short-form citations is given in the Bibliography.

Introduction

1 Comte claimed that the development of human thought could be conceived in terms of the growth of religious, metaphysical and positive or scientific outlooks.

2 Notably by Francis Fukuyama in *The End of History and the Last Man* (London: Hamish Hamilton, 1992).

3 For this interpretation, see, for example, John Gray, *False Dawn: The Delusions of Global Capitalism* (London: Granta, 1998).

4 A general introduction to the topic, with a selected range of key primary sources, is offered in Claeys and Sargent, *The Utopia Reader*. On some definitional problems, see Fátima Vieira, 'The Concept of Utopia', in Claeys, *The Cambridge Companion to Utopian Literature*. The best general survey of the field as a whole remains Manuel, *Utopian Thought in the Western World*.

5 On this theme, see Martin Foss, *The Idea of Perfection in the Western World* (Princeton: Princeton University Press, 1946).

Chapter 1

1 Hesiod, *Works and Days* (Oxford: Oxford University Press, 1988), p. 40.

2 This phrase was coined in the mid-17th century to describe revolution in England at that time.

3 For a late 19th-century attempt, by a utopian author, to prove the story, see Ignatius Donnelly, *Atlantis* (2nd ed., London: Sidgwick & Jackson, 1970).

4 Plutarch, *Life of Lycurgus* (New York: Random House, n.d.), p. 57.

5 Ibid., p. 61.

6 Ibid., p. 73.

7 See Z. S. Fink, *The Classical Republicans* (Chicago: Northwestern University Press, 1945); Elizabeth Rawson, *The Spartan Tradition in European Thought* (Oxford: Clarendon Press, 1960); Eric Nelson, *The Greek Tradition in Republican Thought* (Cambridge: Cambridge University Press, 2004).

Chapter 2

1 This reputedly occurred in some forms of Catharism, Albigensianism, Lollardy and Anabaptism. A good general account of these traditions is in Gordon Leff, *Heresy in the Later Middle Ages* (2 vols, Manchester: Manchester University Press, 1967).

2 On the chronology of the imagery of heaven, see, in particular, McDannell and Lang, *Heaven*.

3 Ibid., pp. 174, 214.

4 An enumeration of functions is provided in Gustav Davidson, *A Dictionary of Angels* (New York: The Free Press, 1967).

5 John Milton, *Paradise Lost* (London: Longman, 1968), Bk 1, l. 680–84.

6 For the development of this theme, see Ernest Tuveson, *Redeemer Nation: The Idea of America's Millennial Role* (Chicago: University of Chicago Press, 1968).

7 See Gerrard Winstanley, *The Law of Freedom and Other Writings* (Cambridge: Cambridge University Press, 1983), p. 84.

8 Ibid., p. 268.

9 Cohn, *The Pursuit of the Millennium*, p. 149.

Chapter 3

1 For one such example, see the claim of Krishan Kumar, *Utopia and Anti-Utopia in Modern Times* (Oxford: Basil Blackwell, 1987), p. 19, that 'Christian civilization may be unique in giving birth to utopia'.

2 Recent work includes Seligman, *Order and Transcendence*, and Jacqueline Dutton, 'Non-Western Utopian Traditions', in Claeys, *The Cambridge Companion to Utopian Literature*.

3 U. Ghoshal, *A History of Hindu Political Theories* (Oxford: Oxford University Press, 1922), p. 12.

4 Lewis Henry Morgan, *Ancient Society* (London: Macmillan & Company, 1877), pp. 530, 536.

5 The classic statement being Friedrich Engels's *The Origin of the Family, Private Property and the State* (1884).

6 *The Qu'ran* (Oxford: Oxford University Press, 2004), p. 7.

7 *Mo Tzu: Basic Writings* (New York: Columbia University Press, 1970), p. 22.

8 Zhang Longxi, 'The Utopian Vision, East and West', in *Utopian Studies*, 13 (2002), pp. 7–17, from which the examples used here are chiefly drawn.

9 This theme is explored comparatively in Qingyun Wu, *Female Rule in Chinese and English Literary Utopias* (Syracuse: Syracuse University Press, 1995).

10 Shiping Hua, *Chinese Utopianism: A Comparative Study of Reformist Thought with Japan and Russia 1898–1997* (Washington DC: Woodrow Wilson Center Press, 2009), p. 18.

11 For example in *The Laws of Manu* (New York: Dover Publications, 1969), pp. 13–14.

12 See, for example, Seiji Nuita, 'Traditional Utopias in Japan and the West', in David W. Plath, ed., *Aware of*

Utopia (Urbana: University of Illinois Press, 1971), pp. 12–32, and Yoriko Moichi, 'Japanese Utopian Literature from the 1870s to the Present and the Influence of Western Utopianism', in *Utopian Studies*, 19 (1999), pp. 89–97.

13 These are introduced in Aziz Al-Azmeh, 'Utopia and Islamic Political Thought', in *History of Political Thought*, 11 (1990), pp. 9–19.

14 Patricia Crone, *Medieval Islamic Political Thought* (Edinburgh: Edinburgh University Press, 2004), p. 318.

15 Richard Walzer, ed., *Al-Farabi on the Perfect State* (Oxford: Clarendon Press, 1984), p. 231.

16 Antony Black, *The History of Islamic Political Thought* (Edinburgh: Edinburgh University Press, 2001), p. 53.

17 Daniel G. Brinton, *The Myths of the New World* (Philadelphia: David McKay, 1896), p. 105.

18 Bruce Lawrence, ed., *Messages to the World: The Statements of Osama Bin Laden* (London: Verso, 2005), p. 166.

19 F. R. Wingate, *Ten Years' Captivity in the Mahdi's Camp* (London: Sampson Low, Marston & Company, 1892), p. 6.

20 See Gould, 'The Utopian Side of the Indian Uprising', in David W. Plath, ed., *Aware of Utopia* (Urbana: University of Illinois Press, 1971), pp. 86–116.

21 For millenarianism in the former, see, for example, Jonathan Spence, *God's Chinese Son: The Taiping Heavenly Kingdom of Hong Xiuquan* (London: HarperCollins, 1996).

22 See Julius K. Nyerere, *Ujamaa: Essays on Socialism* (Oxford: Oxford University Press, 1968).

23 For an introduction to these developments, see Pordzik, *The Quest for Postcolonial Utopia*, and Bill Ashcroft, 'Remembering the Future: Utopianism in African Literature', in *Textual Practice*, 23 (2009), pp. 703–22.

24 For example, Zhang Longxi, 'The Utopian Vision, East and West', in *Utopian Studies*, 13 (2002), pp. 1–20.

Chapter 4

1 Quoted in Colin Davis, 'Thomas More's *Utopia*: Sources, Legacy and Interpretation', in Claeys, *The Cambridge Companion to Utopian Literature*.

2 More's approach to this issue, however, is hardly straightforward. His original Latin title was *Libellus vere Aureus nec minus salutaris quam festivus de optimo reipublicae statu deque nova Insula Utopia* ('A pamphlet truly golden no less beneficial than enjoyable concerning the republic's best state and the new Island Utopia'). It was also simply first called 'The Best Condition of a Society'.

3 On the context, see, in particular, Davis, *Utopia and the Ideal Society*.

4 Thomas More, *The Complete Works of Thomas More*, Vol. 4: *Utopia*, eds Edward Surtz and J. H. Hexter (New Haven: Yale University Press, 1965), p. 21.

5 Ibid., p. 61.

6 Ibid., p. 74.

7 Ibid., p. 72.

8 Ibid., pp. 77, 89.

9 Ibid., p. 83.

10 Ibid., p. 76.

11 See Claeys, *Imperial Sceptics*.

12 For example, J. H. Hexter in *More's Utopia: The Biography of an Idea* (Princeton: Princeton University Press, 1952), pp. 33–42.

13 Thomas More, *The Complete Works of Thomas More*, Vol. 4: *Utopia*, eds Edward Surtz and J. H. Hexter (New Haven: Yale University Press, 1965), p. 11.

14 Ibid., pp. 150–51.

15 Ibid., p. 152.

16 See the account in J. C. Davis, 'Utopianism', in J. H. Burns, ed., *The Cambridge History of Political Thought 1450–1700* (Cambridge: Cambridge University Press, 1991), pp. 329–46.

17 Karl Kautsky, *Thomas More and his Utopia* (London: A & C Black, 1927), p. 159.

18 Thomas More, *The Complete Works of Thomas More*, Vol. 4: *Utopia*, eds Edward Surtz and J. H. Hexter (New Haven: Yale University Press, 1965), p. viii.

19 See, most notably, Quentin Skinner, *The Foundations of Modern Political Thought* (2 vols, Cambridge: Cambridge University Press, 1978), and George M. Logan, *The Meaning of More's Utopia* (Princeton: Princeton University Press, 1983), pp. 139–40.

20 For example, W. E. Campbell, *More's Utopia and his Social Teaching* (London: Eyre & Spottiswoode, 1930), p. 140.

Chapter 5

1. The classic account here is Adams, *Travelers and Travel Liars*.

2 An extensive catalogue of such reputed peoples is provided in John Block Friedman, *The Monstrous Races in Medieval Art and Thought* (Cambridge, Mass.: Harvard University Press, 1981).

3 Christopher Columbus, *The Book of Prophecies* (Berkeley: University of California Press, 1997), pp. 67–8, 71, 77, 291. See, generally, Tzvetan Todorov, *The Conquest of America: The Question of the Other* (Norman: University of Oklahoma, 1999).

4 Peter Martyr Anglerius, *De Orbe Novo* (2 vols, London: G. P. Putnam's Sons, 1912), Vol. 1, pp. 62, 139; Girolamo Benzoni, *History of the New World* (London: W. H. Smith, 1867), p. 15.

5 See, generally, Anthony Pagden, *The Fall of Natural Man: The American Indian and the Origins of Comparative Ethnology* (Cambridge: Cambridge University Press, 1982), and Robert Berkhofer, *The White Man's Indian: Images of the American Indian from Columbus to the Present* (New York: Vintage, 1978). Graphic representations are reprinted in Hugh Honour, *The European Vision of America* (Cleveland: Cleveland Museum of Art, 1975).

6 Peter Martyr Anglerius, *De Orbe Novo* (2 vols, London: G. P. Putnam's Sons, 1912), Vol. 1, pp. 64, 90; Christopher Columbus, *The Journal of his First Voyage to America* (London: Jarrolds, 1925), p. 67.

7 Tacitus, *Historical Works* (London: J. M. Dent, n.d.), Vol. 2, p. 314.

8 Peter Martyr Anglerius, *De Orbe Novo* (2 vols, London: G. P. Putnam's Sons, 1912), Vol. 2, p. 274.

9 Quoted in Levin, *The Myth of the Golden Age*, p. 61. Rebellious natives sometimes parried this obsession by pouring molten gold down the throats of captured Spaniards; see Girolamo Benzoni, *History of the New World* (London: W. H. Smith, 1867), p. 73.

10 As is claimed by Enrique Dussel in *The Invention of the Americas* (New York: Continuum, 1995), p. 32.

11 The first printed work in English on 'Armenica', drawn from Vespucci, appeared at Antwerp, *c.* 1511 – where More's *Utopia* was conceived in late 1515 (Richard Eden, ed., *The First Three English Books on America* (Birmingham: 1885, p. xxv).

12 Peter Martyr Anglerius, *De Orbe Novo* (2 vols, London: G. P. Putnam's Sons, 1912), Vol. 1, pp. 103–4. See also William Brandon, *New Worlds for Old: Reports from the New World and their effect on the development of social thought in Europe, 1500–1800* (Athens, Ohio: Ohio State University Press, 1986) and Stelio Cro, *The American Foundations of the Hispanic Utopia* (2 vols, Tallahassee: Desoto Press, 1994).

13 The boldest assert that More 'cannot have helped being acquainted' with the work (H. W. Donner, *Introduction to Utopia*, London: Sidgwick & Jackson, 1945, p. 27).

14 Bernal Diaz, *The Conquest of New Spain* (London: Penguin, 1963), p. 269; Frederick J. Pohl, *Amerigo Vespucci: Pilot Major* (London: Frank Cass, 1966), p. 133.

15 Thomas More, *The Complete Works of Thomas More*, Vol. 4: *Utopia*, eds Edward Surtz and J. H. Hexter (New Haven: Yale University Press, 1965), p. xxxiii.

16 Amerigo Vespucci, *The First Four Voyages of Amerigo Vespucci* (London: Bernard Quaritch, 1893), pp. 8, 11.

17 Garcilaso de la Vega, *Royal Commentaries of the Incas* (Austin: University of Texas Press, 1966), Pt 1,

pp. 254, 271; Pedro Sarmiento de Gamboa, *The History of the Incas* [1574] (Austin: University of Texas Press, 2007), p. 134.

18 Pedro Pizarro, *Relation of the Discovery and Conquest of the Kingdoms of Peru* (New York: The Cortes Society, 1921), p. 35.

19 William H. Prescott, *History of the Conquest of Peru* (London: Swan Sonnenschein, 1889), pp. 15, 21, 23, 27, 29.

20 Notably in Lorraine Stobbart, *Utopia: Fact or Fiction? The Evidence from the Americas* (Stroud: Alan Sutton, 1992).

21 John Phelan, *The Millennial Kingdom of the Franciscans in the New World: A Study of the Writings of Geronimo de Mendieta (1525–1604)* (Berkeley: University of California Press, 1956), p. 66.

22 R. B. Cunninghame Graham, *A Vanished Arcadia: Being Some Account of the Jesuits in Paraguay 1607 to 1767* (London: William Heinemann, 1901), pp. xiv, 22, 201; Philip Caraman, *The Lost Paradise: An Account of the Jesuits in Paraguay, 1607–1768* (London: Sidgwick & Jackson, 1975), pp. 116–17.

23 In the 1530s in Mexico, Vasco de Quiroga founded communities for the Indians that wedded More's ideas with monastic concepts. See Fernando Gomez, *Good Places and Non-Places in Colonial Mexico: The Figure of Vasco de Quiroga (1470–1565)* (New York: University Press of America, 2001), pp. 74–80.

24 John Locke, *Two Treatises of Government* (2nd edn, Cambridge: Cambridge University Press, 1970), p. 319.

25 See Benedict Anderson, *Imagined Communities: Reflections on the Origin and Spread of Nationalism* (London: Verso, 1993).

26 Louis-Sébastien Mercier, *Memoirs of the Year Two Thousand Five Hundred* (Dublin: W. Wilson, 1772), Vol. 2, p. 185.

27 Gabriel Foigny, *The Southern Land, Known*, ed. David Fausett (Syracuse: Syracuse University Press, 1993), pp. 42, 57.

28 Denis Veiras, *The History of the Severambians* (Albany: State University of New York Press, 2006), p. 87.

29 See, generally, J. G. A. Pocock, *The*

Machiavellian Moment. Florentine Political Thought and the Atlantic Republican Tradition (Princeton: Princeton University Press, 1975).

Chapter 6

1 See Fausett, *The Strange and Surprizing Sources of Robinson Crusoe*.

2 Daniel Defoe, *Robinson Crusoe* (London: J. M. Dent, 1906), p. 72.

3 These themes also emerge strongly in some subsequent writings of Defoe on the theme, notably *Serious Reflections During the Life and Surprising Adventures of Robinson Crusoe* (1720; reprinted in Claeys, *Modern British Utopias*, Vol. 1, pp. 113–266).

4 See, generally, Michael Newton, *Savage Girls and Wild Boys: A History of Feral Children* (London: Faber & Faber, 2002).

5 These texts are reprinted in Claeys, *Modern British Utopias*.

6 Rennie, *Far-Fetched Facts*, p. 98.

7 Denis Diderot, *Political Writings*, eds John Hope Mason and Robert Wokler (Cambridge: Cambridge University Press, 1992), p. 39.

8 William Godwin, *Enquiry Concerning Political Justice* (2 vols, London: G. G. J & J. Robinson, 1793), Vol. 1, p. 10.

9 Claeys, *Utopias of the British Enlightenment*, p. 12.

Chapter 7

1 The classic study of the relationship remains Lasky's *Utopia and Revolution*.

2 See James Harrington, *The Political Works of James Harrington*, ed. J. G. A. Pocock (Cambridge: Cambridge University Press, 1977).

3 Claeys, *Utopias of the British Enlightenment*, p. 80.

4 Robert Burton, *The Anatomy of Melancholy* (London: J. M. Dent & Sons, 1932), p. 104.

5 Louis Sébastien Mercier, *Memoirs of the Year Two Thousand Five Hundred* (Dublin: W. Wilson, 1772), Vol. 2, p. 119.

6 Jean-Jacques Rousseau, *The Social Contract and Discourses* (London: J. M. Dent, 1973), p. 181.

7 This is the thrust of the argument in Dan Edelstein's *The Terror of Natural Right: Republicanism, the Cult of Nature, and the French Revolution* (Chicago: University of Chicago Press, 2009).

8 Karl Popper, *The Open Society and Its Enemies* (2 vols, Princeton: Princeton University Press, 1962).

Chapter 8

1 Johann Valentin Andreae, *Christianopolis: An Ideal State of the Seventeenth Century* (Oxford: Oxford University Press, 1916), p. 156.

2 See Richard Sennett, *The Uses of Disorder: Personal Identity and City Life* (London: Faber & Faber, 1966).

Chapter 9

1 The standard account remains Robert Allerton Parker, *A Yankee Saint: John Humphrey Noyes and the Oneida Community* (2nd ed., Philadelphia: Porcupine Press, 1972).

2 Miller, *The 60s Communes*, p. xix.

Chapter 10

1 *New Moral World*, Vol. 4, No. 178 (24 March 1838), p. 175.

2 See Claeys, *Citizens and Saints*.

3 See, for example, Ernest Tuveson, 'The Millenarian Structure of *The Communist Manifesto*', in C. A. Patrides and Joseph Wittreich, eds, *The Apocalypse in English Renaissance Thought and Literature* (Manchester: Manchester University Press, 1984), pp. 323–41.

Chapter 11

1 On its background and development,

see Christopher Lasch, *The True and Only Heaven: Progress and Its Critics* (New York: W. W. Norton, 1991).

2 *Famous Utopias of the Renaissance*, introduction and notes by Frederic R. White (New York: Hendricks House, 1955), p. 240.

3 See Charles Webster, *Utopian Planning and the Puritan Revolution: Gabriel Plattes, Samuel Hartlib and Macaria* (Oxford: Wellcome Institute for the History of Medicine, 1979), p. 4.

4 Claeys, *Utopias of the British Enlightenment*, p. 9.

5 Ibid., p. 47.

6 Grant Allen, *Twelve Tales* (London: Grant Richards, 1900), pp. 45–66.

7 Most of these texts are reprinted in Claeys, *Late Victorian Utopias*.

8 Walter Besant, *The Inner House* (London: Simkin, Marshall & Co., 1888), p. 33.

9 For example, 'Robinson Crusoe' [pseudonym], *Looking Upwards: or, Nothing New* (Auckland, NZ: H. Brett, 1892).

10 William Morris, *News from Nowhere* (London: Longmans, Green & Co., 1899), p. 80.

11 Herman Melville, *Typee* (New York: Library of America, 1982), pp. 149–50.

Chapter 12

1 A recent anthology of such works is Peter Fitting, ed., *Subterranean Worlds* (Middletown: Wesleyan University Press, 2004).

Chapter 13

1 Karl Popper, *The Open Society and its Enemies* (2 vols, Princeton: Princeton University Press, 1962).

Chapter 14

1 Scientologists believe, among other things, that human beings are descended from an alien race.

2 The filming of Wells's works is discussed in Keith Williams, *H. G. Wells, Modernity and the Movies* (Liverpool: University of Liverpool Press, 2007).

Conclusion

1 Rousseau to the elder Mirabeau, 26 July 1767, quoted in Baczko, *Utopian Lights*, p. 22. The reference is to an idealized form of distribution proposed in the system known as Physiocracy.

2 Among recent pronouncements: John Gray, 'The Death of Utopia' in *Black Mass: Apocalyptic Religion and the Death of Utopia* (London: Allen Lane, 2007), pp. 1–35. See also Isaiah Berlin's account of utopia defined as 'a static perfection in which human nature is finally fully realized, and all is still and immutable and eternal' in *The Crooked Timber of Humanity* (London: John Murray, 1990), p. 22.

3 Judith Shklar, *Political Thought and Political Thinkers* (Chicago: University of Chicago Press, 1992), pp. 168–69.

4 Christopher Lasch, *The True and Only Heaven: Progress and its Critics* (London: W. W. Norton & Co., 1991), p. 41.

5 R. Buckminster Fuller, *Utopia or Oblivion: The Prospects for Humanity* (London: Penguin, 1970).

6 See, most notably, Richard Wilkinson and Kate Pickett's *The Spirit Level: Why More Equal Societies Almost Always Do Better* (London: Allen Lane, 2009).

7 A sequel is Ernest Callenbach's *Ecotopia Emerging* (Berkeley, Calif.: Banyan Tree Books, 1981).

Bibliography

In addition to this selected listing, further relevant works are mentioned in the Notes.

Adams, Percy G., *Travelers and Travel-liars, 1660–1800* (Berkeley: University of California Press, 1962)

Albinski, Nan Bowman, *Women's Utopias in British and American Fiction* (London: Routledge, 1988)

Aldiss, Brian W., *Billion Year Spree: A History of Science Fiction* (London: Weidenfeld & Nicolson, 1973)

Alexander, Peter, and Roger Gill, eds, *Utopias* (London: Duckworth, 1984)

Alkon, Paul K., *Origins of Futuristic Fiction* (Athens, Ga.: University of Georgia Press, 1987)

Amis, Kingsley, *New Maps of Hell: A Survey of Science Fiction* (London: Victor Gollancz, 1961)

Armytage, W. H. G., *Heavens Below: Utopian Experiments in England, 1560–1960* (London: Routledge and Kegan Paul, 1960)

—, *Yesterday's Tomorrows: A Historical Survey of Future Societies* (London: Routledge and Kegan Paul, 1968)

Atkinson, Geoffrey, *The Extraordinary Voyage in French Literature before 1700* (New York: Columbia University Press, 1920); Vol. 2, *The Extraordinary Voyage in French Literature 1700–1720* (1922)

Baczko, Bronislaw, *Utopian Lights: The Evolution of the Idea of Social Progress* (New York: Paragon House, 1989)

Bailey, J. O., *Pilgrims Through Space and Time: Trends and Patterns in Scientific and Utopian Fiction* (London: Argus, 1947)

Barkun, Michael, *Disaster and the Millennium* (New Haven: Yale University Press, 1974)

Bartkowski, Frances, *Feminist Utopias* (Lincoln, Nebraska: University of Nebraska Press, 1989)

Beaumont, Matthew, *Utopia Ltd: Ideologies of Social Dreaming in England, 1870–1900* (Leiden: Brill, 2005)

Becker, Ailenne R., *The Lost Worlds Romance* (London: Greenwood Press, 1992)

Berneri, Marie, *Journey Through Utopia* (London: Routledge and Kegan Paul, 1950)

Bestor, Arthur E., *Backwoods Utopias: The Sectarian Origins and Owenite Phase of Communitarian Socialism in America, 1663–1829* (2nd ed., Philadelphia: University of Pennsylvania Press, 1970)

Blaim, Artur, *Early English Utopian Fiction* (Lublin: Marie Curie Skiodowskiej University Press, 1984)

—, *Failed Dynamics: The English Robinsonade of the Eighteenth Century* (Lublin: Marie Curie Skiodowskiej University Press, 1987)

—, *Aesthetic Objects and Blueprints: English Utopias of the Enlightenment* (Lublin: Marie Curie Skiodowskiej University Press, 1997)

Blewett, David, *The Illustration of Robinson Crusoe* (Gerrards Cross, Colin Smythe, 1995)

Bloch, Ernst, *The Principle of Hope* (3 vols, Oxford: Basil Blackwell, 1986)

Bollerey, Franziska, *Architekturkonzeptionen der utopischen Sozialisten* (Berlin: Ernst & Sohn, 1991)

Booker, M. Keith, *The Dystopian Impulse in Modern Literature* (Westport: Greenwood Press, 1994)

Braunthal, Alfred, *Salvation and the Perfect Society* (Amherst: University of Massachusetts Press, 1979)

Buck-Morss, Susan, *Dreamworld and Catastrophe: The Passing of Mass Utopia in East and West* (Boston: MIT Press, 2002)

Claeys, Gregory, *Citizens and Saints: Politics and Anti-Politics in Early British Socialism* (Cambridge: Cambridge University Press, 1989)

—, ed., *Utopias of the British Enlightenment* (Cambridge: Cambridge University Press, 1994)

—, ed., *Modern British Utopias, 1700–1850* (8 vols, London: Pickering and Chatto, 1997)

—, and Lyman Tower Sargent, eds, *The Utopia Reader* (New York: New York University Press, 1999)

—, ed., *Restoration and Augustan British Utopias* (Syracuse: Syracuse University Press, 2000)

—, Lyman Tower Sargent, and Roland Schaer, eds, *Utopia: The Search for the Ideal Society in the West* (New York: Oxford University Press, 2000)

—, ed., *Late Victorian Utopias* (6 vols, London: Pickering and Chatto, 2008)

—, ed., *The Cambridge Companion to Utopian Literature* (Cambridge: Cambridge University Press, 2010)

—, *Imperial Sceptics: British Critics of Empire, 1850–1920* (Cambridge: Cambridge University Press, 2010)

Clarke, I. F., *The Pattern of Expectation, 1644–2001* (London: Jonathan Cape, 1979)

Clute, John, *Science Fiction: The Illustrated Encylopedia* (London: Dorling Kindersley, 1995)

Cohn, Norman, *The Pursuit of the Millennium* (London: Secker & Warburg, 1947)

Cornea, Christine, *Science Fiction Cinema: Between Fantasy and Reality* (Edinburgh: Edinburgh University Press, 2007)

Davis, J. C., *Utopia and the Ideal Society: A Study of English Utopian Writing 1516–1700* (Cambridge: Cambridge University Press, 1981)

Eaton, Ruth, *Ideal Cities: Utopianism and the (Un)Built Environment* (London: Thames & Hudson, 2002)

Eliav-Feldon, Miriam, *Realistic Utopias: The Imaginary Societies of the Renaissance 1516–1630* (Oxford: Clarendon Press, 1982)

Elliott, Robert, *The Shape of Utopia: Studies in a Literary Genre* (Chicago: University of Chicago Press, 1970)

Erasmus, Charles, *In Search of the Common Good: Utopian Experiments Past and Future* (Glencoe: The Free Press, 1977)

Eurich, Nell, *Science in Utopia* (Cambridge, Mass.: Harvard University Press, 1967)

Evans, Rhiannon, *Utopia Antiqua: Readings of the Golden Age and Decline at Rome* (London: Routledge, 2008)

Fausett, David, *Writing the New World: Imaginary Voyages and Utopias of the Great Southern Land* (Syracuse: Syracuse University Press, 1993)

—, *The Strange and Surprizing Sources of Robinson Crusoe* (Amsterdam: Rodopi, 1994)

Ferguson, John, *Utopias of the Classical World* (London: Thames & Hudson, 1975)

Firchow, Peter Edgerly, *Modern Utopian Fictions from H. G. Wells to Iris Murdoch* (Washington DC: The Catholic University Press of America, 2007)

Fishman, Robert, *Urban Utopias in the Twentieth Century: Ebenezer Howard, Frank Lloyd Wright, and Le Corbusier* (New York: Basic Books, 1977)

Fogarty, Robert S., *American Utopias* (Itasca, F. E. Peacock, 1972)

—, *Dictionary of American Communal and Utopian History* (Westport: Greenwood Press, 1980)

—, *All Things New: American Communes and Utopian Movements, 1860–1914* (Chicago: University of Chicago Press, 1990)

Fortunati, Vita, and Raymond Trousson, *Dictionary of Literary Utopias* (Paris: Honoré Champion, 2000)

Friesen, John W., and Virginia Lyons Friesen, *The Palgrave Companion to North American Utopias* (London: Palgrave-Macmillan, 2004)

Goodman, Percival and Paul, *Communitas: Means of Livelihood and Ways of Life* (Chicago: University of Chicago Press, 1947)

Goodwin, Barbara, *Social Science and Utopia: Nineteenth Century Models of Social Harmony* (Hassocks: Harvester Press, 1978)

—, and Keith Taylor, *The Politics of Utopia* (New York: St Martin's Press, 1983)

Gove, Philip Babcock, *The Imaginary Voyage in Prose Fiction* (New York: Columbia University Press, 1941)

Green, Roger Lancelyn, *Into Other Worlds: Space-Flight in Fiction, from Lucian to Lewis* (London: Abelard-Schuman, 1958)

Guarneri, Carl, *The Utopian Alternative: Fourierism in Nineteenth Century America* (London: Cornell University Press, 1991)

Guthke, Karl S., *The Last Frontier: Imagining Other Worlds, from the Copernican Revolution to Modern Science Fiction* (London: Cornell University Press, 1990)

Hansot, Elizabeth, *Perfection and Progress: Two Modes of Utopian Thought* (Cambridge, Mass.: MIT Press, 1974)

Hayden, Dolores, *Seven American Utopias: The Architecture of Communitarian Socialism, 1790–1975* (Cambridge, Mass.: MIT Press, 1976)

Hertzler, Joyce, *The History of Utopian Thought* (London: Macmillan, 1923)

Hillegas, Mark R., *The Future as Nightmare: H. G. Wells and the Anti-Utopians* (Carbondale: Southern Illinois University Press, 1967)

Hillquit, Morris, *History of Socialism in the United States* (1903) (5th ed,, New York: Dover Publications, 1971)

Holloway, Mark, *Heavens on Earth: Utopian Communities in America 1680–1880* (2nd ed., New York: Dover Publications, 1966)

Holstun, James, *A Rational Millennium: Puritan Utopias of Seventeenth-Century England and America* (Oxford: Oxford University Press, 1987)

Jacobs, Jane, *The Life and Death of Great American Cities* (London: Pelican, 1965)

James, Edward, *Science Fiction in the Twentieth Century* (Oxford: Oxford University Press, 1994)

—, and Farah Mendlesohn, eds, *The Cambridge Companion to Science Fiction*

(Cambridge: Cambridge University Press, 2003)

Jameson, Frederic, *Archaeologies of the Future: The Desire called Utopia and Other Science Fictions* (London: Verso, 2005)

Jean, Georges, *Voyages en Utopie* (Paris: Gallimard, 1994)

Johns, Alessa, *Women's Utopias of the Eighteenth Century* (Urbana: University of Illinois Press, 2003)

Kagan, Paul, *New World Utopias: A Photographic History of the Search for Community* (London: Penguin, 1975)

Kamenka, Eugene, ed., *Utopias* (Oxford: Oxford University Press, 1987)

Kateb, George, *Utopia and its Enemies* (Glencoe: Free Press, 1963)

Kenyon, Timothy, *Utopian Communism and Political Thought in Early Modern England* (London: Pinter Publishers, 1989)

Kumar, Krishan, *Utopia and Anti-Utopia in Modern Times* (Oxford: Basil Blackwell, 1987)

—, *Utopianism* (Buckingham: Open University Press, 1991)

—, and Stephen Bann, eds, *Utopias and the Millennium* (London: Reaktion Books, 1993)

Lasky, Melvin, *Utopia and Revolution* (Chicago: University of Chicago Press, 1976)

Leslie, Marina, *Renaissance Utopias and the Problem of History* (London: Cornell University Press, 1998)

Levin, Harry, *The Myth of the Golden Age in the Renaissance* (Oxford: Oxford University Press, 1969)

Levitas, Ruth, *The Concept of Utopia* (Syracuse: Syracuse University Press, 1990)

Loxley, Diana, *Problematic Shores: The Literature of Islands* (London: Macmillan, 1990)

McCord, William, *Voyages to Utopia* (New York: W. W. Norton, 1989)

McDannell, Colleen, and Bernhard Lang, *Heaven: A History* (New York: Vintage, 1988)

McKnight, Stephen A., *Science, Pseudo-Science, and Utopianism in Early Modern*

Thought (Columbia: University of Missouri Press, 1992)

Manguel, Alberto, and Gianni Guadalupi, *The Dictionary of Imaginary Places* (New York: Harcourt, Brace, Jovanovich, 1987)

Mannheim, Karl, *Ideology and Utopia: An Introduction to the Sociology of Knowledge* (New York: Harcourt, Brace & Co., 1936)

Manuel, Frank, *The Prophets of Paris* (New York: Harper & Row, 1965)

—, ed., *Utopias and Utopian Thought* (Boston: Beacon Press, 1965)

—, and Fritzie P. Manuel, eds, *French Utopias: An Anthology of Ideal Societies* (New York: Schocken Books, 1971)

—, and Fritzie P. Manuel, *Utopian Thought in the Western World* (Cambridge, Mass.: Belknap Press, 1979)

Margolis, Jonathan, *A Brief History of Tomorrow* (London: Bloomsbury, 2000)

Markus, Thomas A., *Visions of Perfection: Architecture and Utopian Thought* (Glasgow: Third Eye Centre, 1985)

Meacham, Standish, *Regaining Paradise: Englishness and the Early Garden City Movement* (New Haven: Yale University Press, 1999)

Miller, Timothy, *The 60s Communes: Hippies and Beyond* (Syracuse: Syracuse University Press, 1999)

Morton, A. L., *The English Utopia* (London: Lawrence and Wishart, 1952)

Moylan, Tom, *Demand the Impossible: Science Fiction and the Utopian Imagination* (London: Methuen, 1986)

—, *Scraps of the Untainted Sky: Science Fiction, Utopia, Dystopia* (Boulder: Westview Press, 2000)

Mumford, Lewis, *The Story of Utopias* (New York: Viking Press, 1950)

Nicolson, Marjorie, *Voyages to the Moon* (London: Macmillan, 1948)

Nordhoff, Charles, *The Communistic Societies of the United States* (1875; new ed., New York: Dover Publications, 1966)

Noyes, John Humphrey, *History of American Socialisms* (1870; new ed., New York: Dover Publications, 1966)

Oved, Yaacov, *Two Hundred Years of American Communes* (New Brunswick, N. J.: Transaction Books, 1988)

Parrinder, Patrick, *Shadows of the Future: H. G. Wells, Science Fiction and Prophecy* (Syracuse: Syracuse University Press, 1995)

Parrington, Vernon, *American Dreams: A Study of American Utopias* (New York: Russell & Russell, 1964)

Passmore, John, *The Perfectibility of Man* (London: Duckworth, 1970)

Pfaelzer, Jean, *The Utopian Novel in America 1886–1896* (Pittsburgh: University of Pittsburgh Press, 1984)

Pinder, David, *Visions of the City: Utopianism, Power and Politics in Twentieth-Century Urbanism* (Edinburgh: Edinburgh University Press, 2005)

Pohl, Nicole and Brenda Tooley, eds, *Gender and Utopia in the Eighteenth Century* (London: Ashgate, 2007)

Polak, Fred, *The Image of the Future* (2 vols, New York: Oceana, 1961)

Pordzik, Ralph, *The Quest for Postcolonial Utopia: A Comparative Introduction to the Utopian Novel in the New English Literatures* (Oxford: Peter Lang, 2001)

Rees, Christine, *Utopian Imagination and Eighteenth-Century Fiction* (London: Longman, 1996)

Rennie, Neil, *Far-Fetched Facts: The Literature of Travel and the Idea of the South Seas* (Oxford: Clarendon Press, 1995)

Roberts, Adam, *Science Fiction* (London: Routledge, 2000)

Roemer, Kenneth, *The Obsolete Necessity: America in Utopian Writing, 1888–1900* (Kent, Ohio: Kent State University Press, 1976)

Rosenau, Helen, *The Ideal City: Its Architectural Evolution* (New York: Harper & Row, 1972)

Rottensteiner, Franz, *The Science Fiction Book: An Illustrated History* (London: Thames & Hudson, 1975)

Sargent, Lyman Tower, *British and American Utopian Literature, 1516–1975* (New York: Garland, 1988)

Sargisson, Lucy, Contemporary Feminist Utopianism (London: Routledge, 1996)

Seed, David, ed., *A Companion to Science Fiction* (Oxford: Blackwell, 2005)

Seligman, Adam B., ed., *Order and Transcendence: The Role of Utopias and the Dynamics of Civilization* (Leiden: E. J. Brill, 1989)

Shklar, Judith, *After Utopia: The Decline of Political Faith* (Princeton: Princeton University Press, 1957)

Snodgrass, Mary Ellen, *Encyclopedia of Utopian Literature* (Oxford: ABC-Clio, 1995)

Sobchak, Vivian, *Screening Space: The American Science Fiction Film* (2nd ed., New York: Ungar, 1987)

Sutton, Robert P., *Communal Utopias and the American Experience: Secular Communities, 1824–2000* (Westport: Praeger, 2004)

Tafuri, Manfredo, *Architecture and Utopia: Design and Capitalist Development* (Cambridge, Mass.: MIT Press, 1979)

Taylor, Keith, *The Political Ideas of the Utopian Socialists* (London: Frank Cass, 1982)

Thrupp, Silvia, *Millennial Dreams in Action: Studies in Revolutionary Religious Movements* (New York: Schocken Books, 1970)

Tinker, Chauncey, *Nature's Simple Plan: A Phase of Radical Thought in the Eighteenth Century* (Princeton: Princeton University Press, 1922)

Trahair, Richard C. S., *Utopias and Utopians: An Historical Dictionary* (London: Fitzroy Dearborn, 1999)

Tuveson, Ernest, *Millennium and Utopia: A Study in the Background of the Idea of Progress* (Berkeley: University of California Press, 1949)

Venturi, Franco, *Utopia and Reform in the Enlightenment* (Cambridge: Cambridge University Press, 1971)

Wagar, W. Warren, *Terminal Visions: The Literature of Last Things* (Bloomington: Indiana University Press, 1982)

Walsh, Chad, *From Utopia to Nightmare* (London: Geoffrey Bles, 1962)

Wegener, Phillip E., *Imaginary Communities: Utopia, the Nation, and the Spatial Histories of Modernity* (Berkeley: University of California Press, 2002)

Williams, Keith, *H. G. Wells, Modernity and the Movies* (Liverpool: Liverpool University Press, 2007)

Picture Credits

Index